AF520975

INDIA BOOKVARSITY

LOTUS CHOICES

Editor: Mahendra Kulasrestha

'Subhas Bose was a votary of violence while I am a devotee of Ahimsa. But what does it matter? He was a great patriot. He laid down his life for the country. He had no use for parochialism and caste distinction.'

—*Mahatma Gandhi*
A week before his assassination,
on 23 Jan. 1948

Judgment:

No Air-crash No Death

by Lt. Manwati Arya
and
Ram Kishor Bajpai

'There is nothing that lures me more than a life of adventure away from the beaten track, and in search of the unknown. To this path I call my countrymen.'

—*Subhas Chandra Bose*

Lt. Manwati Arya

Lotus
PRESS
4263/3 Ansari Road,
Darya Ganj, New Delhi- 110 002

JUDGMENT

NO AIR CRASH NO DEATH

A closest to definitive study of
Netaji Subhas Chandra Bose's
Last Forty Years' Life

by:

LT. MANWATI ARYA,

Rani Jhansi Regiment, Ex. I.N.A.

and

RAM KISHOR BAJPAI

JUDGMENT

No Aircrash No Death

© Authors

ISBN : 978-81-8382-226-8

First Edition : 2010

Published by: **Lotus Press**

4263/3, Ansari Road, Darya Ganj,
New Delhi- 110002
Ph.: 32903912, 23280047
E-mail: lotus_press@sify.com

Laser Typeset by Upasana Graphics, Delhi
Printed at Anand Sons, Delhi.

Editorspeak

Verdict, at Last

Unlike Gandhiji's, Netaji's unusual contribution to freedom movements has not yet been recognised. The former's way was non-violent manipulation of people's power; the latter's the manipulation and use of the ruler's enemies' powers in one's own nation's interests. Both were new as concepts in world polity, and while the former drew wide attention and admiration because it seemed to have succeeded in India, the latter failed, owing essentially to the fact that the Axis powers did not succeed either in the west or the east—had it been otherwise, the tables would have completely turned. And for this reason Netaji as well as his I.N.A. went down the hill, although his reputation as a patriot rose high in an equal proportion, which remains undiminished till date—and will remain so for ever. It is important that Gandhiji himself called him a 'Prince among Patriot, and there is no reason to distust his honesty. I would also dare to say that had he been alive, the Congress and Nehru Government would not have given Netaji the shabby treatment they continue to give him even after his—and Nehru's—death. It reflects the nation's morale which even Gandhiji's tremendous influence could not change.

Non-violence is fine and definitely better than violence, but it is still in the stage of exprimentation, and has not been established as an absolute value, successful in all kinds of situations. Gandhiji carried out the first experiment, Martin Lunther King another, and many more have to be undertaken by Gandhiji's followers—which they seem to have conveniently forgotten. It is well known that Gandhiji supported fighting with the raiders in Kashmir; and C. Rajagopachari argued that he 'did not advocate a pacifism that rejected national borders and that he actually preferred armed resistance for good causes when there was no reasonable chance for non-violent resistance'.

Be that as it may, the Netaji chapter in current Indian history has been an undiluted shame for the whole country. No one clearly knows what happened to him after the so called plane-crash in June 1945, and despite the two enquiries—the Shah Nawaz and Justice Khosla's—both instituted during the Gandhian Congress governments, nothing was finally established. Meanwhile, stories of Netaji travelling as a Baba were rampant, which one could take or leave as he desired. A third, Justice Mukherjee Commission, was instituted under a non-congress government, which has now submitted its report, which has been rejected outright by the present Congress government, just in one sentence, without giving any reason. This is high insolence and gross insult of democracy!

Well, an unknown Netaji and I.N.A. soldier, Manwati Arya, at out request penned her first book on the subject, which we published in 2008 under the title 'Patriot: The Unique Indian Leader'. It was unexpectedly well written, so we persuaded her to pen down one more, which she started working upon despite her great age—88. But since misfortune follows everything concerned with Netaji, she had fractures, etc., preventing her to work further. But then again, help came from unexpected sources, and one absolutely unknown person to her, Ram Kishor Bajpai, appeared like an angel to undertake the work. Thank you, Mr. Co-author, to have done it so remarkably well! You have served a significant national cause in a significant way.

Here is perhaps the first book on the subject, updating the Netaji chapter upto the exact present, in a most comprehensive as well as interesting manner. The material it provides is from all possible sources, and its examination is perfect. It underlines what should be taken as certain, and indicates what more remains to be done. But the general outline of the last forty years of Netaji's life has been drawn quite clearly: that he left for the Soviet Union in that month, was perhaps also jailed in Irkutsk, left after Stalin's death m 1953, reached India via China, stayed here disguised as a Sadhu—in Lucknow, Naimisharanya, Ayodhya, and Faizabad, where he died in 1985 at age 88—that he read lots of the best books and magazines of the world (I would like to organise a library of these and also perhaps auction them), he wore a monkey cap and talked from behind a curtain, smoked wildly, etc., etc., etc....

Ah, and yes, I was thrilled when I read that in Lucknow he stayed at A.P. Sen Road, when I worked in that city and visited this lanelike road quite often to meet friends living there in a flat.

One more episode: A Sarvodaya leader named Mahavir Bhai, native of the city of my birth, Etawah in U.P., who became famous in the J.P. movement in which over 700 dacoits surrendered, in 1972, told me about his visiting Netaji as Gumnami Baba, in some detail, which I found quite thrilling as well as intriguing.

Let me say that I am highly pleased at the completion of this book. Now I want another, for which I've been trying for some time, by the grandchildren of Netaji—describing what they feel/think about their situation. My friend Dr. Vinod Verma, a frequent visitor to Germany, has been trying to get in touch with the family, but without any response. May be, she may succeed one day—Insha allah!

Is anyone of you — Anita, Martin Pfaff, Peter Arun, Thomas Krishna, and Maya — listening? God—if you really exist—bless them!

Amen!

Foreword

Ram Krishna Tailang

President
Swatantrata Sangram Adhyayan Kendra

Temperamentally I have been a peace-loving person and Gandhiji suited me the best, but it is also true that since my adolescence I have been renting my ears to listen keenly the stories of revolutionaries including the valiant deeds of Netaji Subhas Chandra Bose. I have also noticed that Netaji's activities during our freedom struggle were so entwined with the advent of independence from the British and the sense of sacrifice that one who had ever any occasion to see him could not forget him and held his memory as a piece of holy touch. The remembrance of such incidence was always described with pride and a special glow on the face. It was always a pleasant feeling for me to converse with such glowing faces and listen to their memories attentively. To me such persons were so charming and fascinating that my inner interest in revolutionaries went on increasing and this interest brought me slowly but steadily in the sphere of history.

An INA sepoy Ram Nath Singh was an almost daily visitor to me and his stories related to the INA's aggression and commandership of Netaji told me repeatedly as if I was his devotee. Another such example I would like to recall with honour. It is related to a respected revolutionary comrade Shiv Kumar Misra who remained very close to me till his death in December 2006. Comrade Misra had accompanied Netaji to Makoor

(District Unnao in Uttar Pradesh) where a Provincial Youth Conference was held on May 7 to 9 1938. Comrade Misra and a staunch supporter of Netaji, Pt. Vishambhar Dayal Tripathi, travelled for three days with Netaji in the scorching heat of May from one village to another to oppose the land revenue policy of the British and later on succeeded in achieving a revenue concession. The hidden agendum of the Makoor Conference was to activate young and old revolutionaries as a separate forum within the Congress. Here as antithesis to Congress slogan — All Powers to Congress — Netaji coined a new slogan — All Powers to the People. Revolutionaries like Batukeshwar Dutta, Raj Kumar Sinha, Yash Pal, Vijay Kumar Sinha, Yogesh Chatterjee, Ram Dularey Trivedi and others attended the Makoor Conference. Comrade Misra used to describe this incidence with vibrant, joyful and enthusiastically elated eyes. The love for Netaji in him was love for the country and it implied solemn and exclusive devotion which infused in him the spirit of sacrifice for the motherland.

Like many such persons the same sort of experience was repeated in wholesale as and when I was meeting respected Lt. Manwati Arya. It was a surprise for me to witness her increasing involvement in social service on every passing day. Her treasure of strength and the sense of social commitment were unending and for this she attributed credit with gratitude to those days which she lived in closeness to Netaji.

In this background I have also observed that Netaji was the only freedom-fighter who wrote his assessment fearlessly and boldly about our freedom struggle very early in 1935. He was also **the first to challenge the mightiest empire of the world militantly with an army.** His dreams for India were so complete and perfect that **he also pioneered the planning for the industrial**

and economic development of the country which would be a requirement after achieving freedom. **Netaji's idea of organising a women's army named as Rani Jhasni Regiment, completely managed by women, was the most innovative idea in the military history of the world.** His decisions regarding Indian National Anthem, Indian Flag, secular-socialist republic, etc., were honorably acceptable to the framers of Indian Constitution later on. And above all, the slogan 'Jai Hind' popularised by him has become a permanent salutation of India.

I, like lakhs of Indians, do believe that Netaji did not die in the alleged plane accident on August 18, 1945 and his story did not end there. **I also feel that he could not get his due and dignified place in our history as he deserved.** The new facts highlighted and decided by the Justice Mukherjee Commission of Inquiry, the documents dug out from the Russian archives and the facts contained in the declassified files are potent proofs which have definitely created a genuine pressure to reassess the role of Netaji and his INA in the history of our freedom struggle.

As I have read many leaves of this book, I am convinced that **the book is alive with some unknown incidents and thoughts related to Netaji.** I feel great pleasure and especially thankful to respected Lt. Manwat Arya and Shri Ram Kishor Bajpai who have jointly undertaken to discuss new aspects of the story of Netaji whose concept of the 'Second Front' for freedom movement was definitely one view which has been ignored by the historians. This and like this many other incidents and thoughts surely deserve to be interpreted afresh. I hope that more serious efforts to review the role of Netaji in our freedom struggle will be undertaken in the light of new facts now available to us by the future scholars.

Being elder and respected in our present society' Lt. Manwati Arya has left a very deep impression upon us and with this remarkable book she has been successful in presenting herself as a new historian of the freedom struggle. Along with her Shri Ram Kishor Bajpai has achieved new credentials by interpreting the documents with keen insight and critical view without being prejudiced to any of the past or present authors.

I must congratulate both Lt. Arya and Shri Bajpai, the former for devotion to the cause and the latter for a discerning view of story of our greatest hero Netaji Subhas Chandra Bose.

Kanpur

Novermber 10, 2009

Prologue

In the deep down recesses of the memory-lane of my childhood when I peep, I hear utterances of my father in praiseworthy words for Netaji who was then illegally incarcerated in Mandalay Central Jail of Burma, now Myanmar. I was then 5-6 years old. This was the first introduction of Netaji to me. In the physical process of my growing up from childhood to adolescence to youth, Netaji had slowly but firmly become my ideal and hero. That great respect for him in me resulted in my preparation and participation to dedicate myself for the cause of my motherland. I began actively taking part in the freedom struggle by joining the Indian Independence League (IIL) as I was then living in Burma where I was born, brought up and educated. In March 1943, I with my parents had come from Maymyo in Upper Burma to Rangoon (now Yangon) and it had provided me with a direct opportunity to meet my hero face to face in the office of the IIL located there. It was actually a working plan prepared and proposed by me for the involvement of all classes of women in our freedom movement which brought me close to him.

Not only today but in those days also, Netaji was a legendary personality. Actually, **he was always greater than his achievements, because his determination was followed by unexpectedly novel and strong action** and his dedication was characteristically self-sacrificing. The appraisement of his personality could be judged by his equally devoted and diehard followers who, drawing inspiration and motivation from him prepared themselves to sacrifice their all in response to his call at the altar of the motherland. I was always thrilled and electrified by the exhortations of Netaji to devote and dedicate myself for social and political cause throughout my life, till today. In fact, the more closely I could know him, the more convinced I became because he was a real worshipper, with his whole passionate being, of Mother India.

I need hardly explain why I could not believe in the so-called story of his death. **It was my firm belief, based on potent logical reasoning**—which has been elaborated in detail in the coming pages—**that Netaji did not die in that alleged air crash.** My sentimental as well as intuitional feelings have always supported me to maintain my faith intact in his, may I call it sacredness—which had sometimes gone to the extent of adoration. Netaji's participation in international politics and in India's freedom struggle was and is essentially historical from many points of view. He told us that the mightiest empire can be challenged forcefully by the oppressed people. His pioneer role in this regard was a **trendsetter which resulted in the form of the achievement of freedom of many countries,** beginning just after the Second World War.

I have most keenly, to the best of my ability, perused the functioning of the Justice Mukherjee Commission of Inquiry (JMCI) and was hopeful that it would be able to resolve the mystery of his disappearance fully and finally. Though it did achieve success on a few points which could provide us with some very potent new clues, but we still need many such clues to conclusively settle all the issues related to the subject. Yet it is my strong feeling that an objective evaluation is still the need of history, **in order to counter the international conspiracy to erase the memory of the Indian people for Netaji** and his contributions to the freedom movement and national development. And, therefore, I yearn that the inquiries and investigations, in the shape of researches and discussions, **must continue—because most of the secret papers related to Netaji will be available to us only in the future,** some 10-15 years ahead.

With these sentiments and commitments I have collected some material related to the subject and have desired to present them, along with my views, in this book. But my age has become a hurdle and my body quick to adopt sickness. It has been a handicap for me in doing further work, particularly travelling to collect facts as also writing. There has also been pressure from the publishers to complete the book at the earliest. It was suggested that I pass all my notes to someone who could edit them. But it was not possible as the notes were scattered and irregularly noted in many of my diaries. And physically I am not in a position to move from Kanpur.

In these circumstances, during a courtesy visit I met Shri Ram Kishor Bajpai, who offered his services to assist me in completing the book. I have seen him while functioning at various social forums with a vibrant spirit of selfless dedication. With a militant trade unionist background, proficiency in journalism and reading habits, with his keen interest in philosophy, Vedic Science, political history and youth for social development, etc., he is a multi-dimensional personality. I knew that he was the most suitable person for me if he undertakes my job of writing. My publishers also gave me the green signal to coopt him as my co-author.

During the writing of the book, Bajpai has certainly proved his worth. He has assisted me to my fullest satisfaction. In highlighting my views, his sincerity towards me has been perfect and his commitment, treatment and approach towards the subject have been commendable—which I hope my readers will also appreciate.

Lastly, I have to state that the present book has been written without prejudice and a pre-occupied mind. The facts narrated in it have been supported by documents and records. I would also like to thank Shri A.J. Sehgal, my publisher, for this assignment to me at this age and reminding me every month about it.

I must also acknowledge my thanks to many of my friends who have been interested in the writing of this book, and blessings to my children for their optimistic support all through these days.

Kanpur **—Manwati Arya**

September 19, 2009

Co-author's Note

With a deep sense of duty and high resolve I accepted to become the co-author of the present book with the most revered freedom-fighter Lt. Manwati Arya of Rani Jhansi Regiment, a wing of the Indian National Army led by the legendary Netaji Subhas Chandra Bose. My unconditional and voluntary offer to assist her was an obligatory duty because I could observe in her a deeprooted and burning desire to express her views on Netaji's disappearance at this advanced age of 89, she felt restrained to undertake this project herself due to gerontological reasons. She gave her immediate consent and asked me to write under her guidance on the basis of the material collected by her. For this purpose she had negotiated the matter with the publishers who were totally unknown to me. I could not argue with her though I felt that it implied an immediate constraint imposed on me by circumstances through her towering personality. Understanding the seriousness of the matter to undertake it quickly, I was left with no alternative except to accept her blessings by becoming her co-author. Her recommendations in this regard for me were approved by the publisher Mr. A.J. Sehgal of Lotus Press, New Delhi.

I am aware that an invitation to write a book is always a challenge, but there is a distinct honour, too, in it. To some it may mean that the writer has an exceptional knowledge in a specific field or has command over the subject of the book, superior to others. The ideas of the author are responded to by the readers in two ways — positively and negatively. Both ways the author's analysis and interpretations may either entertain and enlighten the reader or motivate and inspire him to formulate a new understanding. But to me it has been a learning process with an adorable woman like the respected Lt. Manwati Arya. Only a few years ago, I came close to her when I got an opportunity in the Servants of the People Society, Kanpur Centre, to organise a week-long *Youth Friendship Camp* in collaboration with an internationally reputed organisation *South Asia Fraternity*. During the Camp she was the Chairperson and I was her Working President. This was an occasion when I could observe and understand Lt. Manwati Arya, her person, her unbounded dedication to Netaji and the INA, and her affectionate way of functional behaviour.

Although she was helpless and restless for a few months in the middle of 2008 due to her two bone fractures, she could consciously retain her sharpness and exactness on the matters related to Netaji because of her deep involvement. She has guided me pace to pace and during this period, I could feel that her restlessness was really the anxiety to express her own views on Netaji's disappearance, so that posterity could learn the truth and further continue to unravel the mystery when new facts will come out from the secret and archival documents. According to her, the report of Justice Mukherjee Commission of Inquiry (JMCI) has opened new vistas by clearly deciphering a few mysteries related to Netaji's disappearance. It is actually the distant view, now not visible, but **out of her warrior spirit and long struggling experience, Lt. Manwati Arya has seen in her extensive mental view over the series of events and over a stretch of time, when**

only justice will prevail, goodness will exist and real ideals will be materialised.

The book is divided into three parts. The first twelve chapters deal with those facts and incidents which narrate the story of the other side and are contrary to the alleged death story of Netaji. The next nine chapters are interpretations of the findings of the JMCI. The appendices are doucuments which support our submissions and, legally speaking, are evidences which can be relied upon.

As regard the propoundings in the book, we have tried to make a simple and direct presentation, maintaining the chronological order of incidents. The description is informative and assertive. We have discussed only those points and opinions which are well recorded and available to us for verification. The book begins with the story of the birth of the mystery and thereafter, the spontaneous reactions of the then prominent leaders and newspapers. Various intelligence reports gathered by different national and international agencies, which are now open for examination, narrate the other story which is totally different to that propagated by the Government. The role played by Col. Habibur Rehman has also been analysed in the light of new facts. When all the facts are cumulatively put together, the truth starts emerging. Likewise, **the betrayal of Shah Nawaz Khan has many other faces which now disclose that the mystery of Netaji was not treated in the natural way but was twisted to serve the vested interests of certain politicians.**

We have considered with an open mind some psychological and behavioral aspects to understand the story from all other possible angles. For example, Netaji had left the country with a definite purpose—to accelerate the pace of freedom struggle. A

'Second Front' was in his mind and it has never been taken seriously by the politicians and historians till now and, therefore, this part of the book is perhaps the most original, enlightening, and is presented to the readers for the first time in its right perspective.

The mystery related to Netaji's disappearance was almost dead but it was revived in the last decade of the last century **as a denied and disputed letter written by Netaji was discovered in a Russian archive**. Not only this letter but many other such documents were dug out from the archives of the Russian Federation, United Kingdom and National Archives of India, which provided new clues to decipher the mystery. The circumstances and developments which resulted in the formation of the JMCI are described in the book, with details of other related backgrounds. Though the Government has rejected the findings of the JMCI without assigning any reason for it, there are many new points which require new approach for tackling the issue afresh and in a different manner, and which may be difficult to digest. Among these there are many personal memoirs of Lt. Manwati Arya about Netaji, the most unusual patriot of our motherland.

From the core of my heart I express my high regards to my friend and advisor Dr. Shiv Kumar Dixit, my respected elder Dr. P.N. Pandey, Shri Deepk Malviya of the Servants of the People Society (SOPS), Shri Vijay Swarup Gupta, a senior colleague in trade union and theater, Shri O.S. Shukla, DGM, DSCL, and late Shri Prakash Gupta, Advocate, for their encouragement and motivation. I am definitely lucky to secure moral support from respected Shri Vishnu Tripathi, veteran journalist, Shri Saket

Gupta, Advocate, Shri Kuldeep Saxena, Editor, 'Vivek-Shakti', theosophist Shri Virendra Agnihotri, Shri Naushad Alam Mansoori (SOPS), Shri G.K. Bajpai, Officer, Central Bank, Smt. Divya Arya and Shri Dinesh Arya, Officer, Punjab National Bank. The tiresome job of reading the parts of handwritten and untyped manuscript and advising valuable amendments at the initial stage was volunteered by honourable ex-Principal Shri Ram Krishna Tailang, a reputed historian, respected Shri Niranjan Bharti (SOPS), ex-Government Official, Shri Prem Ratna Gupta, ex-Officer, SBI, Shri Vivek Bajpai, Senior Executive, SBI, Vijay Mishra, journalist and satirist, and my affectionate nephew Satyam Bajpai. Regarding books and other material I am grateful to Shri Surendra Nath Chitranshi, Assistant Editor, 'Subhas Prabha', Sardar Harminder Singh, Shri Yogesh Srivastava, poet and critic, and my vigorous friend Shri Manoj Kapoor. To get access and support on the internet and computer I have been obliged according to my convenience by Shri Purnendu Sahai, Secretary, 'Puratatva Mitra', and Kamlesh Bajpai, a professional in Graphic Arts and my beloved grandsons Masters Manan and Chandan.

And last but not the least, I could venture this great project on the great patriot only due to the kind consideration of my name by Shri A.J. Sehgal, Lotus Press, Delhi, on the affectionate recommendation of respected Lt. Manwati Arya whose blessings are my real wealth.

19, *State Bank Colony*
Barra-3
Kanpur-208027 **—Ram Kishor Bajpai**
September 19, 2009

CONTENTS

THE OTHER SIDE OF THE STORY

1

The Air-crash: A Black Lie

The most provocative if not the most important incident was Radio Tokyo broadcast on August 23, 1945, when a great and perennial mystery took its birth. The broadcast declared: *"Mr. Subhas Chandra Bose died in a Japanese hospital from injuries received in an air crash. Mr. Bose, the Head of the Provisional Government of Azad Hind, left Singapore on August 16, 1945 by air for Tokyo for talks with the Japanese Government. He was seriously injured when his plane crashed at Taihoku airfield at 14.00 hours on August 18. He was given treatment in a hospital in Japan where he died at midnight. Lt. General Tsunamasa Shidei was instantly killed and Colonel Habibur Rehman, Bose's adjutant, and four others were injured in the crash."*

The Government of Japan and its Imperial Headquarters of Army in Tokyo did not issue any official announcement relating to the death of Netaji Subhas Chandra Bose and Lt. General Tsunamasa Shidei. Assuming that their silence in the case of Netaji might have been a diplomatic consideration, hiding the news of the death of

Lt. General Shidei, who was a very senior army commander and was recently deputed as Deputy Chief of Staff of Quantung Army, was creating a doubt-situation.

Now it is an open fact that the mystery-pregnant news was drafted on August 21, 1945 by S.A. Ayer, who was the Publicity and Propaganda Minister of the Provisional Government of Free India, and the head of the Azad Hind Rashtriya Bank. Ayer was a journalist by profession. He was posted as special correspondent in Bangkok with the Reuters News Agency before joining the INA in 1942. After his arrival in Tokyo from Saigon with the Japanese Colonel Tada, he was asked to write this news draft. Ayer had been with Netaji only upto Saigon on August 17, 1945. He had not been in Taipei, the Formosan city where the alleged air accident took place. He prepared the news at the behest of the Japanese authorities. This news was relayed verbatim by international newspapers via Domei News Agency. Ayer was neither an eye witness nor was he having any reliable source to counter-check such an incident, but he had drafted the news as he could make it from the Japanese officials' information.

It had also been consternating that the authorities in Taipei, where the so-called air crash was said to have taken place, issued no statement for about a week before the local intelligence department circulated a press-release on August 25, 1945. On the basis of this news-release, this particular news was published in *Taiwan Shin Pao*, the only daily newspaper in those days published from Taipei. At the time of the visit of the Mukherjee Commission to Taipei, no such record was available. This new item was almost similar as drafted by Ayer. Its wording was as under:

"The Chief of Independence Movement of Free India, Netaji Subhas Chandra Bose, desirous of a discussion with the Japanese authorities took a plane from Shonan (Japanese name for Singapore)

en-route Tokyo on August 16. The plane crashed in the vicinity of Taihoku, Taipei airport, at 2 o'clock in the afternoon on August 18. Mr. Bose sustained severe injuries and was sent to the local hospital for treatment. He died at 0 (zero) or 24th hour—the junction of August 18 and 19. On the same plane, there were Col. Habibur Rehman, a senior aide, also badly burnt, Lt. General Shidei, a Japanese military officer, who died on the spot and four other officials who were either severely or slightly injured."

The news of Netaji's death delivered a blow to everyone who heard or read it. Admirers of Netaji were deeply shocked as to them he was a symbol of the revolutionary stream of life and his critics were jolted as to them he was not merely a great freedom-fighter but really a Karmayogi, a man with perfect action. It was Saturday on August 25, 1945, when a reputed Indian newspaper of Congress leanings *The Hindustan Times*—highlighted its news item *Reported Death of Subhas Bose* — by quoting its source to Japan's Domei News Agency via its London reporter as under:

"The Japanese news agency on Thursday announced the death of Mr. Subhas Chandra Bose in a Japanese hospital from injuries received in an air crash, says a London report. The Japanese news said, 'Mr. Bose, the head of the Provisional Government of Azad Hind, left Singapore on August 16 by air for Tokyo for talks with Japanese Government. He was seriously injured when his plane crashed at Taihoku airfield at 14.00 hours on August 18. He was given treatment in a hospital in Japan, where he died at midnight.'"

Understanding well the impact and implications of this news *The Hindustan Times* also added that the death of Mr. Subhas Chandra Bose reported by the Japanese, if true, relieved the British authorities of a difficult problem, but undoubtedly caused a great pain in the hearts of millions of Indians, as written by Preston Grover, the Associated Press of America's staff correspondent. At the same time many Indians questioned whether the Japanese cooperated by giving him an opportunity to go underground and escape punishment for opposing the Allied Forces.

Another renowned south Indian newspaper *The Hindu* adopted an indirect approach while publishing this news. It gave the heading *London Indians Skeptical* — and based its news on the reports of evening newspapers of London. Covering the death story of Netaji it wrote that *"The death of Subhas Chandra Bose was a front page news in the early editions of all the three London evening newspapers today. With its top column report of the accident the 'Evening Standard' published a photograph of Mr. Bose and 'Evening Star' recalled the chief incidents in Mr. Bose's stormy career. The news was received with surprise and a certain amount of skepticism in the Indian quarters in London. Mr. V.K. Krishna Menon, secretary of India League, said, 'We cannot comment on his death.'"*

'Bose Dead, Story Not Believed in London' was the heading of a separate news-item published in '*The Hindustan Times*'. It pointed out that such reports were also released by the Japanese about two years ago when Netaji had disappeared from Germany. But he reappeared in Tokyo to perform his life's most effective role. Supporting the logic of the news it said that *"Opinion expressed is that the Japanese reports savour too much of imitation, that the timing is too good to be entirely fortuitous and that Subhas is probably seeking an easy way out with intentions of not returning to India."* The news quoted several renowned Indians residing in London that they were awaiting proof to know the truth about the story of the plane crash.

Netaji's elder brother and freedom-fighter Sarat Chandra Bose was confined in Coonoor jail when the plane crash news stormed through the newspapers in India. After reading it he was shocked and his immediate comment was that *"today's 'Indian Express' and*

'The Hindu' brought the heart-rending news of Subhas' death as a result of an aeroplane crash. Divine Mother! How many sacrifices have we to offer at your altar!"

Gandhiji's immediate reaction was recorded as *'Subhas Bose has died well, he was undoubtedly a patriot though misguided.'* The second most popular leader of India, Jawaharlal Nehru, expressed his sentiments as: *"I always had great regard for him in spite of our mutual differences. I earnestly pray that the departed soul may rest in peace."* But the founder of the Benaras Hindu University and one of the most respected freedom-fighter Pandit Madan Mohan Malviya did not believe in the news of his death in the plane-crash story. He was bold enough to advise the family members of Netaji *"not to perform the Sraddh ceremony, but hold mild prayers."* Gandhiji now amended his first statement a little and supported Malviyaji's advice when he was asked again to react.

After assessing the increasing popularity graph of INA's image and its contribution to India's liberation struggle amongst the people all over the country, Jawaharlal Nehru, like Gandhiji, also amended his previous stand. While briefing the press on September 11, 1945 Nehru said, *"I have received a number of reports which have put me in great doubt and I disbelieve the authenticity of the news."*

It was the time when in India hectic preparations were being undertaken for the success of the general session of the All India Congress Committee (AICC) scheduled to take place on September 21, 1945 under the presidentship of Maulana Abul Kalam Azad, who conveyed his firm reaction on the news of Netaji's death by declining to include his name in the list of those for whom obituary tributes were to be paid in the session of the AICC. With full confidence Azad said: *"The circumstances in which the news has reached us and the sources responsible for its announcement don't make it certain that Netaji is in fact dead. His name, therefore, should not appear in the obituary list of those who died since the last session of AICC"* which was held before the Quit India Movement of 1942.

In support of Netaji's death in plane-crash the United Press of America had released a graphic account of his death based on the interviews of those Japanese who had survived in the plane-crash accident. As the authentic story about the death of Subhas Chandra Bose a report was circulated on November 23, 1945 by the Chinese Central News Agency. This report was based mainly on the narration given by Miss Chen Pee Sha, a Formosan nurse who claimed that the body of Netaji was immediately cremated after his death. Like this report, another sensational news came from Hongkong that the plane in which Netaji was travelling and which was alleged to have been crashed at Taipei airfield, was seen in Hongkong on the very next day of the reported accident.

There was confusion and Netaji's death story was being rejected by many, and leaders like Gandhiji, who was making his sharp reactions against such death-supporting news items and views. Adamantly, he said on December 30, 1945: *"If someone shows me the ashes even then I will not believe that Subhas is not alive."* He again repeated the same version in different words on January 2, 1946 and said, *"I believe Subhas is still alive and bidding his time somewhere."* He wrote in *'Harijan'* on February 3, 1946: *"The hypnotism of the INA has cast a spell on us. Netaji's name is one to conjure with. His patriotism is second to none. His bravery shines through all his actions."* He emphasized his belief that *"Subhas is not dead. He cannot die that way."*

The INA personnel and associates of Netaji had a deep understanding that their strutted and fretted leader had disappeared and their job now was to maintain the valiant tempo of the INA's freedom struggle till the reappearance of Netaji. These sentiments and emotions had been witnessed by Lt. Manwati Arya in a very peculiar happening at a meeting of Indians in Rangoon on November 25, 1945. She was present in that meeting of the members of Indian Independence League and ex-INA personnel where almost everyone had taken for granted that Netaji had disappeared with a definite plan. Every speaker in the meeting was endorsing the feelings of the audience. The most peculiar point in the meeting was that the central chair on the dias was kept vacant considering as if the spirit of Netaji was occupying it. Every speaker coming over to the dias was registering his formal and warm salutations to that vacant chair with full dignity and awareness as if Netaji was himself present on that vacant chair.

This and many more such happenings and statements created a rippling effect in India and abroad of doubt regarding the reality of the news of the death of Netaji. Presiding over such a boisterous meeting, in Singapore on January 23, 1946, which was the 49th birthday of Netaji, K.P.K. Menon imitated Netaji and shouted the famous slogan *'Chalo Delhi'* and declared with full confidence that Netaji was hiding and would *"come to India as the first president of a free country."* A renowned barrister of Calicut in South India settled in Malaya since 1927, Menon had opened a branch of Annie Bseant's Home Rule League in Rangoon. Menon also firmly informed the audience that *"the British are making frantic efforts but they will not find Netaji."* The self motivated Menon also said that *"Netaji is alive, our great leader Mahatma Gandhi confirms this belief of ours."*

Like K.P.K. Menon, almost everyone in those days had been mentally attuned to convince himself and others to take the side of Netaji and INA. Gandhiji himself was repeating the same sentiments as and when he had to face such questions. After his meeting with the stalwarts of the INA's leadership, Shah

Nawaz Khan and P.K. Sehgal, Gandhiji expressed his inflexible views that *"I still believe in my heart of hearts that Netaji Subhas Chandra Bose is still alive."* He became emphatic on March 30, 1946 when he said, *"There is strong evidence to counteract the feeling that Subhas was dead."*

The views of Gandhiji and others were being taken seriously by intelligence agencies. The Indian Intelligence Bureau was incited and it expressed its motive on February 19, 1946 that *"Our pressing anxiety is to get the truth whether Bose is actually and permanently dead. Government wants to know where they stand over the matter in view of the claims by Gandhi and others in India that he is still alive."* Exactly similar considerations were going on at the office of the British intelligence. It raised its doubt in its report dated March 1, 1946 and observed that *"if the plane-crash is a deception plan it is one which has been extremely carefully and ingeniously organised."*

By this time the elder brother of Netaji, Sarat Chandra Bose, became certain that the plane-crash story was not to be believed. His understanding was not due to emotional and fraternal reasons but to him it was a matter of objective rationalism because available proofs were telling their own story. With certainty he hinted before the news agency United Press, on July 22, 1946, that he was led to believe that Netaji Subhas Chandra Bose was alive. He further expressed that the story of the plane-crash connected with Netaji's death was a myth.

The comments raising doubts on plane-crash story were acclaimed by the INA personnel and followers as a logical conclusion but these statements provoked the resentment of those who were aware of the political impact and implications of such doubt to confuse the public at large. It was the main reason why in October

1946 Jawaharlal Nehru had burst out and angrily conveyed his dismay in clear words that *"I don't think there is slightest justification for the belief that Shri Subhas Chandra Bose is alive."* Mentioning the rationale of his understanding he said, *"For some months after the news of his death, I was rather doubtful of its veracity. Later when Colonel Habibur Rehman gave me a detailed eye witness account of the accident which resulted in death, I became convinced of it. No piece of news has come to me since then, or has appeared in the press that has shaken that conviction."*

Nehru's statement was quoted in the Indian Council of States by Ahmad Jaffar who raised a question on October 31, 1946. He asked if the interim Government of India had any evidence whether Bose was dead or alive. The question was simple and direct but it became mysterious when a responsible person like Vallabhbhai Patel, the then Home Minister, cryptically replied in one word, *'No'*. Another member Sardar Mangal Singh thought it better to seek a second clarification from the then interim Government of India and questioned if the Government made any enquiry whether Netaji was dead or alive. This time again Patel replied in the negative but added one sentence that *"Government are not in a position to make any authoritative statement on the subject."* It was such a reply which denied the negativity of 'No' and further confirmed that Nehru's statement was his own comment. But Sardar Mangal Singh wanted to be specific, so he again raised the question for the third time on November 6, 1946, and he sought the clarification from the Government with reference to the statement of its Prime Minister. Very quickly on the next day the reply was given and it repeated that *"Government are not in a position to make an authoritative statement on the question."* It made clear that the Government of India was indifferent and it was doing nothing to resolve the mystery.

Right from August 23, 1945, when the news of Netaji's alleged death was broadcasted from Radio Tokyo, the news had been either endorsed or denied in such a manner that the people had no option but to accept it as a mystery which was becoming deeper and deeper on every passing day. Regarding the incidence of plane-crash at Taihoku on August 18, 1945, several enquiries had been conducted by different governments' intelligence agencies. But their conclusions had not been flawless. It created pressure on the Government of India to investigate the matter on its own but Nehru had been opposing because it involved some very difficult knots which would get knottier only in the future. **He was also very touchy because he was quite close to realising his dream and he did not want either to wait or to shatter it for an uncertain furute. Netaji was definitely his rival who was sharing the same dream but with a difference. Therefore, Nehru avoided any investigation on this matter for a sufficiently long time.** There had been some other very definite reasons which he never wanted to be discussed in public and it also resulted in his reluctance to appoint or conduct a sincere enquiry.

Inspite of these facts and circumstances, there had been some common points in the story of Netaji—either it was concerned from the point of view of accident or from the disappearance angle. About one week before Netaji's alleged plane-crash, he was present at Seremban near Singapore in the office of the Provisional Government of Free India (PGFI), popularly known as PGI, which was situated on Thomson Road in a very spacious bungalow. It was also a common point from all sides of this story that he formulated his strategy and prepared himself to face the recent situation after two atom bombs which were dropped on two Japanese cities, Hiroshima and Nagasaki, on the 6th and 9th August, 1945. The worst of the worse happened when the Soviet Union declared war against Japan on August 9, 1945.

Netaji was well aware of the Japanese compulsions and was in constant touch with higher rungs of the Japanese authorities. In this connection the Japanese ambassador in Thailand, Tsubogami, sent a letter to Netaji through a special envoy, Tadamoto Negishi. The contents of the letter contained a message-cum-information and also an advice that the Japanese Government had finally accepted the Postdam Declaration, issued on August 12, 1945, in a summit meeting of the Allied Powers in the presence of Winston Churchill, Joseph Stalin and Truman. The Japanese convinced the Allied Forces that their Emperor's position will have to be kept intact as it was, and they would surrender and accept all the conditions. Tsubogami informed in the letter that *"the Emperor will issue an order for the people of Japan to surrender"* and the orders of the Emperor not be disobeyed by anyone. Therefore, Netaji was advised to pull himself out before the issuance of final orders for the surrender of the Japan.

The pace of events was now very fast. Netaji was convinced that in these circumstances the question of further fighting had lost its relevance, and he was also sure that at this juncture it would be impossible for his Subhas Brigade to continue guerrilla warfare in furtherance of his plan to free India. And, more so, because guerrilla warfare would require a separate planning and point to point strategy for its successful execution. Now he was required to wait for some time to reconsolidate his forces for any action against the British forces.

Under such adverse circumstances in his preoccupied mind, Netaji was calculating the evacuation plan for his Rani Jhansi Brigade. This brigade was one of the most ambitious and pioneer adventure in the military history of the world, where a complete regiment was organised and controlled by women themselves. This experiment had begun just about two years before, i.e., on October 10, 1943, and it had proved very positive, with encouraging results. Netaji was, therefore, very emotional for the safe and successful evacuation of this brigade from Singapore before the arrival of the British army. After issuing his guidelines to carry out safe deportation of all the girls and women of the Rani Jhansi Brigade in Singapore, he entrusted the job to Captain (Miss) Janaki Thevar, the second person to command the Rani Jhansi Regiment in Rangoon.

On August 14, 1945 Netaji was formally intimated by his Japanese counterparts that the declaration of surrender could be pronounced on the next day. As the situation was changing rapidly, so he decided to consult and seek the opinion of his associates available at that time in Singapore an emergency meeting was convened. It was attended by Colonel Habibur Rehman, S.A. Ayer, Major General S.C. Alagappan, Major General Mohammed Zaman Kiani, A.N. Sarcar and G.R. Nagar. Current developments were narrated by Netaji himself. The meeting was informed that Japan had agreed to surrender and the process could begin shortly. Describing the consequences and complications of the Japanese surrender, he expressed his willingness for the INA's surrender before the Allied Forces in Singapore if his colleagues would agree about it. After a brief discussion, it was unanimously decided that Netaji should escape his arrest to avoid the Allies' vindictive action. Netaji rejected this advice and said that the worst they would do was to put him against the wall and shoot him, and he was prepared for it. He emphasized that the sacrifices made by the INA and the civilians would not go in vain. But he was persuaded that no useful purpose would be served by his surrender as their ultimate aim was a free India. The freedom struggle had to continue and, therefore, his leadership role was also essential. So he must not surrender in any case. The meeting also felt that the question of the INA's surrender would be finalised in consultation with the Japanese authorities.

As per the decisions taken in the meeting, the local Japanese army commander was consulted, but he said that he was nobody to say anything and opined that Netaji should take up this matter at his own level with appropriate Japanese authorities. Netaji agreed to this suggestion and decided first to visit Bangkok where Hachiya Teruo, the Japanese minister designate to the PGI, and Lt. General Saburo Isoda, the Chief of Hikari Kikan, the Japanese military organisation liasioning with the PGI, were present. In Bangkok he would consult his other Japanese associates, who were actually co-travellers in his struggle, and then he would go to Tokyo. Thus Netaji asked his INA colleagues to proceed to Bangkok.

Netaji and other officials of the INA were desirous for a separate surrender of the INA in Singapore, so they had to come back to Singapore, and therefore, they were required to carry a small luggage and some basic documents concerning the INA's strength at various points in South-East Asia. After reaching Bangkok along with S.A. Ayer and Col. Habibur Rehman, Netaji met his INA Chief of Staff Major General J.K. Bhonsle and proceeded to contact Hachiya, Isoda and his deputy, Kagawa. They held a conference and discussed the INA and the Japanese plans of surrender. Hachiya, who spoke English, informed Netaji that there was no definite information about the surrender-plan and they were not appropriate authorities to take any final decision. He expressed his wish that he too was very anxious to know the details. Hachiya proposed that all of them should proceed to Saigon to meet Field Marshal Count Terauchi

Hisaichi, who was a close relative of Japan's Emperor and who was expected to possess detailed information.

Considering the call of time two planes were immediately engaged. Netaji, Habibur Rehman, Pritam Singh, S.A. Ayer and the Japanese interpreter Negishi left in one plane and Hachiya, Isoda, Gulzara Singh, Debnath Das and Abid Hasan travelled in another. At Saigon it was found that the local situation was so tense that it was not conducive to undertake further journey to Dalat, which was about ten kilometers away from Saigon and where Terauchi's headquarters were stationed. They decided that only Hachiya and Isoda would go to Dalat and Netaji with all his associates would wait in Saigon at the house of Narain Das who was representing the Indian Independence League, the parent body of Indian organisations in East Asia.

Hachiya and Isoda came back very soon from Dalat. They conveyed the gist of their discussions to Netaji that due to failure of wireless links, Terauchi could have no contact with Tokyo and therefore he too was helpless to offer any advice, particularly on the question of the INA's separate surrender. They also conveyed the advice of Colonel Yano Muraji, the Chief of India Section that this matter had to be discussed directly with the Government of Japan in Tokyo.

Upto this point of the story there was almost nothing to dispute. The doubts about the plane-crash began onwards. The most widely circulated story was that Netaji was advised by the Japanese authorities that he alone should leave Saigon immediately by the bomber plane which was coming from Manila and going to Daren in Manchuria via Tokyo and which was almost packed with passengers and luggage. In the beginning Netaji was unwilling to accept this advice, but when the delicacy of the deteriorating situation was explained to him, he consulted his colleagues. He told them that a bomber plane was ready to take off immediately and the Japanese were ready to spare one seat for him, so he had to go alone. His associates advised him to bargain with the Japanese and to exercise his pressure so that he would not have to travel alone. Netaji discussed the matter with the Japanese and one more seat was spared. He asked Habibur Rehman, *"Aap chalengey?"* and further desired that S.A. Ayer and Gulzara Singh should accompany him to the airport with their luggage, and in case of more vacancies, they would also be accommodated to travel with him.

They left immediately for the aerodrome where they found a plane almost ready to take off. A senior Japanese commander and expert on Soviet Union affairs, Lt. General Tsunamasa Shidei, who had been deputed as Deputy Chief of Staff, Quantung Army, came from inside the plane to welcome Netaji. In a hurried manner the luggage was loaded. Netaji, who was in his khaki shirt, trousers, INA cap and badges, spoke to S.A. Ayer and Gulzara Singh, *"Well, Jai Hind, I will meet you later,"* while entering the plane followed by Habibur Rehman. The other co-travellers in the plane included the Pilot Warrant Officer Aoyagi, Associate Pilot Major Takizawa, Lt. Colonel Tadeo Sakai, Lt. Colonel Shiro Nonogaki, Major Taro Kono, Major Ihato Takahachi, Arai, one engineer and two radio operating officers.

The plane reached Tourane, on the south of Vietnamese coast, at about 7 p.m. Netaji and other officers rested there in a hotel in the town. In the morning of August 18, 1945 the plane took off after unloading some military equipments including arms and ammunition to reduce the load of the plane. It had to skip its scheduled landing at Heito due to a radio message that the Russians were advancing rapidly. The plane landed at 2 p.m. at Matsuyama aerodrome in Taihoku where the spectacular mountains — Szshou, Mu-zhy and Bi-jra stood beside the beautiful river Keelung. At the aerodrome the scene looked devastated as nothing was usual due to recent bombings. At 2.30 p.m. the plane was again ready to take off as its refueling was over and Major Kono's doubts for starboard engine behaving oddly, were twice checked by Major Takizawa to ensure that nothing was wrong.

Minutes after its take off the plane crashed and a perennial mystery took its birth.

—o—

2

Doubts in Documents

"I wonder if the Japanese announcement of Subhas Chandra Bose's death in an air-crash is true. I suspect it very much, it is just what should be given out if he meant to go underground." These words were the spontaneous reaction of the Indian Viceroy Archibald Wavell on August 23, 1945, after listening to Radio Tokyo broadcast about the death of Netaji Subhas Chandra Bose. Wavell recorded his sentiments in his diary. He asked his House Member Robert Francis Mudie to take up the matter and prepare a detailed note as to what steps had to be taken to initiate the trial of Netaji and his INA associates.

Mudie took the Viceroy's instructions seriously and did his home work, especially considering those angles which would entangle Netaji and his colleagues to bring them to a trial. But it was his disappointment as he could not get anything illegal as such even after extending the definition of war criminal. Mudie was also worrisome that Netaji's popularity and performance were at a very high climax and, therefore, any action against him including even his detention would arouse people's feelings which might turn into violent demonstrations against the British Government and its officials.

In his note to the Viceroy, Mudie mentioned with rationales that if a trial would be initiated against Netaji the consequences would be worrying for the British. He expressed quite emphatically that contrary to the British propaganda and according to the disclosures made by the INA personnel in particular and Indians in general to the British interrogators and intelligence agents, Netaji was not regarded as a puppet of the Japanese Government. It was the general perception that Netaji was maintaining his relations and dealings with the Japanese on equal terms. He was being firmly acknowledged as an intelligent and independent-minded person. His straightforwardness and his clean image had been acclaimed by both his friends and foes.

Mudie commented in his note that Netaji's personality had become more glamourous since his second term success in the election of the President of Indian National Congress in 1939 inspite of the open opposition of Gandhiji. His resignation from the post of Congress President in April 1939, his escape from Kolkata in 1941, his broadcasts from Radio Berlin and Tokyo between 1941 and 1945, and his leadership of the INA and such other equally great landmarks had given boost to his increasing popularity. Thus, Mudie suggested that any action against Netaji was not advisable either legally or politically.

He also considered whether a summary trial to hang Netaji was feasible. In his consideration Mudie submitted his firm opinion that such summary trials were not feasible in India in current circumstances. He stated in his note that the Burmese Government was holding the same opinion and was not prepared to undertake any harsh measure to implicate Netaji in order to punish him. The situation in Singapore for this purpose was equally alarming because Netaji was regarded as an icon in the whole of East Asia and any sort of action against him was bound to create enormous problems.

Actually Mudie's note was a detailed study for the British Government to assess that a penal action against Netaji had to be initiated or not. The British authorities were keenly willing to inflict a deterring punishment on Netaji. In this connection, detailing his suggestions, Mudie further submitted in his note that even a quick military execution was not a solution at this juncture. It would be very difficult to defend such military action because such execution might create a wrong impression amongst the army soldiers and more particularly on British Indian soldiers who might take it as a feigner on the part of the British to avoid the issue of Indian independence.

To this point Mudie submitted his views with an impression as if in his belief Netaji did not die in the plane-crash. What he advised in the conclusion of his note was very surprising as it hinted a clear indication about the whereabouts of Netaji. Like his boss Viceroy Wavell, he was not at all doubtful about the plane-crash story but was sure that Netaji was alive and might be in custody somewhere in Russia. Mudie suggested that *"in many ways the easiest course would be to leave him where he is and not ask for his release.* ***He might, of course, in certain circumstances be welcomed by the Russians.*** *This course could raise fewest immediate political difficulties, but the security authorities consider that in certain circumstances his presence in Russia would be so dangerous as to rule it out altogether is not possible."*

By March 1946 the British view was firm and certain that Netaji was hiding somewhere in Russia

The view of Mudie was not accepted by the then British Government of India. The Commander-in-Chief Claude Auchinleck ordered to set up a special section at his military headquarters. He desired the trial of the INA personnel and this special section was assigned the job to initiate and prepare details for the trials. Auchinleck was more anxious to maintain discipline in the army and in his decision a deterrent punishment was justified for those soldiers who joined the INA and fought against the British army. Understanding unfavourable public opinion on the action of Auchinleck, the Joint Secretary of War Department, Mason, clarified that the patriotic motive of the INA personnel would be taken at its face value and its members would be treated as prisoners of war.

Very soon there were demonstrations, strikes and violent agitations all over the country and the British could realise that their action was not only against the pubic opinion but it was also provocative for its army personnel. Indian leaders including Gandhiji and Jawaharlal Nehru, who had always been uncomfortable with Netaji, had changed their minds and quickly jumped on the INA bandwagon. Gandhiji began to praise Netaji as a *Prince among Patriots.* Nehru said, *"Netaji Subhas had set an example of courage and passionate devotion to the cause of Indian freedom, which will live long in Indian history."* Nehru decided to put on his old lawyer's robe and committed to plead in favour of the INA. Even Muslim League leader Mohd. Ali Jinnah requested the British Government to treat the INA personnel leniently.

In this changed scenario of the country Field Marshal Auchinleck was compelled to amend his previous stand and declared that no more INA personnel would be tried on the major charge of waging war against the King of England. He also explained that only those who committed *'acts of gross brutality'* would be brought before the courts. Auchinleck was actually issuing statements to save his face. He was ready to take an about-turn stand when he said that the number of cases against the INA personnel would go only between 20 to 50.

In these circumstances the British Indian Government could not dare to declare in definite words regarding the death or disappearance of Netaji. There was no public statement but the Government was very cautious and careful in collecting the informations related to Netaji. Their intelligence units and secret services were engaged knowing the latest on the matter. The intelligence reports were very clearly hinting that Netaji had crossed over to the Russian territory and now they firmly believed that he did not die on August 18, 1945 in the plane accident.

Immediately after the World War II two teams of intelligence were engaged to probe into the death story of Netaji. The first team was headed by Intelligence Bureau Director P.E.S. Finney. In this team a top ranking Indian Police Officer Rai Bahadur Bakshi Badrinath had joined. But Bakshi Badrinath was called back and was deputed to investigate the Royal Indian Navy mutiny, which was an after effect in sympathy with the INA personnel as one of its most important reason. The team also included W.F.W. Davis, Kalipada Dey and A.K. Roy. Another five-member team was constituted from Intelligence Assault Unit of the 7th Independent Division of Allied Land Forces, Siam.

The first team was disappointed when they visited Bangkok and Seremban near Singapore where all the documents had been burnt. The team was informed by the German Embassy in Bangkok that they had burnt their archives including all documents related to Netaji.

In their extensive search the Intelligence Assault Unit in Bangkok could trace out a file containing three classified telegrams exchanged between Field Marshal Count Terauchi Hisaichi of Southern Army Command in Saigon and Lt. General Saburo Isoda, Chief of Hikari Kikan, the military organisation responsible for liaisoning with the INA. The file was related to *'T'* which was a code name given to Netaji.

The first telegram contained a short message that, *"Today at 17.00 hrs.. (August 17, 1945) 'T' with Lt. General Shidei and others left here for Tokyo via Formosa and Diren. Inform Indian communities of this."*

'Top Secret' marked the second telegram which was dated August 20, 1945 and it read, *"'T' while on his way to the capital, as a result of an accident to his aircraft at Taihoku at 14.00 hrs. on the 18th , was seriously injured and died at midnight on the same date. His body has been flown to Tokyo by the Formosan Army. I have thanked the Formosan Army for their kindness. Further I have asked the proof of his death in the plane accident — remains, photographs etc. be collected. As for the centre (Tokyo), I am getting Staff Officer Col. Tada who leaves Saigon on the 20th to take up an appointment maintained in handling the matter."*

The third telegram was sent after the announcement of the news of the death on Radio Tokyo and it was dated August 24, 1945. There was an instruction to Hikari Kikan to inform all Indians about the death of Netaji. It read, *"Please ensure that Indian communities are informed of the Domei despatch regarding 'T's' death."*

All these three telegrams in one file were deliberately left out after burning all other documents only to create confusion and to support the death story of Netaji. There was no doubt that the above noted file was left out to deceive the Allies and it was definitely a part of the plan of Netaji's escape.

When the Intelligence Bureau sleuths reached in Saigon in early October, 1945, they found that all the records including the arrival and departure registers related to aircrafts had been completely destroyed. The team could only get a simple misleading statement from the Japanese Air Force Staff Captain Yoshida that for the journey of Netaji *"the aircraft used was a K-21 heavy Bomber (Sally) and the final destination was Tokyo."*

The Intelligence Bureau team could get success in rounding up Major E. Bhaskaran Menon who was a very close associate of Netaji. Major Bhaskaran never believed in the plane-crash story and when specially questioned by the Intelligence Bureau team, he said, *"...before leaving for the aerodrome in Bangkok Netaji called the members of his personal staff and gave them presents in a very emotional manner and the four iron boxes containing gold ornaments brought from Rangoon were taken along with him when he left after bidding them good-bye."*

The statement of Major Bhaskaran contained several *'whys'* in it. Why Netaji became emotional and why the presents were given to his personal staff? But the most consternating *'why'* was that if he was going to thank the Japanese Government for the help rendered to him and to work out the surrender plan of the INA then what was the purpose of those four ornament-full iron boxes which contained about 50 pounds of gold ornaments.

On October 5, 1945 the Intelligence Bureau and the Intelligence Assault Unit submitted their reports which were prepared by Philip Finney. It stated: *"The general opinion among the Indians here (in Bangkok) is that Bose is not dead but has probably managed to evade Japanese control and has made his way to some place occupied by the Russians."*

In 1997 when Netaji's centenary was being celebrated along with the 50th anniversary of Indian independence, John Major, the then Prime Minister of United Kingdom, was approached with a request to permit to scrutinise the files and documents related to Netaji. These papers were preserved in the Indian Records Office. Such queries in India remained either unanswered or a dilly-dallying reply was given, but unlike Indian Government, the British reply said specifically that because of diplomatic sensitivity some files will not be declassified for at least another 50 years. In the British reply one sentence was very important from the point of view of Netaji's disappearance. It read: *"There is a fear that releasing this information will effect friendly relations with other countries. Subhas' relationship with the Axis Powers after the war was a huge issue."* Now that important sentence came and it said: *"Nehru, Indian and British governments just did not know how to handle him."* Here the open mention of the name of Nehru had disclosed many things. Dragging the name of Nehru by the British was really a strong support to Netaji's diehard followers.

The head of the Rani Jhansi Regiment, Lakshmi Sehgal, during her cross-examination before Mukherjee Commission said that American intelligent sleuths had *"followed a man whose description matched with that of Netaji up to the Russian border."* This and such other statements reflected two impressions — one, that Netaji had not met with death in the so-called plane-crash accident, and two, that there were other nations and their governments who were keenly observing the activities of Netaji for one or the other reason. As a matter of fact, Netaji was an international personality and his efforts for the freedom of India were very wide as he was challenging a world power and a mighty army and that too from a foreign land. Netaji was also aware about the role of some nations including United States in the field of international affairs.

After analysing some declassified files and their documents possessed by the United States, the scholars found that the American Strategic Service Office was following the activities of Netaji since his escape from Kolkata in 1941 . The United States was a powerful partner of Allied Powers and her war against Japan was direct to the extent that it was the American army which had first touched the Japanese soil under the leadersip of General MacArthur. They were also the first to reach Taipei where the so-called plane-crash accident was said to have taken place. The advantage of this pioneer action was such that the Americans could gather the first-hand information about Netaji.

The American military wing, the Counter Intelligence Corps, popularly known as CIC, headed by Colonel Figges, interrogated several INA personnel including Habibur Rehman, the only Indian to accompany Netaji in his so-called last journey. The gist of American inquiry regarding Netaji was that the plane-crash story was untrue. According to the US version, the plane-crash theory could not be relied upon because there will be no documentary proof, no direct evidence and the Japanese statements were altogether misleading.

It had also come to our notice that America's most notorious Central Intelligence Agency, known as CIA, reported that Netaji was alive even in 1964. The CIA had also shared its reports in 1945-46 with the British intelligence agencies which said that Netaji was not only alive but he was planning his comeback to India. The exchange of information between the US and UK secret agencies on the subject of Netaji was not only an example of sharing information at intelligence level, but there was also a tradition that the Americans handed over the fugitives to its friendly countries without insisting on observing legal formalities. In 1945 Habibur Rehman and S.A. Ayer etc. were brought to India on a simple request of the British authorities. The system of American secret reports was to pass on the collected information to their ally's government only after a simple request made by the concerned government though they were providing the information to their allies after censoring it at their level. This system was so quick that the American Secretary of State and the corresponding authority of the ally's government were receiving the informations simultaneously.

—o—

3

Habibur Rehman's Dilemma: The Truth Behind his Oath

In his last authentic and undisputed long message to John A. Thivy on August 17, 1945 before undertaking his flight from Saigon to Tokyo or perhaps for an unknown destination the strong-willed and pugnacious Netaji wrote: *"I am writing to you on the eve of a long journey by air and who knows an accident may not overtake me."* Although these words did not clearly indicate that these were otherwise shrouded and contained a mystery or a prophesy, yet Netaji's associates and the INA's personnel very clearly read between the lines, that their unquestionable leader was not willing either to bend or to relax before his enemy. He had simply executed his secret plan which he was discussing with some of them for the last few days before this mysterious journey. They prepared themselves to understand that their beloved leader had left for a long distant place which was beyond East Asia and which was going to become unapproachable to them. Even for Allied Forces his place was farther and out of their speculation.

The INA people also believed that the story of the air accident was only to cover the safe passage for their great leader. The incident of air crash was believed but with doubts and presumptions, and it was also disbelieved but with demurs and assumptions. Netaji could thus overcome those who knew him and even more the others who opposed him. Now onwards this story of air crash was not an enigma or a private secret. It was also not limited to utterances or behaviour of some persons to suggest the problem involving inherent paradoxes or apparent contradictions. As time passed it became a perennial mystery. Its mysteriousness excited wonder and curiosity on the one hand and surprise and confusion on the other. Every effort to explain or to understand the plane-crash story of Netaji's death ended either with the feeling of hopefulness and positivity or terminated in the intermingling of defeat and exasperation.

The mysteriousness of the plane-crash story frustrated many because it had such puzzles in it which more often went beyond one's capacity to explain or discover the truth therein. It had been always against human nature to acknowledge something which was beyond understanding and, therefore, new and again new angles had come before us to interpret the story. The questioned plane-crash story was conundrum for some as its answers involved such problems which could only be solved in speculative thinking. This exercise exposed many because between death and disappearance of Netaji a riddle rested in the centre, which had been more serious a tragedy than merely a sincere effort to unveil the mystery.

Colonel Thakur Singh of the INA deposed before the Khosla Commission on March 3, 1971 that the INA's Major General A.C. Chatterjee had informed him that we wanted to accompany Netaji wherever he went, but we were told by the Japanese that it would not be possible to disguise a group of men except Netaji alone. He could only be dissembled and would be kept away from the enemy. When asked why only Habibur Rehman was accompanying Netaji, the Japanese said that he too would be left behind at the last stage.

But A.C. Chatterjee was right that if anyone else would also have joined Netaji, we could have perhaps got the true story.

It was an admitted fact that Habibur Rehman was the only Indian who went along with Netaji when he was last seen off. Contrary to his importance from the evidence point of view, Habibur Rehman was not believed as he did not provide a final conclusion. He rather gave birth to such questions which made the plane-crash story more ticklish and oversensitive. Even very intelligent persons and expert investigating agents could not get any leading clue or information out of Habibur Rehman's mouth.

One of the most distinguished among his INA fellows, Lt. Colonel Habibur Rehman belonged to a very aristocratic family. His father Raja Mansur Ahmed Khan was a dignified member of the British army. His own eagerness to join the army had a psychological impact on his father. His desire was fulfilled in 1936 when Habibur Rehman was very young, still in his teens. In 1942 he was participating enthusiastically in the war against Japan on the Burma front where he was made a prisoner of war by the Japanese Imperial Army. In his prison camp he was exhorted by Captain Mohan Singh and Major Iwaichi Fujiwara to join the first-INA organised by Mohan Singh to fight for the freedom of India. Habibur Rehman was quickly won over and was initiated to contribute his services for his motherland. He was assigned a job and deputed as the Commandant of Officers' Training School, INA.

After the arrival of Netaji in Japan the INA was reorganized and because of his talent and strong commitment to the struggle to achieve freedom of India Habibur Rehman was successful in winning the confidence of Netaji also. He got quick promotions and became Lt. Colonel. He could also get an opportunity to be deputed on a prestigeous position as Aide-de-Camp to Netaji. When Major General J.K. Bhonsle was supervising the INA forces in Malaya and Singapore, Habibur Rehman took over the charge of Chief of Staff in February 1945 and continued in this position till August 15, 1945, when he was asked to accompany Netaji.

Commenting on the character of Habibur Rehman, Shah Nawaz Khan said that he was cool, calm, solid as rock and a dedicated follower of Netaji and the most selfless worker for Indian independence. Khan also told the Khosla Commission that *"Rehman was so devoted to Netaji that he would not have hesitated even for one minute to sacrifice his life for him and any order or instruction given to him by Netaji, he would faithfully carry it out, even at the cost of his life."*

The air-crash incident provided us a bitter-sweet experience as Habibur Rehman remained the sole credible witness. His leanings and performances in the INA had been sincere and faithful and his loyalty towards Netaji was unflinchingly solid. Inspite of this glaring and positive background his statements on Netaji's death story were taken as maneuvered and misleading. Each sentence of Habibur Rehman was examined critically not because he was doubtful but because he was bent upon confirming the death of Netaji. His utterances irked many but he was never taken to task or challenged even by the INA people.

It was the general feeling that while not revealing the truth, Habibur Rehman was not self-motivated or selfish, **but he would have been an oath-bound person to maintain a secret**. Between the years, in 1945-46 he became a very important person and his importance was never misunderstood, though according to some of Netaji's followers, he played a dubious role. He was bitterly criticised for his changing versions and conjectural answers, but none dared to outcast him because it was everyone's belief that whatsoever objectionable role he was playing, he was simply following the instructions of Netaji. Habibur Rehman's commitment and dedication was above board and he was also the hopeful beginning point of that thread which could have led the diehard followers of Netaji to a happy end.

A brief and precise statement was issued under the signature of Habibur Rehman on August 24, 1945 describing the details of the incident and the injuries received by Netaji in the plane-crash. It said: *"Netaji got out of the plane from the left side from the front. I followed him. We had to pass through the fire in doing so. As soon as I got out, I saw that Netaji's clothes were on fire from head to foot. I rushed to help him to remove the clothes. By the time his clothes were removed, he had sustained severe burns on his body in addition to a serious head injury received during the crash."*

Even the believers of the story as narrated by Habibur Rehman were also surprised as to why after the incident he opted to remain in Tokyo since his arrival on September 1, 1945 till his arrest on September 29, 1945 by the American military organisation, the Counter-Intelligence Corps (CIC). After locating him the CIC interrogated him first on September 24, 1945. Habibur Rehman was perhaps aware that his presence in Tokyo would be helpful in propagating the story of the plane-crash and death of Netaji. During his interrogation conducted by a team of the CIC headed by Colonel Figges, Habibur Rehman told them that on August 16, 1945 he accompanied Netaji on a proposed trip to Tokyo, the capital of Japan. The purpose of their visit was to negotiate with the Japanese Government the role of the INA in the current circumstances but the plane in which they were travelling crashed at Taihoku, Taipei, and Netaji was killed.

Replying to a question in his cross examination, Habibur Rehman said that he was not rendered unconscious after the plane-crash. He could notice that the interior of the plane broke into flames at the nose and tail. Due to the terrific crash the canopy overhead of the plane was broken and it was through this opening that those who were not too seriously injured or instantly killed, escaped from the burning plane.

In his reply to a specific question, Habibur Rehman told the CIC team that he had no knowledge as to how Netaji escaped or was removed from the plane. He said that he noticed upon alighting from the plane that his own coat was blazing. He removed his coat immediately and then saw Netaji lying by the plane with his clothing afire. He then went to the aid of Netaji and removed his burning clothes. He further said that he could now know that Netaji had received serious injuries on his head and neck in addition to severe body burns. According to Habibur Rehman, Netaji recovered sufficiently to carry on a conversation and complained of the pain in his body and asked him to request the medical authorities to check his blood pressure.

Colonel Figges submitted the report of interrogation to the General Headquarters, US Armed Forces Pacific. Considering the importance of Habibur Rehman's statement, he forwarded his report to the Commander-in-Chied of India and the Director of Military Intelligence for further perusal. Colonel Figges expressed his own views in the report that he himself did not feel very confident of the outcome of the interrogation. He commented that then he had reason to believe that the Japanese Government had submitted information based on the statement of Habibur Rehman, but he felt very strongly that this evidence could not be regarded as conclusive.

On the request of the British military authorities, Habibur Rehman and S.A. Ayer were brought to Delhi on December 23, 1945 by a military plane of the United States. They were handed over to the Combined Services Detailed Interrogation Centre (CSDIC) the Red Fort in Delhi. The CSDIC was an Allied's counter-intellignce international body. Since his arrival in The Red Fort, Habibur Rehman was interrogated regularly for about one month by the Commandant of the S. Section, B.C. Chakraborty, and his senior, Colonel Stevenson. In the report of the CSDIC it was stated clearly that the only available evidence of Netaji's death was the statement of Habibur Rehman, and when he was subjected to questions, he failed to give satisfactory answers to all the questions and he did not deliver the truth.

After analysing all available information and reports it was obvious that Habibur Rehman told lies and the Japanese Government had concealed the facts. The CSDIC's report said that the replies of Habibur Rehman were nothing more than a product of conspiracy regarding the movements of Netaji on August 18, 1945. There was other information with the CSDIC leading to different conclusions, including that there was no plane accident or even if there was one, Netaji had escaped death.

There was another controversy—related to Netaji's wrist watch. As described in the Dissentient Report submitted by Suresh Chandra Bose, a partially burnt wrist watch in square shape was given to him by Jawaharlal Nehru, who told him that the watch was brought by Habibur Rehman. Narrating the story of the watch, Nehru had told him that Habibur Rehman had got the watch from Captain Dr. Taneyoshi Yoshimi, who removed it from the body of Netaji after his death in the Nanmon (South Gate) Military Hospital. Habibur Rehman was susscessful in bringing the watch to India. In the Red Fort, Delhi, the watch was passed on to Shah Nawaz Khan who handed it over to INA's defence counsel Bhulabhai Desai, and finally it was given to Nehru.

Anuj Dhar has said in his book *'Back from the Dead'* that *"Dr. Yoshimi had flatly denied that he had ever passed on any watch to Habibur Rehman, leave alone his removing one from Bose's body."*

Netaji always wore a distinct round-rimmed Omega gold watch till his disappearance. Again to quote Anuj Dhar: *"He was so much attached to this present by his parents that he would refuse to part with it even in jails."* Netaji never wore a square watch. Anuj Dhar writes: *"He did have a number of other watches. Many square watches were gifted to him by Joseph Lural, the President of Philippines. He had all those distributed among the INA officers, including Habibur Rehman and Shah Nawaz. Both of them were wearing these watches when they were brought to the Red Fort as prisoners."*

The issue of the burnt watch was raised by Netaji's nephew Dwijendra Nath Bose before the Khosla Commission. In this context Dwijendra's statement according to Anuj Dhar was that *"The mark left by fastener on the leather strap was not where it would have been in case it was worn by his uncle. So whoever wore it had a bulkier wrist than Bose."*

During his interrogation by the CSDIC, Habibur Rehman said that Netaji was not wearing a wrist watch. When he was asked about his own watch which was gifted to him by Netaji, he said, *"I had it with me at the Red Fort, but someone stole it."* According to Netaji's close acquaintances, Habibur Rehman would have passed his own watch only to justify his version of the story of the plane-crash.

Digging in her memory lane Lt. Manwati Arya says that Netaji had gifted a square-shaped watch to Lt. Lavanya Chatterjee, the staff nurse in the INA's Medical Corps in Maymyo. Lt. Lavanya lost her watch as it fell in the toilet ditch and when it came to the notice of Netaji, she was provided with another watch of the same type.

In its conclusion the report stated that Habibur Rehman's deposition deserved to be rejected categorically. It dissatisfied the British authorities who ordered to reinterrogate Habibur Rehman. Again interrogation sessions were held by the CSDIC. This time a protracted questioning method was applied on Habibur Rehman but no desired results were obtained. Habibur Rehman went to the stage of resentment while being interrogated but he did not divulge anything worth it and he became more adamant regarding the death of Netaji. This time the interrogation was conducted by Major Hayat Khan who could not change Habibur Rehman's earlier attitude, which, according to Khan, was known as cleverish denials under the cloak of forgetfulness. The findings of this second interrogation with Habibur Rehman were submitted to British-Indian Government on March 25, 1946, with similar comments and conclusions as in the previous report of B.C. Chakraborty.

The Intelligence Bureau again expressed its dissatisfaction and ordered a third interrogation of Habibur Rehman. The Bureau also sent its own guidelines with a specific questionnaire and instructed the CSDIC on April 2, 1946 to conduct the interrogation according to these instructions. The CSDIC again took Habibur Rehman in their custody and began their questioning sessions according to new guidelines. In this interrogation Habibur Rehman showed his cooperation and maintained a low profile. He was afraid of something worst might happen to his person during the sessions of repeated questioning.

Habibur Rehman told them most humbly that he had volunteered all the information which he had in his possession. He said that it would not at all have been difficult for the authorities to verify the truth of his statements if investigations were taken up on the spot. He charged the Government that except worrying him for nothing, they appeared to have taken no steps to arrive at a definite conclusion regarding the death of Netaji Subhas Chandra Bose. He strongly felt that whenever some irresponsible person made some sort of statement in the press with the intention to keep up the spirit of the ex-INA personnel, the Government got unnerved and someone rushed on to him with a new volley of questions. Thus there was no change in the version, and without any change in the attitude of Habibur Rehman and his statements the CSDIC submitted its report on June 9, 1946.

Other INA officials were also detained for interrogation by the CSDIC. Netaji's Confidential Secretary Major E. Bhaskaran who had never believed is the plane-crash theory to determine the death of Netaji, once pressurised his co-detainee Habibur Rehman to tell the truth. **After many denials he said at last,: *"It is a word of honour I have given to Netaji, don't question me further."*** Almost the same experience was repeated with Colonel Pritam Singh who met Habibur Rehman in Delhi during his detention in Kabul Lines, Delhi Cantonment. His experiences were narrated by Pritam Singh before the Mukherjee Commission on July 22, 2000 that *"Habibur Rehman did not tell us anything about the alleged plane-crash. Nor did we dare to ask him about that. It might be that he was under such an oath of secrecy to Netaji that he would not divulge anything even on pain of death. Such was our loyalty to Netaji. Even if heavens fall, we would not do anything against his wishes."*

After his delayed release from detention Habibur Rehman was bombarded and harassed with the questions and queries of many persons whenever one could get an opportunity to meet him. The impact of such public interrogations and questionings was very serious on Habibur Rehman. Perhaps it resulted in his migration to Pakistan though he took an excuse for his migration that some of his close relatives were killed during riots by those people for whom he had fought under the leadership of the great Netaji. Besides this excuse it was a fact that his native place was the territory of Pakistan. But most of the INA people knew that Habibur Rehman opted for Pakistan to avoid future interrogations which could be initiated by the new Government of India to explore the truth of the plane-crash story.

But there had been another better reason for his migration to Pakistan. According to Captain Lakshmi Sehgal, the head of Rani Jhansi Regiment, all Muslim members of the INA whose native places were in Pakistan, had collectively appealed, under the joint leadership of Major General Mohammad Zaman Kiani and Habibur Rehman, to Jawaharlal Nehru to permit them to live in India and serve India. In an interview to *Dainik Jagaran* on June 14, 2000 **Lakshmi Sehgal said with a heavy heart that Nehru declined their appeal and asked them to treat Pakistan as their country and serve it.**

The impact of such feelings was very deep in the young mind of Habibur Rehman. He almost broke all his INA's connections and relationships. He not only migrated to Pakistan but also accepted Pak Army's offer to lead tribal and other irregular forces which later on infiltrated in Kashmir in 1947 at the time of Maharaja Hari Singh. Being a most trusted Pathan soldier he was assigned very senior civilian positions in Pakistan and was a favourite of General Ayub Khan. He retired as Brigadier from the army and was popularly called in Pakistan as Brigadier Raja Habibur Rehman. It was only after about a decade when he agreed to come to India with some strict conditions to depose his evidence before the Shah Nawaz Committee. His condition was to submit his statement in black and white and he was not ready to face any questioning under the procedure of cross-examination. Thus he came to India simply to submit a written statement personally after putting his signatures before the Shah Nawaz Committee and he did it on April 9, 1956.

Habibur Rehman was given VIP treatment in India. Shah Nawaz Khan himself went to Pakistan High Commission in Delhi to welcome Habibur Rehman and brought him to the venue of the Committee. At this moment there appeared a sensational news in a newspaper published from Kolkata. It said that Habibur Rehman had denied his presence at the moment of death of Netaji. This news item warmed up the environment of the country but, as expected, Habibur Rehman adhered to his old view in his written statement. It was a great relief to the Government of India and particularly to Prime Minister Jawaharlal Nehru who always believed in the version of Habibur Rehman.

In his written statement submitted before the Shah Nawaz Committee, Habibur Rehman showed his dutiful presence at all points, particularly covering Netaji's journey from Saigon on August 17, 1945, to the handing over ceremony of the ashes of Netaji at Renkoji Temple on September 9, 1945 in Tokyo. He also expressed that he performed his duties to the best of his capabilities. After submitting his written statement before Shah Nawaz Committee he returned to Pakistan and thereafter he never visited India.

T. Hayashida was the Japanese to accompany Habibur Rehman when the alleged ashes of Netaji were carried from Taipei to Tokyo. In his visit to Pakistan in 1965 Hayashida met Habibur Rehman in Rawalpindi. While they remembered their old days, Habibur Rehman told Hayashida that *"Netaji Subhas Chandra Bose was the greatest revolutionary that the Indian sub-continent had produced in the present century.... The flame of freedom lit by him is still burning and will continue to inspire the freedom fighters all over the world for all times to come."* This comment could be taken as an example to assess the sentiments and respect towards Netaji which Habibur

Rehman had in his mind. In a similar incident in 1975 the General of the first INA, Mohan Singh, who had inducted Habibur Rehman in the INA, got an opportunity to meet him. Mohan Singh was having a critical view regarding Netaji but he was interested in knowing the truth. He discussed his curiosity with Habibur Rehman and tried to excite his sentiments. **On this occasion Habibur Rehman broke down and said that he was duty-bound to follow the orders of Netaji,** and *"beyond this I do not want to say anything."*

The Khosla Commission was told on March 3, 1971 by Colonel Mahboob Ahmed: *"What used to happen normally when we sat together and the topic came around about the death story of Netaji and we wanted to know from Habibur Rehman. When the story started, **he would come to a stage when he would be weeping like a child** and sthen we gave up asking about this from him."* There were many examples like this when in private questionings Habibur Rehman very clearly hinted that he was obeying orders and that was all. The family members of Netaji were having identical experiences about the sentiments of Habibur Rehman.

There was a very interesting comment from Mahatma Gandhi when he met Habibur Rehman. He said: *"Rehman just gave me a soldier's statement. I know the Guru was not telling the truth and the Chela was also not telling the truth."* When the Mahatma was asked for proof of his belief that Netaji was alive, he said, *"he possesses it"*, ascribing it to his inner voice which had been the most reliable phenomenon in his way of life. According to his close followers, this inner voice was Gandhiji's secret and divine information service system, which he used to receive from his conscience from time to time and he had always firmly believed in it.

In the revolutionary history of India in general and Bengal in particular, there was a sacred tradition and practice of taking a quasi-religious oath that each revolutionary was required to undertake in order to maintain the confidentiality of some specific information against all odds. It was a sort of ritual but its depth was extended upto the centre of the heart and its strength was greater than all the morals and ideals of the mind.

Netaji's nephew Dwijendra Nath and Aurobindo also underwent such ritualistic oaths when Netaji was planning his 1941–escape in Kolkata. The British authorities applied all their torturing methods on Dwijendra Nath when he was in their custody in Lahore Fort but they could get nothing. Deposing on such matters, Dwijendra Nath told the Khosla Commission in August 1972 that he would not divulge anything as he was oath-bound.

According to Pradip Bose, a veteran journalist and the younger brother of Aurobindo, there was almost total similarity in the behaviour of Habibur Rehman and my elder brother who did not open his mouth about the secret of the 1941– escape even to his family members till his death in 1988.

Upholding the sanctity of such oath which was certainly not limited to Netaji's family and persons like Habibur Rehman, there were many examples when other INA personnel adhering to their commitment not to disclose the secret even at the cost of their life. Colonel Gurubaksh Singh Dhillon wrote in his memoirs in the book *'From My Bones'*, that two majors of the INA's Secret Service, Maghar Singh and Ajmer Singh, were being interrogated in Delhi's Salimgarh Fort and were *"daily tortured but they refused to disclose any information about the INA and the Japanese disposition. When they felt that they might not be able to keep their secrets under daily torture, they snatched a guard's rifle one night and committed suicide."*

The second in command of Shah Nawaz Khan's Subhas Brigade, Colonel Thakur Singh narrated almost similar experience regarding Abid Hasan Sarfrani before the Khosla Commission on March 3, 1971. Thakur Singh said: *"Abid Hasan had come from Germany with Netaji in a submarine and had been in my regiment for training. I asked him how Netaji had come from Germany, I piled him with drinks. And when I thought he was full, I put him this question. He threw his glass and the bottle and said even if the British had cut him into pieces, he would have not revealed the fact."*

Thakur Singh recalled the days of incarceration in the Red Fort with Habibur Rehman and said that *"Habib and I were kept in the Red Fort for a month longer than others because the British wanted to know from Habib where Netaji had gone and I was kept because I had organised a special regiment."* Further explaining the determination of Habibur Rehman, he said, *"One day Habib said that Mahatma Gandhi may go on making all kinds of statements but he would never tell the truth about Netaji's whereabouts."*

Habibur Rehman had remained consciously adamant on his version even if some delicate situation was created in ordinary conversation. At some point testifying before the Mukherjee Commission on April 4, 2000, Captain Bipul Kumar Sarcar belonging to the INA Secret Service said that he questioned to provoke Habibur Rehman that there were no burns-effected scratch marks on his shirt and on his palms. He reacted sharply and said that he had understood the hidden motive of the question and he said, *"Sarcar, you are too intelligent and after he extracted a promise from me that I would not disclose to anybody for 30 years."* Sarcar said that he did not disclose this conversation as per promise for 30 years.

One of Netaji's staunch follower, Sunil Krishna Gupta alias 'Sukrit', was in Delhi when Habibur Rehman came to India to submit his statement before the Shah Nawaz Committee. Gupta along with Amar Majumdar met Habibur Rehman at Pakistan High

Commission just minutes before he left with Shah Nawaz Khan. They could draw the attention of Habibur Rehman to a recent news item published in Lahore's *Civil and Military Gazette,* which quoted him as saying that Netaji did not die in the plane-crash. They also asked him many other questions related to Netaji. Firstly, Habibur Rehman spoke nothing but expressed through a gesture that he had not made any such statement. Gupta then asked him why did he not contradict the news. In reply to this question, Habibur Rehman said that the newspapers had always misquoted him. Gupta, who was about twice older than Habibur Rehman, asked him, *"Why have you not sent a protest when the news was published or have you sent any kind of contradiction till now?"*

Habibur Rehman replied that he *"punctiliously avoided the reporters because they have always misquoted him."*

Gupta asked him again, *"Why did't you give a fitting rejoinder?"*

"Oh, they will again misquote me. They were being so anxious to demolish a story which had no basis. Let them declare that Netaji is dead. It would be a double gain," he said.

Gupta asked surprisingly, *"Why it would be a double gain?"*

"Keep it to yourself, will you? One, we shall get Netaji amongst us. Two, the people who are trying to establish the plane-crash story will be exposed," replied Habibur Rehman.

In this connection a reference was made to Major E. Bhaskaran Menon, Netaji's Confidential Secretary, who said that some time before his death in 1991, Habibur Rehman tried to contact him but this could not materialise. This raised a doubt. Would Habibur Rehman have told something, and whether that something would have been different from his previous versions? Perhaps this question was better answered in absolute negative by Shiela Sengupta, sister of Aurobindo Bose. She strongly felt that, *"Habib Bhai would not have done that, come what may, just like my brother Aurobindo,"* who kept mum on the events of Netaji's escape from Kolkata in 1941 and disclosed nothing till his death.

Habibur Rehman was considered by some people as a good person because he obeyed the instructions of Netaji. But to others he was charged that he had given undue importance to his oath of secrecy. Actually the oath of secrecy was related to the safe passage for Netaji's disappearance only. Now that condition was time-barred but the truth had not been revealed and the mystery continued intact since August 18, 1945. Many documents were discovered by many diehard followers of Netaji and some new truths had come before us. These documents had made Habibur Rehman's versions more doubtful.

In her earlier book—*'Patriot, The Unique Indian Leader Netaji Subhas Chandra Bose'* — Lt. Manawati Arya has treated Colonel Habibur Rehman as a most trusted officer of the INA who had to play a double role. Commenting on the performance of Habibur Rehman she has very firmly asserted: *"On the one hand he pretended to turn a traitor to Netaji by joining the Allied Forces secretly and pretending to help in their plan to do away with Netaji in an air crash done purposely with the help of the vanquished Japanese Army. On the other hand, he remained faithful and loyal to Netaji and helped him to escape safely by taking the risk of burning his hands and parts of his body to give evidence of Netaji's death due to severe burns in the air crash accident."*

—o—

4

Betrayal for Power and Pelf

The conventional image of Netaji during the freedom struggle of India was iconic and he was regarded as an object of uncritical devotion even by his competitors. Describing his love for the country, his apolitical boyhood friend Dilip Kumar Roy wrote in his book '*Netaji, the Man, His Reminiscences*' that *"in fact, the more closely I came to know him, the more convinced I became that it was because he was an authentic mystic at heart, that he could worship with every fibre of his passionate being the essence and aura of Mother India."* After the end of Second World War when the INA soldiers and officers were brought to India for their trial in the Red Fort, Delhi, Netaji's personal magic of leadership aroused a very special popular loyalty and enthusiasm among the people for his statesmanship and the INA's commandership. His charismatic personality and patriotic contributions evoked great delight and admiration among the people.

This was also the time when his death-mystery was being discussed by one and all in the country and he was also expected to reappear at any time. In this connection several kinds of opinions were being expressed and various rumours being circulated through mouth to mouth. It was a common belief that the investigations undertaken by the intelligence sleuths concluded that Netaji would have escaped to Soviet Russia. But there was none to confirm it. There was also an awe in a soft low indistinct sound among his followers that Netaji might have been held up as a prisoner either in Russia or in China. These suspicions and disseminated opinions about Netaji from discernible sources were painful.

The British Government of India and more particularly the interim Government which took oath on September 2, 1946 *"to bear true faith and allegiance to King Emperor George VI and his heirs and successors"* formed under the first Indian Prime Minister Jawaharlal Nehru, gave a very cold response to initiate any action to decipher the truth about Netaji. It became clear to the supporters of Netaji and the members of the INA that the Congress Party and the Nehru Government had adopted an anti-Netaji policy, to banish steadily the contributions of Netaji and his struggle against the British rule for the independence of the country. This disgraceful policy was equally targeting the INA and its personnel. The soldiers and officers of the INA were tactfully refused their re-induction in the army of free India and they were also not granted, till as late as 1972, the status of freedom-fighters. Netaji's portrait was banned for hanging up in public places including offices and army-mess halls. In a confidential memo dated February 11, 1949, under the signature of Major General P.N. Khandoori, the Government recommended that *"The photos of Netaji Subhas Chandra Bose be not displayed at prominent places, Unit Lines, Canteens, Quarter Guards or Recreation rooms."* There were no official functions to celebrate Netaji's or the INA- related important dates and incidents. Lt. Manwati Arya remembers that during her talks on All India Radio she was always briefed by her programme-producers, without fail, about the national policy to be careful and not mention any reference of the INA including the name of Netaji in her discourse on AIR.

It was almost evident that Nehru was consciously reluctant to utilise his position as the head of the Indian Government to unravel the mystery of Netaji's death. Actually it was an apparent fact that the Gandhian wing of the Congress Party, now led by Nehru, had always been uncomfortable with Netaji. He was not appreciated even when he became the President of the All India Congress Party and was equally disliked when he was out of the Congress. Recently, Suman K. Chakraborty, a correspondent of CNN-IBN television channel, opined that it is *"indeed surprising that the Government which has spent more than Rupees 200 crore in a year on advertisements of eminent Indian personalities does not consider Netaji worthy enough to be on the list."*

Thus it became crystal clear that on account of the political rivalry with Netaji many in the Congress Party and particularly Jawaharlal Nehru always tried to maneuver with an intense passion to downplay the importance of Netaji and the INA. This view has been endorsed by the reputed historian Dr. R.C. Majumdar in his book — *'History of the Freedom Movement in India'*. Dr. Majumdar wrote in 1948 as under:

"The universal sympathy was expressed all over India for the INA officers who were tried for treason in the Red Fort at Delhi in 1946 which gave a rude shock to the British Government. It clearly demonstrated that Indians of all shades of opinion put a premium on the disloyalty of the Indian troops to their foreign masters and looked upon it as a true and welcome sign of nationalism. The honour and esteem with which every Indian regarded the members of the INA, offered a striking contrast to the ill-concealed disgust and contempt for those sepoys who refused to join the INA and remained true to their so-called salt. The British came to realise that they were sitting on the

brink of a volcano which may erupt at any moment. It is highly probable that this consideration played an important role in their final decision to quit India in 1947. So the members of the INA did not die or suffer in vain, and their leader Netaji Subhas Chandra Bose has secured a place of honour in the history of India's struggle for freedom."

Dr. Majumdar had gone further positive favouring Netaji when he wrote in the same book that ***"the contribution made by Netaji Subhas Chandra Bose towards the achievement of freedom in 1947 was no less, and perhaps far more important than that of Mahatma Gandhi**, and I hope true historians and all lovers of truth now accept this view."*

The views of Dr. R.C. Majumdar were subsequently corroborated by the former Chief Justice P.B. Chakraborty of Calcutta High Court in 1956 when the ex-Prime Minister of United Kingdom, Clement Attlee, visited Kolkata. While expressing thanks for the publication of Dr. R.C. Majumdar's book, Justice Chakraborty responded in his memoirs to the publisher in his letter dated March 30, 1976 in the following words:

*"When I was acting as Governor of West Bengal in 1956, Lord Attlee, who gave India freedom by putting an end to British rule, visited India and stayed in the Raj Bhawan, Kolkata, for two days. I had then a long talk with him about the real grounds for the voluntary withdrawal of the British from India. I put it straight to him like this: 'The Quit India movement of Gandhiji practically died out long before 1947 and there was nothing in Indian situation at that time which made it necessary for the British to leave India in a hurry. Why did they then do so?' In reply **Lord Attlee cited several reasons, the most important of which were the activities of Netaji Subhas Chandra Bose which weakened the very foundations of the attachment of the Indian land and naval forces to the British Government**. Towards the end I asked Lord Attlee about the extent to which the British decision to quit India*

was influenced by Gandhiji's activities. On hearing this Attlee's lips widened in a smile of disdain and he uttered slowly, putting strong emphasis on each single letter.: 'MI-NI-MAL'.

Since 1950 the INA's personnel began to put their demand before the Government of India to investigate the so-called death of Netaji and if he had not died in the plane-crash as it was generally believed, then the government would have to find out his whereabouts. But the Government of India's dilly-dallying and deaf-mute policy delayed the matter. In those years just after the Second World War there were "war criminals' trials" and thus the international situation was very complicated. It was secretly discussed among Netaji's supporters that his name might have been included in the list of war criminals and therefore, any kind of pressure was not applied in the matter of Netaji's death or disappearance by his supporters.

A close associate of Netaji, Debnath Das, could not maintain his patience and wrote a private letter dated March 27, 1953 to some of his colleagues and supporters. He wrote in the letter that *"It is beyond our comprehension to think why the Government of India have chosen not to set up an Investigation Commission ... There was a historical necessity too in case everything was done according to the plan, for Netaji's remaining underground for obvious reasons only to appear at the historical moment for shaping India's destiny."* Debnath Das also expressed his regrets for his veterans in the INA who took up governmental assignments and were sabotaging Netaji's cause. In his letter he even named such seniors as S.A. Ayer, J.K. Bhonsle and A.M. Sahay who openly supported and took up the side of the Government.

Suresh Chandra Bose has mentioned in his *'Dissentient Report'* the statement of Nehru in the Parliament on September 29, 1955, while replying to a pressing question repeatedly raised by H.V.

Kamath. Nehru said, *"In a matter of this kind, the only enquiry, that is to say, satisfactory enquiry that can be made is by the Japanese Government. The matter is in Japan, the whole thing is there. We cannot impose ourselves or an Enquiry Committee on the Japanese Government. Of course, if they choose to enquire we will gladly cooperate and give such help as we can."* Nehru also told his decision that in such cases any enquiry was not possible for his Government as the whole matter relating to Netaji involved many foreign territories.

Testifying under oath before the Khosla Commission on this issue, the Delhi Congress President in 1958-59, Jagdish Kodesia, disclosed on March 1, 1971: *"...from the records of the Parliament it was seen that always a stereotype reply was coming when questions were put about Netaji. The feeling among various Congress leaders was that Panditji (Nehru) had an aversion for Netaji."* Kodesia himself was holding doubt in the death story of Netaji as he had been in Saigon in 1961 where his doubts were doubled and his inclination not to believe in the plane-crash story, became firm.

Understanding the attitude of Nehru towards Netaji, it was proposed by some of the INA members and their supporters that an unofficial inquiry without the help and funds of the Indian Government should be instituted. There were suggestions that the renowned Justice Radha Binode Pal should be persuaded to lead the inquiry team. Justice Pal was a widely acclaimed and highly honoured international juristic personality whose name and fame was at peak. In Japan he commanded great respect due to his open pro-Japanese gestures while conducting the war criminals' trials. There was confidence among Netaji's followers that if Justice Pal would agree to lead the investigation team not only Japanese co-operation would be easily available but international recognition would also be granted to it. Besides his knowledge of judicial complexities, Justice Pal was well aware of South-East Asian affairs.

With the above idea in mind a meeting was called in Kolkata on September 6, 1955 by the followers of Netaji with only one point agenda, to undertake a decision to appoint an unofficial enquiry committee to unravel the mystery of Netaji. The meeting was presided over by Shah Nawaz Khan who had become popular because of his Red Fort trial by the British. In the meeting Shah Nawaz Khan frankly expressed that Prime Minister Nehru was not ready for any official probe relating to Netaji's mystery. This meeting adopted a resolution to form a public-funded and non-official committee which would be assigned to enquire about the death or disappearance of Netaji. The meeting decided as proposed that Justice Radha Binode Pal would be requested to head the inquiry committee.

According to Anuj Dhar in his book *'Back from Dead'*, this meeting was the last occasion when Shah Nawaz Khan pleaded from the side of Netaji's followers. Dhar writes: *"That was the last time Shah Nawaz Khan was heard to voice his opinion on the side of those who doubted the crash theory."* It was in the records of the Intelligence Bureau's Daily INA Report No. 56 dated February 5, 1946, which informed, *"In the Punjab, the rumour that Bose is alive is also current. Shah Nawaz and Ehsan Qadir (a member of Netaji's Provisional Government) both are stated to have said recently that they greatly doubt the reports of Bose's death."* Shah Nawaz Khan had assured in the Kolkata meeting that he would be careful so that no hurdle could be raised by the Indian Government he would rather manage to obtain some tangible help and assistance for the proposed enquiry committee.

Reacting against this development and decision, the Government of India declared suddenly that it will appoint its own Netaji Inquiry Committee (NIC) headed by Shah Nawaz Khan. The NIC included Netaji's elder brother and former Magistrate

Suresh Chandra Bose, along with a nominee of the West Bengal Government, S.N. Moitra, who was an ICS officer and a former Chief Commissioner of the Andaman and Nicobar islands. Although the notification for the appointment of the NIC was issued on December 3, 1955, but it could begin its functioning only in April 1956.

Everyone was surprised on the choice of Shah Nawaz Khan as the Chairman of the NIC. None could understand this diplomatic move of Nehru. According to some legal experts, Shah Nawaz Khan was a better choice for Nehru than the aggressive and authoritative Justice Pal. Though Shah Nawaz Khan's appointment was hailed as the victory of Netaji's supporters, but no exclamation of greeting was seen either in the Congress or in the INA circles.

The NIC, popularly known as the Shah Nawaz Committee, examined in all 67 witnesses including Indians and Japanese. The NIC report had six chapters which consisted a total of 78 pages. The first chapter discussed — *'Last Plans of Netaji Subhas Chandra Bose'*. The conclusion of this chapter was that Netaji had desired to go to Russia but he could not go. The NIC report said that there were a number of reasons for Netaji to go to Tokyo though his ultimate aim was Russia via Manchuria. With its prejudiced and preoccupied mind the NIC report was keen to express its assumptions that *"there was no time then to contact Russian authorities or to make out a detailed plan ahead. Russia was at war with Japan, and the Russian armies were advancing into Manchuria. Even if Netaji reached Manchuria what would have happened to him, and a few trusted lieutenants whom he wanted to take with him, was uncertain."*

'The Air Crash at Taihoku (Formosa)', *'The Death of Netaji Subhas Chandra Bose'*, and *'Cremation of Netaji's Body'* were respectively the second, third and fourth chapters which were

supported by only those testimonies which were establishing the death story of Netaji, despite the fact that in the opinion of Shah Nawaz Khan himself some of these testimonies had glaring and serious discrepancies and contradictions, the time of death and the date of cremation were also disputed. All these three chapters were concerned with the incidents which took place at Taihoku airport in Taipei city. But the NIC could not visit these places. The NIC decrepitly mentioned its lame reasons, including the lack of Indian diplomatic relations with Formosa for not being able to visit Taipei.

The fifth chapter of the NIC report described inadequately its opinion about the ashes of Netaji's body. It said in feeble words, *"... so although there cannot be absolute certainty, nevertheless, it can be said that in all probability, the ashes kept in Renkoji temple, Tokyo, are the ashes of Netaji Subhas Chandra Bose."*

While presenting the NIC report in Parliament on September 11, 1956, Prime Minister Nehru emphatically said: *"Government feels that the conclusions of the Committee about Netaji's death should be accepted as the evidence adduced in the report is practically overwhelming."* Though it was an alarming fact that till this date the report of the NIC was not signed and agreed to by Suresh Chandra Bose, who by then had not submitted his opinion and he was expected to differ.

Suresh Chandra Bose demanded copies of drafts, reports, and relevant papers, including exhibits and photographs, etc., held by the NIC to be provided to him to prepare his dissent note. He was not denied these in black and white but he could smell that the NIC's documents would not be made available to him. Shah Nawaz Khan was uncomfortable with him since the beginning of the NIC's functioning. And when their differences came to the notice of Nehru, he very cleverly advised them some tips, which included respect for each other's seniority, to avoid making statements to press and not to discuss Committee's secrets with any other person. Nehru shrewdly prompted Shah Nawaz Khan with a motive so that he could use Shah Nawaz Khan politically in his mission to declare Netaji's death in the plane-crash and he succeeded in his latent mission.

Nehru was aware of the fact that Shah Nawaz Khan was keeping malice against Netaji also who had removed him from the position of the Commanding Officer, Kohima front. It was alleged that Shah Nawaz Khan had betrayed the INA's campaign in Kohima by revealing the codes and the military plans of the INA and the Japanese army to his brother who was then an officer in the British Indian army which was fighting in Kohima.

While commanding the No. 2 Division of the INA, Col. P.K. Sahgal, along with a reconnaisance party, was ordered on February 22, 1945 to reoccupy Pyinbin and to join Shah Nawaz Khan, who was heading towards a strategic place known as Mount Popa, where Col. Sahgal could reach on March 17, 1945, after destroying the British posts at Pyinbin. Now it was firmly decided that the occupation of Pyinbin was to be maintained to strengthen the INA's position at Meiktila[1] inspite of the counter attacks and air operations of the Allied Forces. In such fightings Shah Nawaz Khan complained to have lost all his documents, including the marked operational maps, while successfully recovering the INA's vehicles from the control of the British. These documents were very sensitive and the loss of such documents was serious in itself.

Likewise, on another occasion when Shah Nawaz Khan was advised on April 14, 1945 to postpone the INA's offensive role towards Imphal, he became disappointed and on May 17, 1945,

1. Lt. Manawati Arya's birthplace.

during an encounter with the British forces in the vicinity of Sit Pinzeix, he lost his personal diary which was subsequently produced as an exhibit at the time of his trial at the Red Fort, Delhi. INA's senior veteran A.C. Chatterji described the above incidents in his book *'My Memories of INA and its Netaji'*. He wrote: *"Shah Nawaz Khan was informed that the INA and Japanese forces around Imphal have failed to capture it. He was asked to select a new role. He was disappointed and wrote in his diary which was subsequently captured by British forces that he wanted "to attack Imphal.'"*

Shah Nawaz Khan's diary was exhibit *'CCC'* and exhibit *'DDD'*. *'CCC'* contained categorical descriptions as to how he was actively involved in the preparation and continuation of the war against the British. He also mentioned in his diary the specific accounts of his participation in the war in Singapore, in Rangoon in the vicinity of Mount Popa Kyaukpadaung and his attack on Imphal. He narrated the details of preparations to move three battalions of the INA to Ukhrul. The exhibit *'DDD'* described the details of the actual operations fought by the INA. It also contained a graphic account of the events and included the names of the officers including Netaji.

Shah Nawaz Khan was suddenly asked to report in Burma and some loyal officers of the INA were placed with him for reporting his conduct to Netaji. This fact was also in the notice of Nehru that Shah Nawaz Khan was not allowed to meet Netaji during his last four months' stay in South-East Asia. It is said that the order of Court Martial was pending against Shah Nawaz Khan but it could not be carried out as the war suddenly came to an end. The INA members alleged that as a matter of fact Shah Nawaz Khan had opted for Pakistan's citizenship. He belonged to a large Muslim family of Janjua Rajputs in Rawalpindi, with his familial links to Northwest Frontier area. **As Nehru was aware of his vexatious rift**

with Netaji, he was virtually highjacked by him from Pakistan and patronised by assigning him the position of a Deputy Minister in the Cabinet of the Government of India.

Shah Nawaz Khan had entered the Dehradun Military Academy in 1933 and he was 58th Indian cadet in his batch to receive commission in the British Indian army. He told the Court at Red Fort at the opening session of his trial: *"I will not be wrong to say that I was hypnotised by his (Netaji's) personality and his speeches. For the first time in my life I saw India through the eyes of an Indian."* He was disappointed by the British who brought him to Singapore: *"so late in the fight, only to be ordered to lay down my arms and surrender unconditionally. I consider it to be extremely unjust to myself and to my sense of honour as a soldier."*

Shah Nawaz Khan was ordered to proceed to Farrer Park at the centre of Singapore on February 17, 1942, when the British Indian Army surrendered along with 5/14 Battalion. His reaction was: *"I had a feeling of being completely helpless, of being handed over like cattle by the British to the Japanese and by the Japanese to Mohan Singh."*

As against the British so against the Japanese, Shah Nawaz Khan had resentments including that they provided inferior equipment, grossly inadequate supplies to the INA. The Japanese were reluctant to seek the assistance and help of its Indian ally INA. According to Shah Nawaz Khan, it was only this Japanese approach and treatment that prevented the INA and the Japanese army jointly capturing Imphal in India.

Before the Red Fort trial Shah Nawaz Khan was not as popular as he became later in India. His imitative nature was closely observed by S.A. Ayer in his book — *'Unto Him Witness'*. Ayer wrote that he began to think that in Shah Nawaz Khan *"he saw Bose-like qualities."*

In praise of the INA, Shah Nawaz Khan wrote in his book '*INA and its Netaji*': *"While the INA was on the offensive, there was not a single occasion on which our forces were defeated on the battlefield, and there was never an occasion when the enemy, despite overwhelming superiority in men and material, was able to capture any post held by the INA."*

Such adulatory comments for the INA by Shah Nawaz Khan were exposed when it was known that ten men from his 2nd Battalian in the INA were seized on suspicion of spying for the British, tied to trees, bayoneted and left hanging till they died. Another incident narrated that three battalions of Subhas Brigade, usually called as the 1st Guerrilla Regiment of their best men in the INA, were given under his command. Some Hindus in the INA were upset by his apparent partiality. Then Netaji said, *"We are in a majority. We can afford magnanimity. The time will come when they will think themseleves as Indians, not as Muslims, but at this stage we should try to avoid any little thing that might hurt their feelings."*

This background of Shah Nawaz Khan had a bad impact on his INA colleagues. It was a fact that he served the British with the desire — '*May the umbrella of the British Government remain over our heads forever.*' (सरकारे बर्तानिया की छतरी हमारे सर पर हमेशा कायम रहे।) His father and grandfather had also aspired in the same way when they served the British Indian Army as Jamadar, Subedar and Subedar Major. The same spirit Shah Nawaz Khan maintained when he joined the INA due to the compulsions of his circumstances. He was showing the same sort of loyalty now to Nehru. When it came to the notice of Suresh Chandra Bose, it was intolerable to him. Commenting on this issue Anuj Dhar, the author of '*Back from Dead*' writes: *"Nehru's jibe worsened the relations between the two."*

Suresh Chandra Bose was compelled to prepare his *'Dissentient Report'* by his memory, personal notes and some of his background papers as Shah Nawaz Khan practically denied him the opportunity to scrutinise the NIC's documents. He was also compelled to publish his report from his own resources. **Suresh Chandra Bose said very frankly that Shah Nawaz Khan was a traitor to Netaji by supporting Prime Minister Nehru.** He also wrote that the conclusion reached in the NIC report that Netaji had died, was clearly against the oral and documentary evidences. He called Shah Nawaz Khan as a dark specimen of an unparalled treachery to Netaji.

Criticising Shah Nawaz Khan's way of functioning as the Chairman of the NIC, Suresh Chandra Bose said in his dissent report that Shah Nawaz Khan relied on such evidence and witnesses which were at all not authentic and truthful. Discussing in his dissent report one of such witness named Mir Ghulam Dastgir, who was an Indian expatriate in Tourane, a Vietnamese city where Netaji was supposed to have spent the night of August 17, 1945 in a hotel; Dastgir told the NIC that he was asked by Mr. Suziko, the Japanese Administrator of Tourane, to meet Netaji who was expected to arrive there. On the basis of this witness the NIC report confirmed Netaji's visit to Tourane whereas Dastgir very plainly admitted that he could not see Netaji at Tourane.

Another dubious witness before the NIC was General Harukei Isayama, who was the Chief of General Staff of the Formosan Army at Taipei at that time. Isayama could not explain as to why he failed to receive Netaji and General Shidei at the airport of Taihoku on August 18, 1945, where they welcomed General Shidei's successor General Tanaka, who had gone there some days after the alleged plane-crash.

According to Suresh Chandra Bose in his *'Dissentient Report,* Shah Nawaz Khan had *"continued calling for new witnesses and examining them not with the intention of arriving at the truth, but to fill up the gaps in the evidence and for explaining and reconciling discrepant and contradictory statements that stood in the way of his coming to the conclusion that the plane had crashed and that Netaji had died."* Thus the modus-operandi of Shah Nawaz Khan was to pick up selective passages from the statements of witnesses and utilise these statements to bridge up the gaps, with the intention to make the plane-crash story somehow believable.

Suresh Chandra Bose raised serious doubts in the circulated story of death. He observed: *"There are six persons who are alleged to have received injuries along with Netaji and who were also taken along with him to the same hospital for treatment. It was strange to note that except Col. Habibur Rehman, none of the five others had any knowledge of Netaji's death, nor had any one of them even seen his dead body, though he is said to have died in the same hospital."*

There had been material discrepancy between the witnesses as to who travelled in which vehicle and who arrived first at the hospital and who took them? The NIC report did not try to establish the exact indentities of nurses and medical attendants at the hospital where the plane-crash injured were alleged to have been treated.

The dissent report of Suresh Chandra Bose, published separately in November, 1956, also pointed out that *"although Lt. Colonel Shiro Nonogaki, the Japanese Air-force Staff Officer of the Burmese Army, had named two staff officers who came on the receipt of the information when Netaji was alive, but the named Staff Officers Colonel Miyata and Major Nagatomo said that they arrived after Netaji had died."*

Regarding the five photographs supplied by the Japanese Government, three photographs showed the wreck of the plane near

Taihoku airport. One showed a bandaged Habibur Rehman sitting in the hospital and the last one showed Netaji's body fully covered with a cloth. In his *'Dissentient Report'* Suresh Chandra Bose assumed: *"I am definitely of the opinion that no better photographs than these four could be available to the Japanese Government — as a plane crashing with Netaji in it; as Netaji with injuries and burns near a crashed plane; as Netaji being treated in a hospital for those injuries and burns; as a dead Netaji in a hospital; as the dead body of Netaji being cremated and being put inside a furnace of a crematorium were not available to the Japanese Government for being photographed, because such incidents did not take place at all, and therefore, it was not possible for them to obtain these photographs."*

A former-officer of the Ministry of External Affairs and an M.P., Dr. Satyanarayan Sinha, disclosed before the Khosla Commission that *"the photograph of an aircraft published by the Shah Nawaz Committee was similar to the photograph which was published in 'Taihoku Nichi Nichi Shimbum' newspaper some time in October, 1944."*

It is also astonishing as to why these photographs were entertained as conclusive evidence by Shah Nawaz Khan, whereas these photographs were rejected summarily by Justice G.D. Khosla on the ground that these photographs could not be admissible as legal document as there was none to endorse the authenticity of these photographs.

The NIC report was also criticised because its Chairman Shah Nawaz Khan could not understand the contradictory information mentioned in the death certificate of Netaji. He rather preferred to ignore and overlook these points. There were two doctors who claimed that the certificate of death of Netaji was issued by them. Dr. Yoshimi was very firm when he said, *"On August 18, 1945 I had issued a medical certificate in respect of the deceased person, writing his name in Japanese Katakana as Chandra Bose — and giving the cause of death as 'burns of the third degree'."* Another Dr. Tsuruta also claimed that actually it was he who had certified Netaji's death 'due to heart failure'. For Shah Nawaz Khan it did not matter as to who issued the death certificate and what would be the legal implications of two death certificates of the same person.

On the question of the death of General Shidei who accompanied Netaji, it was a great surprise as to why Shah Nawaz Khan relied on those two papers which subsequently were declared as *'fraud'* by Justice G.D. Khosla. One of these papers was an anonymous 1947 application for the posthumous promotion of General Shidei which appeared to have been forwarded by the Chief Korean and Manchurian Affairs Section, also called First Demobilisation Section. The other paper was the enclosure of the above noted application which was a brief description of the career of General Shidei by the Japanese Foreign Ministry.

It was a bewildering truth that the **Japanese Government had never shown any interest to conduct even a cursory inquiry for the alleged plane crash at Taihoku, where along with Netaji its most important General had also died.** On this count two lame arguments of General Isayama were quoted by Shah Nawaz Khan. Isayama said, "*...since the aeroplane in question did not belong to Formosan Army, the headquarters of the Formosan Army had no responsibility to hold inquiry into the matter.*" He further said, "*It was the duty of Commander Ando, his boss, within whose area an air crash took place, to inquire and report to the higher authorities. In this case, a report was submitted to the Imperial headquarters by my Staff Officer Lt. Col. Shibuya through me.*" Shah Nawaz Khan also mentioned in his report that not only the Japanese Government denied having received any such report purported to have been sent by Shibuya, who also denied the knowledge of any such inquiry or report prepared by him. Shibuya said, *"The responsibility of holding it lay with the Air Division concerned."*

There are several fallacies which were exposed by Suresh Chandra Bose in his *'Dissentient Report'*. The role played by Shah Nawaz Khan in preparing the NIC report was a setback for the demand to find out the whereabouts of Netaji. Now in the changed scenario many more facts have seen the light of day, and it can be said with certainty that if Shah Nawaz Khan would have not betrayed and would have remained loyal to Netaji, the mystery would have been solved.

Shah Nawaz Khan's report and his character has been critisized by the subsequent inquiry commissions instituted by the Government of India as well as by various authors who wrote their memoirs of Netaji. Lt. Col. Ehsan Qadir, who was a member in Netaji's Provisional Government and who opted for Pakistani citizenship, wrote in his diary that *"this Shah Nawaz had created communalism in the INA by inciting Muslim members of the INA."* Like Qadir many others expressed their displeasure against Shah Nawaz Khan because a rarest of rare opportunity was lost, a national and international hero was betrayed, an obligatory duty was stopped in its performance and once again a Brutus was victorious. Thus Shah Nawaz Khan lied against Netaji, against the INA, against the people and finally, against himself, only to secure a cosy and comfortable berth in the Nehru Government — with lots of facilities and perks including a high stature in the society and the world at large.

—o—

5

Netaji's Secretive Nature

The legends and myths related to Netaji's death story oscillated between two opposite adherents. At the time of the end of World War II there was one group consisting of some INA personnel and their Japanese associates who propogated, with their full strength, the death of Netaji in the Taipei plane-crash. At the other side were those British, American and other intelligence agents who always doubted and never confirmed the so-called death story of Netaji.

Later on this classification took a different shape. Now one side was represented by most of the INA personnel and their sympathisers who had a firm faith that Netaji had actually disappeared and not died and his disappearance was an elaborate subterfuge to divert and confuse the Allied Powers from the then current view according to prevailing political circumstances. According to these people, it was their well founded conviction that Netaji would reappear at an opportune moment as he had done successfully in his earlier disappearances. The other side consisted of some prejudiced members of the Congress Party and the Government of India led by Jawaharlal Nehru who endorsed the version of Habibur Rehman because of their political convenience, inspite of the knowledge that **all investigations conducted by either British or American intelligence agencies had concluded that Netaji might be still alive.** Nehru was also adamant not to undertake any further investigation to inquire into the disputed death of Netaji. Nehru was well aware that the results of different investigations by the intelligence sleuths had some inherent dubitations in their inquiry panel as well as process. All these investigations in their incertitude never confirmed the plane-crash theory and therefore, provided a life-dose to the mystery of Netaji's death or his planned disappearance.

The image and personality of Netaji had always been emotionally fascinating and intellectually captivating. Some new books and articles doubting and not confirming the death story had been written and circulated almost every year for the last six decades. The result of these new books and research papers along with the magical influence of Netaji's personality was so miraculous that whosoever spoke or wrote about his return or his reappearance anywhere and in any form, it was listened to with curiosity, respect and reverence. The opposite views were always either rejected or ignored.

The characterisation of Netaji's unparalleled personality by intellectuals was most positive. His name, fame and the role of the INA in India's freedom struggle became a very inspiring story. Netaji's multifaceted activities and his motivating achievements were told and retold to inspire the people at large. Judged by the yardstick of a common man's reasoning and logic, Netaji had been regarded as a super human personality. His persona in the eyes of the pubic was a magnificent fusion of many sterling qualities which had created in him an impregnable character. He was a combination of a positive thinker, a serious philosopher, a scarifying patriot, a dreamy and delightful social reformer, a sincere philanthropist, a shrewd politician, a revolutionary freedom-fighter, a great warrior, an enchanting orator, a well-versed statesman, a practical acumen, a skilled diplomat, a competent organiser, a disciplined military commander, and a complete man of virtues, qualities and attributes in one body, so to say, a **supernatural man.**

In the minds of the people, the stature and strength of Netaji's image had created a ray of very strong hope and positivity in every heart. There had been a general view that Netaji would come back any day and when he would appear in public, all problems which the country and its people were facing, would get their appropriate redressal. And thus the mystery of his disappearance became deep to deeper and which is still continuing.

Although there was absolute darkness and no exact or distant clues were visible to lead to know the whereabouts of Netaji, if he had not died; yet a desire with expectation of his reappearance was kept alive in the minds of those who loved him and also in those who doubted it. This is why in all the three official attempts to unravel the mystery by the Indian Government, there had been two disappointing. The Netaji Inquiry Committee headed by Shah Nawaz Khan and the Khosla Commission headed by Justice G.D. Khosla conducted their proceedings with a preoccupied mind to support the line and policy of the Governments in India led by the Congress Party and thus to justify by hook or crook the plane-crash theory. It was only the Mukherjee Commission headed by Justice M.K. Mukherjee, which again raised the hopes of the people and firmly concluded, with arguments based on legal documentation and juristic reasonings, that **Netaji might have died by that time because of the average age-factor but not in the alleged plane-crash.**

Considering the specific reasons of hope and inspiration among the people to maintain the mystery for such a long period we are reminded of those incidents of disappearances and reappearances which were related to the early life of Netaji. Narrating one such incident in her earlier book, Lt. Manwati Arya writes:

"During the summer vacation of 1914, while studying for his Inter Arts in the Presidency College at Kolkata, after coming home to their Kolkata house for the holidays, he suddenly disappeared to join his boyhood friend Hemant Kumar Sarkar[1]*. In a pre-planned programme of roving and visiting places of pilgrimage in search of a spiritual Guru and religious truths to fulfil with Hemant without informing anyone at home, at an age of barley 17 years. His home people at Kolkata and Cuttack became very much worried and made frantic searches to locate him but all in vain. They had to remain in suspense hoping against hope for his return. After spending about two months in visiting the famous places of pilgrimage such as Gaya, Benares (Varanasi), Vrindavan, Mathura, Haridwar, Rishkesh, etc., he came back to his parents in Cuttack."*

Netaji's biographer Durlabh Singh has also confirmed this dramatic incident in his book. He writes that Netaji was deeply absorbed in the ideas of eternal peace and salvation. This religious and spiritual thinking resulted in his disappearance in 1914 when perhaps he decided once for all to forsake the pleasures of the world. This disappearance was so well planned and managed that he could not be traced until he himself appeared suddenly at his Cuttack

1. Hemant was a link Subhas had with so-called *"Neo Vivekanand group"* who was devoted to working for a *"synthesis between religion and nationalism"*. The leading person of this group was a student of Calcutta Medical College, Suresh Chandra Banerjee (later Doctor). Both Dr. Banerjee and Hemant were leaders in the freedom struggle. Hemant lived in Calcutta and visited Cuttack during school holidays. Hemant had also shared the value-system Netaji acquired from the writings of Sri Ramkrishna and Vivekanand.

residence's drawing room where his mother and other family members were surprised to see him.

About the secretive nature of Netaji, his nephew Dwijendra, who was the son of his elder brother Satish Chandra Bose, told the Khosla Commission in reply to a question, that once he had gone to Jaipur to serve cholera patients without informing anyone. He was keenly searched but was found only when he himself came back. According to Lt. Manwati Arya, the place name *'Jaipur'* in this incident is not the capital of Rajasthan but a small town in Orissa.

Narrating another popular incident known as the great escape of Netaji in 1941, Lt. Manwati Arya writes:

"At 1.30 a.m. of 16/17 January, 1941, when all the members of the family including the servants were fast asleep and even the CID men on the roadside were snoring under their blankets, Subhas Chandra Bose disguised as Mohammad Ziauddin, a Travelling Inspector of the Empire of India Life Assurance Co. Ltd., quietly slipped out of the house and was driven away by Sisir towards Bararee...

"Subhas Bose had left a number of letters bearing different dates and addressed to different people, to be posted gradually according to their dates after his departure, to give an impression that he was writing letters as usual from his seclusion. He had also left a number of slips roughly scribbled in a casual manner, informing his inability to meet anyone as he was observing complete silence in connection with his meditation...

"Aurobindo and their eldest uncle's son Dwijendra who were politically active with Subhas Bose, were advised to be seen around his room as usual to make a show of attending to the needs of their uncle in normal course. His meals served in 'thali' by the cook used to be pushed behind the screen in front of his room and the emptied 'thali' removed

from the same place after some time. On the secret departure of Subhas Bose, Ila[1] *had to consume the meals quietly from behind the screen leaving the emptied 'thali' in the usual place to prove that he had taken his meals as usual.*

"This drama of usual routine of Subhas Bose in seclusion engaged in Sadhana or Meditation, to bluff the people and the CID men on constant watch, continued for nine days till he was expected to have crossed the Indian border safely."

After his successful escape from Kolkata, Netaji lived a secretive life for about 10 months adopting different names and changing different places and countries until he reached Berlin. He made his public appearance only when he spoke on Radio Berlin in November, 1941. He launched a radio programme in the name of Azad Hind Radio (Free India Radio) which broadcasted in several Indian languages on a regular basis.

Netaji's another nephew, Pradip Bose, a veteran journalist has described in his book *'Subhas Bose and India Today'* the modus operandi of Netaji's disappearance in January 1941 as told to him by his elder brother Aurobindo. Pradip quotes his brother in his own language: *"I see a strange similarity in the pattern of the story of his escape from India in 1941 and his 'planned escape' to the Soviet Union in August 1945. At least seven-eight members of the Bose family knew about some aspects of his escape from India. As Subhas came to the conclusion that if all of them pretended that they did not know anything about his escape, then at least some of them would be arrested, interrogated and even tortured to get on to the truth. To avoid such a possibility he constructed a story of his withdrawal from worldly affairs in order to meditate in an undisturbed environment. He withdrew behind a curtain and only one person, his nephew Aurobindo, was*

1. Niece of Netaji.

allowed to enter into the 'prohibited area' late in the evening to know about his requirements. While Aurobindo knew that Subhas had left Calcutta on 17th January 1941, he told the police that he had seen Netaji on 25th January, as Subhas had asked him to do. On the 26th January an announcement was made that he was no longer in his room. Aurobindo was a 'viable witness' observing that he saw Subhas Bose on the 25th night, while actually he had already crossed the Indo-Afghan border."

Like the above story of Netaji's escape, Pradip Bose expressed his opinion that *'at least five or six persons in the Provisional Government of Azad Hind knew that Netaji was planning his escape to the Soviet Union after the end of the war but only one person Habibur Rehman was chosen to fly with him. He was the sole Indian witness to the event of his death. Or, was it yet another non-event as vouched for by Aurobindo on the earlier occasion?"*

Sitanshu Das, a veteran journalist associated with the Indian Express Group of newspapers, wrote, in his research book *'Subhas: A Political Biography'* that *"at least eight members of his family knew that he was planning to leave Calcutta, but they too were not fully aware. In the Forward Bloc only a small group knew of his desire to leave the country — but not all knew how the plan would be executed. An outer ring of sympathisers presumably included Sardar Baldev Singh, industrialist, who was later to be independent India's first Defence Minister, and according to one report, Akali leader Master Tara Singh and some members of the Shiromani Akali Dal Executive Committee. Directly involved in the proposal was the directorate of the Kirti Kisan Party of Punjab which had agreed to organise his travel through the NWFP tribal territory and then to Kabul ..."*

Before describing another such thrilling and exciting incident related to the secretive nature of Netaji, we have to understand the circumstances of those times which compelled him to undertake a secret plan. By the end of 1942 Netaji was busy in Germany in organising the Indian Legion comprising nearly 4000 trained soldiers and officers. While celebrating the 'Independence Day for India' on January 26, 1943, he addressed a huge gathering in Berlin where hundreds of guests were also invited to witness the function. He spoke: *"The Congress under Gandhiji's leadership has demonstrated that it is possible to paralyse the administration with the weapon of passive resistance. The younger generation in India has, however, learnt from the last twenty years' experience that, while passive resistance can weaken or paralyse a foreign administration, it cannot overthrow or expel it without the use of physical force.*

"There are internal causes which account for my optimism. Among the internal causes, I may say that the campaign led by the Indian National Congress is spread all over India that the princely states are also participating in the all India fight and that the movement has spontaneously developed from passive resistance to active fighting. Among the external causes, I may say that India is not fighting alone this time."

When the above policy statement was being delivered, no one could guess what exactly Netaji meant. Actually his mind was engaged in some new and secretive adventure. Very few among his close circle could infer that Netaji might launch a decisive action against the British. On February 15, 1943, Singapore fell to the Japanese Army and on February 17 Col. Hunt, along with the British Indian troops, surrendered before Major Fujiwara in an impressive ceremony held at the Farrer Park, situated in the heart of the Singapore town.

By this time Netaji had done his home work well and succeeded in securing Hitler's suggestion that in view of the spectacular success of Japan on South-East Asian front, Netaji would have to shift himself to that region. Both agreed that it would take at least another one or two years before Germany herself could gain a direct influence in India to effectively assist the Indian freedom-fighters, whereas Japan could contribute help more strongly within a few months, if suitable measures were undertaken by them. Both also conformed to take up the matter with the Japanese Government. This understanding between Netaji and the Fuhrer was not enthusiastically supported by the German Foreign Office, but due to the insistence of Netaji, it was reluctantly approved.

Netaji was maintaining very cordial relations with the Japanese officials in Berlin. Col. Yamamoto Bin, the Japanese Military Attache in Berlin, was a good personal friend of Netaji and the Japanese Ambassador Lt. General Oshima Hiroshi was in acquaintance with Netaji since October 1941, when he was diplomatically approached and was fully convinced to contribute his services to provide Japanese aid for the Indian independence movement against the British. In the light of new military developments in South-East Asia, a series of meetings were held and finally the Japanese Government had given its green signal agreeing in principle that Netaji would be welcomed in Japan and would be given all possible support for his activities in furtherance of the Indian freedom movement.

Now the secretive part of Netaji's life was again on the test as at one end he was required to hide his intentions and programmes of shifting his activities from Germany to Japan, and at the other, he had to reach Japan which was almost the other end of the earth, passing through an area which was under the control of the enemy.

He was given several pieces of advice by his supporters as to how he had to implement his entire programme. Some of his advisors suggested that he could use an aeroplane belonging to the Lufthansa Company to travel to Japan via Soviet Union. This suggestion was not acceptable to the Japanese Prime Minister Hideki Tojo, on the ground that this would amount to a breach of trust between Soviet Union and Japan. Col. Yamamoto offered that he should travel by an Italian plane but Hitler himself warned Netaji against an air journey, which could compel him to a forced landing in the British territory. Journey by ship was also opposed because, in Fuhrer's opinion, Netaji was a too important personality and his life could not be endangered by such experiments. **Hitler suggested that he could place at his disposal a German submarine which would take him to Bangkok or any other suitable destination through a longer route via the Cape of Good Hope**. But the Japanese Naval Command objected to such a voyage under the pretext that its internal regulations did not permit any civilian to travel on a warship in wartime. Counterfoiling the Japanese objection Adam von Trott responded immediately that *'Subhas Chandra Bose is by no means a private person, but Commander-in-Chief of the Indian Liberation Army'.* Trott was virtually the head of the Indienreferat in the German Foreign Office and a former Rhodes scholar at Oxford; he was deeply involved in the pro-Allies, anti-Hitler Black Orchestra conspiracy. He was close to David Astor, head of the pro-German *"Cliven set"* in pre-1939 England,

All these discussions between the governments of Germany and Japan were conducted close-mouthly and in a concealed manner, though there had been involvement of many persons who belonged to different nationalities, languages and positions. And finally it was decided to carry Netaji upto a certain undisclosed place in the east and for the further journey, the responsibility was assigned to the Japanese Naval Authorities.

Before undertaking this secret journey, Netaji handed over his job, including the leadership of the Indian Legionaries in Germany to A.C.N. Nambiar, under the pretext that he was to go on a prolonged journey. A.C.N. Nambiar showed leaning towards communism and his first wife Suhasini, Sarojini Naidu's younger sister, was also a communist. He was appointed Bose's deputy in the Free India Centre in Berlin and was close to Adam Trott. By profession Nambiar was a journalist and was known to Netaji when he had spent the years of his exile in 1933-36 in Europe. According to the plan, on February 8, 1943 Netaji arrived at the port of Kiel in north Germany where a 77 meter long six-engine submarine U-180 was waiting for him. It was a brand new 1500 ton fastest boat with expert crews under the command of Werner Musenberg. In this perilous voyage his sole Indian companion was Zain-al-Abdin Hasan Saffrani, better known in the INA as Abid Hasan. He was also known in his close circle as *'Jai Hind Saffrani'* because he had coined the most famous slogan of India — Jai Hind. Abid Hasan reached Kiel separately without knowing his destination and he was informed of the itinerary only after the commencement of the journey.

Netaji and Abid Hasan continued to travel towards the east making a wide sweep out into the Atlantic Ocean. Meanwhile, a Japanese submarine left the Penang port on April 20, 1943 under strict orders not to attack or risk detection to the south of south-west of Madagascar. On April 26, after obtaining and confirming the codified signals and identities, both submarines agreed to coordinate. After waiting for a day for the sea to become calm on April 28 1945, a great adventure was undertaken and it was submarine to submarine transfer of the passengers in the annals of World War II in an area dominated by the enemy's air and naval forces. **Netaji and Abid Hasan were transhipped into the Japanese submarine via a rubber raft.**

Travelling across the ocean on May 6, 1943 the Japanese submarine reached safely at Sabang, which was an isolated off-shore islet north of Sumatra in Indo-China region. Netaji was welcomed as per assurance by Col. Yamamoto, who was in Berlin and who was now head of the Japanese liaison group — Hikari Kikan. Netaji's further journey was arranged by plane en-route Penang, Manila, Saigon and Taiwan to Tokyo, where he reached on May 16, 1943. He was given the Japanese name 'Matsuda' supposed to be a VIP.

Narrating before the Khosla Commission about the secret value of this incident, Col. Thakur Singh, who was INA's second in Command with Shah Nawaz Khan, said that Abid Hasan had told him that *'even if the British had cut him into pieces he would not have revealed that fact'* as to how he had completed his voyage with Netaji in submarines provided by German and Japanese naval authorities. For about four months none among Netaji's close circle could know his whereabouts and it was finally disclosed when he addressed a press conference in Tokyo on June 19, 1943 at Imperial Hotel.

—o—

6

Making of the Second Front

Is it not common experience that falsehood not only disagrees with truth but usually quarrels with each other? The great French philosopher Jean Jacques Rousseau who is better known as the *Father of Socialism,* suggested a rationale that *"falsehood has an infinity of combinations, but truth has only one mode of being."* The ramifications of falsehood further create such complexities which oppose each other and finally lead towards darkness. Netaji's mystery had such layers of falsehood which were actually creations of national and international conspiracies against him. If these conspiracies would have been allowed to be investigated then many agreed postulates and established personalities would have been exposed. His mysteries did have secret plans but those were not hypothetical stories. His escape attempts were not as complicated as they were presented. While undertaking such attempts he simply shifted himself to a better or safer place with the purpose of continuing his struggle for Indian independence.

In December 1937 Netaji had gone to his favourite health-resort, Badgastein, in Austria. From Badgastein he went to London in January 1938 where he received the news that he had been unanimously chosen the President of Indian National Congress.

During this visit to England he met with many prominent British leaders of both the Labour and the Liberal parties. Among these leaders were Clement Attlee, Arthur Greenwood, Bevin, Sir Stafford Cripps, Harold Laski, Lord Allen, Lord Halifax and Lord Zetland. It was an opportunity for a President-elect of Indian National Congress to assess the British mood on Indian freedom movement.

Netaji accepted to become the President in the Haripura Session of the Indian National Congress scheduled to take place in the memory of Vithal Bhai Patel, on February 19, 1938. Haripura is located on the banks of Rapti river in Gujerat. Author of the book '*Rediscovering Bose and Indian National Army*', Brig. R.P. Singh, wrote that *"it amounted to his 'Political Coronation' when his car, drawn by 51 bullocks, passed through 51 decorative gates with glamour and glory. One of the youngest president of the Congress, Bose was lustily cheered by the huge gathering on both the sides of the road, when he entered the Pandal with his impressive personality. Everyone who witnessed the ceremony was so completely thrilled that he cherished it as one of the most unprecedented phenomenon of his life."* Earlier on February 3, 1938, Netaji went to Wardha and discussed with Gandhiji in detail, and Gandhiji endorsed his proposed Presidential address which broadly covered all aspects of national issues and laid emphasis on the *"necessity of developing closer relations with our neighbours, viz., Persia, Afghanistan, Nepal, China, Burma, Siam, Malay States, East Indies and Ceylon."* He concluded his speech by saying that *"India freed means humanity saved."*

In his performance in India as the President of Indian National Congress, Netaji did his best to stiffen the opposition of the British. He adopted a policy of no-compromise in view of the changing international situation, particularly in Europe. He began an open propaganda campaign throughout India for his preparation to launch a national struggle for Indian freedom. He was successful in gaining support of the people. His services as the President of the Congress were recognised internationally. Netaji was given honour by publishing his photograph on the front cover of the internationally reputed magazine *'TIME'* in its issue of March 7, 1938.

His policy of stiffness towards the British caused annoyance in the circle known as the Gandhian wing of the Congress. This group was represented by Vallabhbhai Patel, Maulana Abul Kalam Azad, Rajendra Prasad, Govind Vallabh Pant, Sarojini Naidu, Bhulabhai Desai, Dr. Pattabhi Sitaramayya, Shankrrao Deo, Harekrishna Mahtab, J.B. Kripalani, Abdul Gaffar Khan, Jamnalal Bajaj, Jairam Das Daulat Ram, Jawaharlal Nehru, etc. The Gandhian wing was mild towards the British and was looking forward to an understanding with the British Indian Government. Netaji's attempts to launch a national struggle were being silently opposed as the Gandhian wing did not like to disturb the functioning of the Congress ministries and their parliamentary jobs in the provinces. In the beginning Gandhiji himself urged that a national struggle was out of question as the country was not ripe for such a movement.

Netaji was firm in his concept for a non-violent national non-cooperation movement as he was sure that Britain had no choice except engageing itself in the war against Germany. According to Netaji, the circumstances in Europe were providing a rare opportunity for hastening and bargaining for Indian freedom more suitably if an all India struggle was launched. A pact was signed on September 29, 1938 by England, France, Germany and Italy at Munich, the then capital of Bavaria, a State of south Germany. Under this agreement a part of Czechoslovakia was ceded to Germany. It gave a signal to Netaji, who was a very far-sighted scholar of international politics, to be alert to the imminent belligerence between Germany and Britain and the approaching world war. As he had envisaged, the involvement of the British Government in the war against Germany and Italy would be helpful to Indian freedom struggle by way of non-cooperation in the war efforts of the British Government in India from within the country, as well as in launching an armed struggle from outside in collaboration with the countries belligerent to Britain. By collaborating with the countries of different political principles which were rather abhorrent to India, he never meant to deviate from Indian principles.

The Gandhian wing was equally active against such moves of Netaji and they took a tough policy not allowing him to take a final decision till his term of, Presidentship ended. Further, Netaji's declaration to form a national Planning Committee for drawing up a comprehensive plan for industrialization and national development, also annoyed Gandhiji who was vehemently opposed to industrialization.

It was an open fact that Gandhiji was regarded as the most powerful leader of the country, and Netaji had also accepted him in very high esteem and had confidence in his leadership. At the same time, Netaji was aware that Gandhiji had some limitations due to his strict adherence to the *'non-violence'* philosophy. He also realised that a national struggle against the British was not possible as he could not convince Gandhiji, who was not prepared even to listen about the fast changing international events and the erupting new crisis for the British. In his book "*The Indian Struggle*' Netaji wrote that due to his rigid convictions —*"Gandhiji would not seize the opportunity for attacking the British Government. It was then that he also realised for the first time that Gandhiji regarded struggle with Britain in near future as outside the domain of possibility."*

Thus the Gandhian wing was now an opposite faction for him and its contentious functioning with its President became known to the public. This resulted in a breach of trust between Netaji and

Gandhiji and the gap was becoming wider. Netaji decided to seek re-election for another term for the post of the President of the Indian National Congress. His candidature was vigorously opposed by Gandhiji. But Netaji won in the contest inspite of some Working Committee members' appeal including Sardar Patel, Dr. Rajendra Prasad, Jamnalal Bajaj, Bhulabhai Desai, Acharya J.B. Kriplani, Jairam Das Daulat Ram and Shankar Rao Deo, in favour of Dr. Pattabhi Sitaramayya. Netaji's clear victory on January 29, 1939 to continue as the Congress President for a second term was the first public defeat of Gandhiji who himself openly acknowledged it in his weekly *'Harijan'* and in Bardoli on January 31, 1939 in a press statement.

On March 11, 12 and 13, 1939, the 52nd Session of Indian National Congress was attended by about two lakh workers at Tripuri, near Jabalpur, Madhya Pradesh. While presiding over the session, Netaji proposed that *'the Indian National Congress should immediately send an ultimatum to the British Government demanding independence within six months and should simultaneously prepare for a national struggle.'* The proposal was not passed due to open and vehement opposition of Gandhiji and other factions including the Congress Socialist Party and the National Front which were functioning within the Congress. Netaji had won the re-election but he could not manage sufficient majority to get his resolution adopted. A perplexing situation arose in the Congress where on every conceivable occasion, the Gandhian wing adopted an obstructionist policy to oppose its President with a view to make it impossible for him to function. The President-elect Netaji was seriously ill at the time. He was brought to the podium on a stretcher. Although Gandhiji himself stayed away from the session, yet his interest was well guarded by his lieutenants who adopted every possible way to obstruct the working of Netaji.

Netaji tried to compromise through direct negotiations with Gandhiji but they proved abortive. On another issue relating to declare his Congress Working Committee, the executive body of the Congress, the Gandhian wing continued their obstructions. For this purpose, on Nehru's consent Govind Vallabh Pant was persuaded to move a proposal to restrict the constitutional freedom of the Congress President to nominate the Congress Working Committee. Further, there were open gestures and press statements that the Gandhian wing was determined neither to accept the leadership of Netaji nor to allow him to control the machinery of the Congress. Tactically, the Gandhian wing was in an advantageous position because it was well organized as one unit under the leadership of Gandhiji. The left wing or the radical elements including the Congress Socialist Party, which lacked a clear revolutionary perspective, were, though instrumental in Netaji's reelection as President due to their numerical majority, but were loosely organised, with many personalities within and without a commanding centre. At this crucial point the Congress Socialist Party opted to remain neutral and the Communist Party of India (CPI) which was called the National Front, also decided to support the Gandhian wing. The CPI was very cautious as the proletarian technique of struggle had been introduced in India and the Communists were not ready to join any non-violent and non-cooperation movement, even if it was launched by Netaji. In these circumstances Netaji did not agree to function as a puppet President and therefore, he opted to resign his Presidentship on April 29, 1939.

Like the Congress Socialist Party, Netaji formed on May 3, 1939 in Kolkata a radical group within the Indian National Congress with a view to rallying the entire left wing under one banner and under one name—*'The Forward Bloc'*. The Forward Bloc was joined by several leaders who had their own following. Among these leaders were Prof. N.G. Ranga, Madurai Annapurniah, Sardar Sardul Singh Caveeshar, Swami Sahajanand Saraswati, Kakani Venkataratnam, Indulal Yagnik, Dhanraj Sharma, Vishambhar Dayal Tripathi, Chandubhai Puranik, Sheelbhadra Yajee, Niharendu Dutt-Mazumdar, Ashrafuddin Chawdhury, Mukundlal Sircar, R.S. Ruikar, H.V. Kamath, Senapati Bapat, Prof. V. Kulkarni, Girdhar Thakkar, K.F. Nariman, Muthuramalinga Thevar, Rajamannar Chetty, T. Kanan, Shankerlal, Trailokya Nath Chakravarty, etc. The immediate objective of the Forward Bloc was to begin an uncompromising struggle with the British imperialism for winning Indian independence. Netaji had two expectations from the Forward Bloc: one, to counter more effectively the Gandhian wing, and second, to activate his followers for any major crises in future. Thus there was no doubt that the Forward Bloc sprang into existence in response to a historical necessity. It was more a necessity of the time because India had to apply its all possible means to secure independence and its people would not be hampered by any philosophical notions like Gandhian non-violence or any sentimentalism like Nehru's anti-Axis foreign policy.

Unlike the Congress Socialist Party and other radical groups within the Congress, the formation of the Froward Bloc was regarded as a serious challenge to the leadership of Gandhiji. It had actually sharpened the internal conflicts within the Congress. The Forward Bloc began its activities in full swing since its very inception. On the initiative of the Gandhian wing, the Congress Working Committee took serious measures to curb the activities of the Bloc in the name of disciplinary action against some of its members. But it only strengthened the morale of the members of the Bloc.

Jawaharlal Nehru wrote in his book '*Discovery of India*' that "*There was a big difference in outlook between him* (*Netaji*) *and others in the Congress Executive, both in regard to foreign and internal matters, and this led to a break early in 1939. He then attacked Congress policy publicly and, early in August, 1939, the Congress Executive took the very unusual step of taking disciplinary action against him, one of its ex-presidents."*

Remembering those days and expressing his deepest convictions Netaji clarified in Shonan (Singapore) in 1943 that *"I have been actively working in the independence movement ever since I left the portals of university in 1921. I have been through all the civil disobedience movements during the last two decades. In addition to this I have been repeatedly put in prison without trial on the suspicion of having been connected with secret revolutionary movements whether non-violent or violent with which I have been familiar. I may also assert, without slightest exaggeration, that there is no nationalist leader in India who can claim to possess the manysided experiences that I have been able to acquire. In the light of this experience I came to the conclusion that all the efforts that we could put forward inside India will not suffice to expel the British from our country. If the struggle at home had sufficed to achieve liberty of our people I would not have been so foolish as to undertake this unnecessary risk and hazard."*

During his campaign to mobilise people's opinion when Netaji was addressing a mammoth gathering of two hundred thousand people at the Marine Beach, Madras (Chennai) on September 3, 1939, he was informed that as per his expectations Britain had declared war against Germany and the Viceroy of India issued an ordinance containing the most stringent powers for the suppression of internal disorder while declaring India a belligerent state with it. On September 6, 1939, Gandhiji had a meeting with the Viceroy Lord Linlithgow and issued a press statement that *'inspite of the differences between India and Britain on the question of Indian independence, India would cooperate with Britain in her hour of danger.'*

Many senior leaders of the Congress supported Gandhiji's views. Against the views of Gandhiji the Forward Bloc firmly decided to mobilise public opinion and compel the Congress for not cooperating with the British in their war efforts. Netaji continued to emphasize anti-British and anti-war propaganda which was supported by the Indian people but it resulted against the Forward Bloc and many of its members were thrown into prison.

The efforts of Netaji were successful and the Congress Working Committee was forced to pass a lengthy resolution. Understanding and assessing the sentiments of the people, the Congress resolution asked the British Government to declare its war aims and stated that if India was granted freedom *"a free and democratic India will gladly associate herself with other free nations for mutual defence against aggression and for economic cooperation."* The resolution also assured an offer of cooperation in Britain's war efforts under certain conditions. In reply to the Congress resolution, the Viceroy of India offered on October 17, 1939 to establish a Consultative Group including Indian representatives to advise the Viceroy on questions pertaining to the war. The Viceroy reaffirmed to grant *Dominion Status* at some future date.

The Viceroy's reply was responded to on October 29, 1939 by the Congress. The people of India were agitated and therefore, the Congress threatened to launch a civil disobedience movement against the British and to resign as Congress ministers in eight provinces. On the other side, the Forward Bloc organised an Anti-Imperialist Conference in Nagpur in October 1939 where public participation was huge. Reacting on the support of the masses for Netaji in the country Gandhiji accepted that after resignation from the post of the President, Netaji's popularity had increased many-fold. **Now the Congress felt the pressure and responded to atone the people's sentiments and it took a tough stand against the British**

Government. As a matter of fact, there was no firmness in the Congress to implement their resolutions. The despondent attitude of the Congress continued for about six months until its annual session at Ramgarh in Bihar.

In the meantime, Gandhiji wrote a letter to Netaji on November 23, 1939 from Allahabad. He showed his deep concern for Netaji and expressed: *"For the time being you are my lost sheep. Some day I shall find you returning to the fold, if I am right and my love is pure."*

But Netaji was firm in his stand and in order to further pressurise the Congress against its compromising attitude with the British, the Forward Bloc and the Kisan Sabha of Swami Sahjananda Saraswati jointly convened the All India Anti-Compromise Conference at Ramgarh on the same dates when the Congress annual session was scheduled to take place. Actually this Conference was a huge demonstration of about 20,000 delegates, almost four times more than the Congress delegates. Netaji wrote in his book *'The Indian Struggle: 1920-1942'* that *"the Congress did not decide anything at Ramgarh about its war policy. For six months its policy had been non-committal, with the result that the British Government had been going on exploiting India for war purposes."* Therefore, it was decided in the Anti-Compromise Conference to immediately launch a fight over the issue of war and of India's demand for independence by observing a National Week beginning from April 6 to April 13, 1940.

At Ramgarh the core group of the Forward Bloc discussed in detail the national and international affairs and approved a plan to seek foreign assistance for an armed uprising in the final phase of India's freedom struggle during the war. Netaji disclosed the rationale of this decision later at his public meeting in Shonan in March 1943. He said that *"the help that our countrymen at home needed and still need is twofold. One moral and the other material. Firstly, they have to be morally convinced that their victory is assured in the long run. Secondly, they have to be given military help from outside. In order to do the first, one had to study objectively the international war situation and thereby find out what the result of the war was going to be. To do the second, one had to find out what Indians outside India could do to help their countrymen at home and also if it was possible to obtain help from the enemies of British imperialism."*

In this speech Netaji spoke with confidence that *"I am now in a position to tell you that both these objectives have been fulfilled. By travelling abroad I could see things for myself and could study the respective positions of the belligerent powers. Thereafter, when I came to the conclusion that the defeat of the Anglo-American powers was assured, I conveyed that information to my countrymen at home. I was delighted to find that my countrymen all over the world were wide awake and anxious to undertake their share of the national struggle. I was also gratified to find that the Axis Powers and Nippon in particular were eager to see India free and they were prepared to render any help that was within their power."*

At Ramgarh it was also decided that Netaji should leave the country to avoid his arrest and detention. As per the official records of the West Bengal Government, Netaji had applied for a passport in October 1939 and desired to visit China. The West Bengal Government had agreed but the British Government expressed suspicion that he might become a foreign agent and thus might foment anti-British activities. Later, Netaji's plan to go out of the country was temporarily stayed. The core group of the Forward Bloc was careful to keep these decisions secret until these were implemented successfully. One of the vice-Presidents of the Forward Bloc, Shankerlal, along with an activist L.K. Sharma was assigned the job to contact the Russian ambassador in Tokyo. According to the plan, Shankerlal visited Japan on a forged passport, but when he came back, Netaji was in Kolkata's Presidency jail, and it had also been doubtful whether he could meet Netaji to share his views with him or had he been successful in his mission?

About the mind of Netaji, there is a reference in the book '*Breakthrough in Burma*', written by Dr. Ba Maw, the deposed Prime Minister under the British Act of 1935, who led Burma to independence on August 1, 1943 under the Japanese rule. In April 1940 Dr. Ba Maw had put some demands before the Japanese authorities to liberate Burma from the British rule. Remembering his meeting with Kuga, the Japanese Consul in Rangoon, and Suzuki, a Japanese secret agent in Burma, Dr. Ba Maw wrote that *"I think it was Kuga who told me that Subhas Bose had asked for the same thing for India, saying that if Japan would not give the help he needed, he would turn to Russia for it, because he was determined to get it somehow. Bose, he said, had asked for ten million rupees and ten thousand rifles, to begin with."*

According to Sitanshu Das, as stated in his book *'Subhas: A Political Biography'*, Netaji *"at the outbreak of the Second World War, had acquired a pre-eminent national standing and was well-known abroad as an Indian leader who could profoundly influence the future course of the freedom struggle."* Netaji was well aware of national and international situations and his decision to form a 'Second Front' outside India was not taken in haste.

Soon after the declaration of war by Britain on September 4, 1939, Gandhiji expressed his views after his meeting with the Viceroy Lord Linlithgow that he was still in favour of cooperation with Britain. After his meeting Gandhiji said in a press conference that there were differences on the question of India's independence and the people in India were not sympathetic to the British, but he would not like to oppose the British Government or the Allied

Powers. Gandhiji, along with many others in India including the radicalist M.N. Roy and the Communists, felt that the Axis Powers were guilty of aggressions which had to be opposed. Although even after repudiating Marxism, M.N. Roy's pro-Allied stand was still influenced by his views of economic determinism, yet he emphasised through his diagrammatic presentation that human affairs were supreme to all other aspects. Whereas Gandhiji's approach was due to his 'non-violence philosophy' and his love for the enemies. Gandhiji issued a statement during the CWC meeting at Wardha on September 14, 1939 that *"I was sorry to find myself alone in thinking that whatever support was to be given to the British should be given unconditionally. This could only be done on a purely non-violent attitude."* He was insisting openly inspite of the well known fact that the Viceroy of India had refused to make a declaration of Britain's war aims or to give assurance of Indian independence after the war or any substantial interim change in the Viceroy's Executive Council. Gandhiji clarified his stand that *"I do not see at the present moment conditions propitious for an immediate launching of the campaign. We are hemmed in with difficulties greater than those we had to face in the past. They are external and internal. The external difficulties are due to the fact that we have declared unmistakably what we want and the Government have also declared their intentions as clearly as possible. Then there is a fact that the British Government are engaged in a World War and, naturally, if we engage them in a fight, we ask for enough trouble."*

Like Gandhiji's views Nehru had his own reasons to cooperate with the British in their war efforts. He was in favour of a more vigorous participation with the British Government only if a National War Council was formed with the representatives of the Congress and its pro-Congress leaders and an assurance to amend the Government of India Act, 1935. It had been disclosed that Nehru desired through his British friends to persuade the Viceroy to make only a hint that India could get a favour after the war and then it would become possible for the Congress to join in the war efforts.

Contrary to the above views on account of the Second World War, Netaji thought that each development of the war situation had to be interpreted either with a view as what effect would it produce on India's struggle for independence, or what India could learn from any of the recently liberated nations, with an overall approach whether or not that would help to strengthen India in its fight against imperialism during and after the war. In his journal *'Forward Bloc'* he wrote on April 27, 1940 that *"During the last four years and particularly during the last eight months, one has noticed that as compared with the old Imperialist powers, a new Imperialist power like Germany has shown far greater dynamism and mobility. Without this dynamism, a revolutionary and unheard of step like the Soviet-German pact would not have been possible. And without this mobility a swift move on Scandinavia which has taken the whole world by surprise, would never have been possible."*

On the issue of national struggle, Nehru came out openly to oppose Netaji and on May 20, 1940 he made a statement that *"launching a civil disobedience campaign at this time when Britain is engaged in a life and death struggle would be an act derogatory to India's honour."* The statement was endorsed by Gandhiji who said, *"We do not seek our independence out of Britain's ruin. That is not the way of non-violence."*

In June 1940 Netaji had lengthy talks with Gandhiji who was absolutely non-committal and firmly advocated that the country was not yet prepared to launch a national struggle on the eve of the war. He told Netaji that if he would launch such a struggle to win freedom for India and if he would get success, he would be the first to congratulate him. Gandhiji's explanation in this regard was published in *'Harijan'* on July 13, 1940: *"He told me in a friendly manner that he would do what the Working Committee had failed to do ... I told him that, if at the end of his plan there was 'Swaraj' during my life-time, mine would be the first telegram of congratulation he would receive. If while he was conducting his campaign I became a convert, I should whole-heartedly acclaim him as my leader... But I warned him that his way was wrong."*

Netaji also met M.A. Jinnah, the President of the Muslim League, and tried to convince him that a national struggle was the real need of the time. Netaji assured Jinnah that he would be acceptable as the first Prime Minister of free India, but Jinnah was adamant for his demand of Pakistan. Netaji's meeting with V.D. Savarkar, the President of Hindu Mahasabha, had not yielded the desired results as he was keen to support the war efforts of the British on the logic that by such support he could secure military training to Hindus by joining the Indian British Army.

At the second All India Conference of the Forward Bloc on June 18, 1940 Netaji proclaimed that *"It is for the Indian people to make an immediate demand for the transference of power to them through a Provisional National Government... When things settle down inside and abroad, the Provisional National Government will convene a Constitutional Assembly for framing a full-fledged Constitution for the country."*

In the meantime, Netaji was secretly planning his escape from India to USSR. According to new disclosures, Sardar Niranjan Singh Talib, editor of Kolkata's Punjabi daily newspaper *'Deshdarpan'*, introduced to him Achhar Singh Cheena who had been a Ghadarite in his early years and had attended a Soviet school for eastern revolutionaries before escaping to Kolkata to live as an absconder on charges of murder. Cheena was also directly known to Netaji as he had met him during the Gaya Session of the Congress in April 1939. Cheena became an intermediary to seek the cooperation and help of the Kirti Kisan Party, a wing of the CPI in Punjab. Cheena was considered trustworthy as he had an identity number, which was a kind of password to contact Soviet foreign missions to secure assistance at the time of need.

Netaji was overcautious in his planning to leave the country and smelled that he was being chased and therefore, he deferred his plan to avoid unnecessary trouble. All of a sudden to divert the attention of the British a day before the Sirajuddaula Day, on July 2, 1940, he decided to launch an agitation against the Hallwell Memorial, which was erected in Kolkata to pay tributes to those British soldiers who had been killed in India. Netaji's trick worked and he was arrested on July 2, 1940, for the last time and it was his eleventh incarceration along with hundreds of his coworkers.

Netaji's arrest resulted in a great commotion among the leaders of all political parties. People gave a favourable reaction. Narrating his reactions Netaji wrote in his book 'that some of the Congress leaders *"began to press Gandhiji to launch the fight, otherwise they would lose all influence and prestige in the country. Others gradually began to join the fight without waiting for his orders. Ultimately, Gandhiji's hands were forced. On September 15, 1940, when the Congress withdrew its offer of cooperation and invited Gandhiji to resume the leadership of the Congress. In October, 1940 Gandhiji declared that he had decided to commence resistance to the British Government's war efforts but not on mass scale ... the Forward Bloc was jubilant that Gandhiji's hands had been forced. Now that both wings of the Congress — the Gandhian wing and the Forward Bloc — were definitely committed to an anti-British and anti-war policy, it was time to consider bigger plans for achieving the independence of India."*

Although Netaji was confined in prison without any trial but due to his prolonged studies, visits and deliberations he was convinced about his assessment of international situation about three things. These were, firstly, that Britain would lose the war and the British Empire would break up. Secondly, inspite of being in a precarious position, the British will not hand over power to the Indian people and the latter will have to fight for their freedom. And thirdly, India will win her independence if she played her part in the war against Britain and collaborated with powers that were fighting with Britain. Netaji's firm conclusion was that *'India should actively enter the field of international politics'.*

With these conclusions Netaji felt that it would be a gross political blunder to remain inactive in prison, when history was being made elsewhere. He explored all the possibilities of being released in a legal manner but he was disappointed. He was also deeply hurt as the Congress Working Committee and the Congress President had failed to voice even a routine protest against his arrest. He wrote to his elder brother Sarat Chandra Bose from the Presidency jail in Kolkata that silence on the part of the Congress reflected its deep rooted hostility towards him and their incapacity to rise above personal vendetta.

On this act of the Congress to ignore Netaji's arrest, Gandhiji wrote in *'Harijan'* that "*...so long as Subhas Babu considers a particular course of action to be correct, he has the right, and it is his duty, to pursue it whether the Congress likes it or not... Even so, if success attends his effort and India gains her freedom, it will justify his rebellion, and the Congress will not only not condemn his rebellion but welcome him as the saviour.*"

As Netaji was determined to get out of prison, he sent an ultimatum to the British Government pointing out that there was no moral or legal justification for detaining him in jail without any trial and that if he would not be released forthwith, he would fast unto death. Netaji's threat was not heard and he had to begin the hunger strike on November 29, 1940. As the popularity of Netaji was touching high peaks, the British authorities got frightened after the seventh day of his fast due to his deteriorating health and they were compelled to release him on December 5, 1940, with a clear intention of re-arresting him after a month or so.

Netaji secured his release with a hidden and specific purpose — to leave the country and organise a Second Front of Indians outside India. According to him, he was on the right path and had commented on this situation that *"Not even my enemies will have the audacity to say that I am capable of doing against the interest of my country. And if the British Government could not demoralise me or allure me, no other power on the earth can do so. Therefore, believe me when I say that if you want any external help in your struggle against British imperialism, the Axis Powers will gladly come to your aid. But whether you need any help or not is for you to decide, and it goes without saying that if you could do without any help, it would be the best course for India. At the same time I should add that if the almighty British Government can go round the world with a begging bowl asking for help everywhere, even from the enslaved and impoverished people of India, there is nothing wrong in our taking help from outside, if we are forced to do so."*

With a very clear motive and planning Netaji disappeared from his residence on Saturday January 17, 1941. It was not a sudden decision. Very quietly he left his home in Kolkata by dodging the secret police which was always on vigil in front of his residence. Explaining the background in this connection a very important disclosure was made by Lt. Manwati Arya that during the first part of 1939, Netaji had studied a bulky police dossier which was secretly maintained by the Kolkata police on his activities. The dossier was obtained by him to know the secret sources of the Government and the methods applied for this purpose. He could get the dossier through one of his colleagues Satya Ranjan Bakshi who edited a journal, *'Liberty'*. Actually this was an opportunity when Netaji could learn that even some very close members of his family and his co-workers were passing information about him. The dossier was brought to him for seven consecutive nights and was being very carefully returned to its place in the police strong-room every morning. The dossier disclosed as to how the police reports relating to him were prepared by the police surveillance about his movements and who provided these.

Netaji's nephew Ashoka Nath Bose also wrote in his book *'My Uncle Netaji'* supporting the disclosure made by Lt. Manwati Arya that *"I know uncle was disagreeably surprised to learn therefrom about the dubious role of some of his so-called co-workers and was also forewarned from a perusal of the dossier about the surveillance of his movements by one of his own cousins. This also proved of incalculable help to him in steering clear of actual and potential enemies while drawing up his plan of escape from India a year later."*

Netaji was actually restless as he was keenly willing to exploit the opportunity of war for India's freedom struggle. He decided to implement his plan by leaving India. Lt. Manawati Arya gives in her book *'Patriot'* the primary description of Netaji's secret escape of 1941 in the following words:

"The plan and arrangements of his adventurous escape were kept strictly secret, even from those who were allowed to meet him. His brother Sarat Bose and the only confidant nephew Sisir were told about his programme merely two days before his exit from the house. Funds for his secret plan were collected intensively by the All India Forward Bloc from all sources and passed on to him. All personal effects giving an

impression that they were belongings of a Muslim gentleman which were purchased secretly and hurriedly by Sisir Bose with the guidance of Mian Akbar Shah, to be packed in a suitcase, an attache and a bed-roll marked 'M.Z.' prominently. He was going to travel, disguised as a Jubblepore-based Moulvi Mohammad Ziauddin, Travelling Inspector of the Empire of India Assurance Co. Ltd. Mian Akbar Shah, a member of Forward Bloc from North-West Frontier Province was to escort him all the way from Kolkata to Peshawar imperceptibly. The clothes of Subhas in Muslim fashion were stitched to his size by a tailor conducted secretly to him for taking the measurement earlier. Sisir Bose, well prepared with instuctions from his uncle Subhas, was to drive the car 'Wanderer', taking him to Bararee in Bihar where Ashok Bose, the eldest son of Sarat Bose, employed as a mining engineer at Dhanbad, lived with his wife. After a day's rest there, he was to board the Delhi-Kalka Mail to change for Peshawar at Delhi."

The popular story of Netaji's escape in 1941 was almost based on the descriptions in the books — *'The Great Escape: My Fifty-five Days With Netaji'* and *'When Bose Was Ziauddin'*, written by Bhagat Ram Talwar alias Rahmat Khan and Uttam Chand Malhotra respectively. He lived with Netaji in Kabul from the last week of January 1941 to March 18, 1941 when Netaji left Kabul. Talwar had been an active worker of the Kirti Kisan Party. Simultaneously, he submitted his reports to the British secret services in India, the Soviet secret service NKVD in Kabul, the Secretariat of the Kirti Kisan Party in Lahore and the headquarters of the CPI in Bombay. Talwar provided safe passage to Netaji from Peshawar to Kabul in January 1941 when he accompanied Netaji.

Some new information is now available through the latest publications of the German Historical Institute, and the Public Records Office, both situated in London, along with some declassified documents available in India's National Archives which narrated a different version. After arriving in Kabul, Netaji presumed that he would get Russian help to secure safe sanctuary in Soviet Union to continue his struggle for freedom. But he was disappointed to find that the Russian ambassador in Kabul was not even ready to provide a visa to travel to Moscow.

It has been a fact that Netaji tried to establish links with the Soviet Union. In June 1939 he was successful in smuggling a letter to the leader of the Communist Party in Great Britain for onward transmission to Moscow. His nephew Amiya Bose, the second son of Sarat Chandra Bose, was a student at Cambridge. He could conceal the letter during his search by the Indian police in Bombay while proceeding to London after his summer vacations. This letter reached its destination. Similarly, in December 1939 Netaji tried to manage to sent another letter to the Soviet Government with his proposal for Soviet help in India's struggle for independence through the Communist Party of India. The letter was included in the agenda of the meeting of the Left Consolidation Committee. After deliberations in the Politburo of the CPI, the proposal of Netaji was returned. P.C. Joshi, a senior leader of the CPI, criticized Netaji and said that the Forward Bloc was a bourgeous reformist formation and a disruptionist agency which had to be opposed.

As per Netaji's plan Achher Singh Cheena along with another activist Ram Kishan was assigned by the Kirti Kisan directorate to contact the Soviet embassy in Kabul. But they failed in their mission as the Soviet officials were unwilling to receive Netaji. They were supposed to pass this information either to Netaji while he was in Kolkata or to the directorate of the Kirti Kisan Party. But Netaji could learn this fact only when he himself had reached Kabul. As a matter of fact Netaji would have been in great trouble if he had not been extra cautious and careful. He was preparing himself for months after the outbreak of the Second World War and was perhaps aware of such hazards. Although the Kirti Kisan Party and its intermediaries promised him some basic support to secure safe sanctuary on the Soviet territory, but actually they endangered him and his plan — yet Netaji had some more cards under his sleeves to play.

In one of his radio broadcasts on July 6, 1944, Netaji explained to Gandhiji as to why he undertook such a terrible risk of leaving India without any sound support and with very little preparation. He said that *"it was the easiest thing for me to remain at home and go on working... It was also an easy thing for me to remain in an Indian prison, while the war lasted."*

Netaji's adventurous journey to cross the Indian frontier was the biggest political sensation not only for the British Government but also for all freedom-fighters of different political parties including the people of India. He was determined to become an active player in the affairs of war in Europe and to use the opportunity to accelerate and hasten India's independence. The directorate of the Kirti Kisan Party in Lahore was directly involved and had assured Netaji regarding all suitable arrangements for his safe passage to Kabul through the NWFP tribal region. Its emissaries were committed to introduce Netaji with full dignity to the Soviet Ambassador for finalising his sanctuary in USSR. Netaji could guess from the activities of Bhagat Ram Talwar, Acchar Singh Cheena, Teja Singh Swatantar and Harminder Singh Sodhi that he could be exposed to perilous risks while in Kabul. He could guess by the behaviour of the Kriti Kisan agents that his planning to enter Soviet Russia had been endangered. He could also understand that he had reposed his faith on persons who were also acting as the Allied's double-cross and were not hesitant to pass on the information of his whereabouts which might have resulted in his arrest.

Bhagat Ram Talwar was assuring Netaji that the Soviet Union had agreed to help India's independence struggle with arms and ammunition including financial support. Talwar was simultaneously maintaining his links with Italian and German diplomats on the same issue for landing Netaji in the Russian territory. **Now it became evident that actually no adequate arrangements had been made by the agents of the Kirti Kisan Party.** The Party viewed the issue with a different angle. They desired to support Netaji for an armed uprising in India with the USSR's help and thus to implement their agenda of militant policy.

The surprising part in this story was that after learning that Soviet Russia unwilling to receive Netaji, Cheena and Ramkishan proceeded to travel was through Soviet Central Asia and did not pass this information to Netaji. This was a very difficult situation which gave lots of physical and mental tension to Netaji. The garrulous and gabby discussions of the Kirti Kisan representatives compelled Netaji to think afresh in the matter.

Netaji was well aware of the condition of post-Versailles Europe. He himself had visited Europe extensively and studied the affairs of all important countries to understand objectively the politics of Europe at that time. In many countries of Europe Netaji had been successful to arouse interest in India's freedom struggle during his visits between the years 1933 to 1936. He was also able to gather first-hand information relating to European incidents and individuals who played important roles. Netaji was definitely competent to acquire a glimpse of the coming events. In his study tour in those years he visited several times countries like Italy, Germany, Austria, Hungary, Czechoslovakia, Poland, the Balkans, Ireland, etc., and well understood the growth of the new forces that were ready to challenge the old order and were effectively functioning within the provisions of the Treaty of Versailles on the one hand and the League of Nations on the other.

In his study tour of Europe, Netaji was entertained by important personalities of Europe. His recognition as a dedicated leader for India's cause was well established. In Rome he was received by Signor Mussolini, the head of the Italian Government, who had also greeted Mahatma Gandhi in 1931 with a warm reception in Italy. As to Netaji's the dictator of Italy had conveyed to Gandhiji also his best wishes for India's movement. In Kabul Netaji could meet Pietro Quaroni, an Italian diplomat with the rank of minister in Italian embassy. Quaroni was fascinated by the views of Netaji and his personality. He proved a very strong link for Netaji to secure a passport in the name of Orlando Mazzotta, an Italian diplomat. Although Netaji was offered an invitation to come to Italy through Quaroni who rose to the rank of a senior minister in the Italian Government after the war, yet Netaji's aim was not limited only to manage a sanctuary for his person, but he was more interested in seeking help to continue his fight against the British for Indian struggle for freedom.

With the assistance of Talwar a Soviet-KGB intelligence agent Mikhael Andrevich Allakherdov, who was popularly known as *'Zaman'* in Kabul, met Netaji but there had been no evidence to suggest whether the Soviet authorities had responded to the request of Netaji or not. The new discovery of declassified documents has revealed that the head of German intelligence body Abwehr's Rear Admiral, Walhelm Franz Cannaris, was personally monitoring the escape affair of Netaji through Bhagat Ram Talwar. Talwar had been liasioning for Netaji with Abwehr. It was also noticed by Netaji that Talwar undertook to provide safe passage only because of monetary considerations. Netaji's stay in Kabul was becoming longer and it was dangerous to his security as the British agents were also alert and were anxious to encircle him.

In these compelling circumstances and concerted efforts by the diplomats of Italy, Germany and Japan, it was finalised that Netaji had to leave Kabul immediately for Berlin. This journey could get the approval of the Russian authorities for managing a short-time stay in Moscow after great pressure by diplomats. Netaji himself was still keen to contact the Russian Government to explore the possibility whether the Russians would accept him.

While implementing his plan Netaji practised well to pretend deaf and dumb when he stayed in Peshawar for about six days. He also learned how to behave like a true Muslim when he left Peshawar for Kabul via tribal areas. In those days it was the time of chilly cold weather which made him sick. But his mission was calling him and he could succed in leaving Kabul on March 18, 1941, almost two months after leaving Kolkata. His further journey to Bokhara in USSR was made through hostile terrain, the lofty mountains of Hind Kush, the cliffs of Tashkurgan, dilapidated ruins of an old city, the holy shrine of Mazar-e-Sharif and one of the world's oldest city Samarkand, popularly known as Tashkent. This strenuous journey was undertaken by car with an Italian diplomatic passport in the name of *'Orlando Mazzotta'* along with a civil engineer Baurat Wenger who coordinated in establishing contacts with foreign embassies. Baurat Wenger accompanied Netaji upto Berlin.

Considering from the security point of view, Netaji travelled from Tashkent to Moscow by train on March 20, 1941. Milan Hauner, the author of *'India in Axis Strategy'*, wrote that Netaji *"would have preferred to collaborate with the Soviets and he certainly tried to approach them during his short stay in Moscow. But he found them inaccessible for political talks."* There has been no evidence that while in his very short stay, Netaji could really contact any important politician or diplomat in Moscow. According to an unauthenticated report, Achhar Singh Cheena, along with an Indian Communist in Moscow, had organised a few meetings with Netaji and senior leaders of USSR's Government with the expectation of Soviet backing for Netaji's plan, but the Russian leadership could not take any decision at that point of time. It has also been said but not confirmed by available documents that Netaji's hope was not lost as he had expressed his gratitude for Soviet leadership in his letter after reaching Berlin to Mikhailovich Molotov, the USSR's Foreign Minister.

Lastly, it was actually the success of German Secret Service *'Abwehr'* and its head Rear Admiral Wilhelm Franz Cannaris, that Netaji landed in Berlin on April 3, 1941 inspite of Hitler's non-committal stand for India's freedom movement and a negative report about Netaji's love for Communism by a Nazi informant Walter Schellenberg, who was the head of Reich Main Security Office, also known as RHSA. Cannaris had activated the then German Ambassador in Kabul, Hans Pilger, to convince the Russian Ambassador V. Kozolov in favour of Netaji. The initiative of the German diplomat resulted in issuing a visa to Netaji, travelling incognito as Italian diplomat Orlando Mazzotta. It had been an interrogative fact that **this visa was issued by the Deputy Foreign Minister of USSR A. Vyshinski himself and the Soviets had not only secretly hosted Netaji in Moscow but had also arranged his onward journey to Berlin.** Cannari's main aim was that Germany ought to support Netaji because a large number of anti-British Indian exiles and prisoners of war were arriving in Germany and they could be utilised for the German cause. And thus Netaji landed in Berlin and was surrounded by a group of officials of German Foreign Office and Working Group of India in Germany but all this looked like a very cool reception for a person of Netaji's stature and calibre.

Maulana Abul Kalam Azad has recorded his sentiments in his famous book *'India Wins Freedom'* in the following words:

"Soon there was one important change in the Indian political situation. Subhas Chandra Bose had, with the outbreak of the war, started a campaign for active opposition to the war efforts. His activities led to his imprisonment, but he was released when he undertook a fast. On January 26, 1941, it become known that he had left India. For over a year nothing was heard about him and people were not sure whether he was alive or dead. In March 1942, all doubts were set at rest when he made a speech which was broadcasted by Berlin Radio ...

"I also saw that Subhas Bose's escape to Germany had made a great impact on Gandhiji. He had not formerly approved many of Bose's actions, but now I found a change in his outlook. *Many of his remakrs convinced me that he admired the courage and resourcefulness Subhas Bose had displayed in making his escape from India. His admiration for Subhas Bose unconsciously coloured his views about the whole war situation."*

In Germany Netaji was well aware that he would not get the favourable situation as he had wished and planned in Kolkata and as he would have been provided in Russia, but to him this was the time when he could openly tell the whole world including the British imperialists as to how India would be liberated. According to him, now it were the Indians outside India who had to be organised as a fighting force which would be powerful enough to attack the British army in India. He was sure that when he would be able to do so, a revolution would break out not only among the civilian population at home which Gandhiji was expected to lead, but also among the Indian army which was standing under the British flag. Thus Netaji's plan was to attack the British Government from both sides — from inside India as well as from outside. Such action would collapse the British Empire and the Indian people would then regain their liberty.

Commenting on Netaji's policy in '*Discovery of India*', Jawaharlal Nehru wrote that there were many trends in public opinion, as was natural in such a vast country and at such a time of crisis. According to him, the *"pro-Japanese sentiment was practically nil for no one wanted to change masters."* Nehru also accepted that *"there was a small group which was indirectly pro-Japanese in the sense that it imagined that they could take advantage of a Japanese invasion for Indian freedom. They were influenced by the broadcasts made by Subhas Chandra Bose."*

Taking up the a point, Netaji replied on his radio broadcast that *"according to my plan, therefore, it is not even necessary to bother about the attitude of Axis Powers towards India. If Indians outside and inside India will only do their duty, it is possible for Indian people to throw the British out of India... Our countrymen at home are hard pressed and they are demanding a Second Front... and I promise you a Second Front, a real Second Front for Indian struggle."*

Some time in 1946, presiding over a function of reception hosted to honour Dilip Kumar Roy, an intimate friend of Netaji, the eminent lawyer Bhulabhai Desai told the audience, and particularly addressing Roy, that like all great men, Netaji was rich in adverse criticism who imputed all sorts of motives to his every act. Referring to the incidents of 1938-1939 when he was one of the members of the Congress Working Committee, Desai confessed that he was also with them, swelling ranks of Netaji's political opponents. He accepted that it was actually the herd instinct which was very difficult to resist. He said, *"I had grown to echo what the coterie in which I moved said against him — that it was a pity he wouldn't toe the line and regrettable that he talked flamboyantly about violence, armed insurrection and so on..."*

Dilip Kumar Roy was surprised to note that Bhulabhai Desai *"had grown overnight into an ardent admirer of Netaji."* In his book

'*Netaji: The Man*' Roy wrote that on that memorable evening Bhulabhai Desai went on to add *"When I was engaged as a defence counsel of the far-famed INA trio, I had, naturally, to scan and make the most of the plans and programmes of Netaji — first, through the evidence of his comrade-in-arms and, secondly, through that of the documents and records testifying to his many sided achievements. Now,* ***the more I came to know of him the more I was impressed till, soon enough, the scales fell from my eyes and I felt deep pangs of remorse for having disparaged him in my cocksure arrogance like*** *an irresponsible debunker of the spirit who has no sense or conception of the deeper soul-values. For it was brought home to me somewhat apocalyptically that here was no cheap firebrand patriot whose nationalism stemmed from blind fanaticism of a one-track mind or whose ardour derived from the megalomania of a self-adulator. Nay* ***he was revealed to me in that awed moment of discovery as a far-seeing statesman, a born realist, a strategist to his finger-tips and an idealist-cum-seer*** *who could not halt or rest on the way because he was haunted by an irresistible, almost mystic, call he had to answer with the last drop of his freedom-hungry blood."*

The change of mind in case of Bhulabhai Desai was not a single case. There had been thousands of cases who knowingly aspired to follow him. Netaji took all possible steps to ensure that his 'Second Front', the Azad Hind Fauz, functioned as a highly disciplined patriotic revolutionary army in consonance with national tradition, valour and spirit of sacrifice as well as the hope and aspirations of the great Indian leaders to prove itself to be a highly motivated and spirited Indian army constituted to serve the nation.

—o—

7

Netaji's Letter Found: New Researches

It had been a controversial matter whether Netaji had written a letter to the Russian Government in November, 1944. According to INA sources, Netaji sent his letter through Yakob Malik who was the Russian Ambassador in Tokyo in those days. On inquiry from the Russian authorities, the reply received was that no such letter had been handed over to the Russian Ambassador. In this connection, the investigating agencies and research scholars were told repeatedly by the INA personnel that Netaji had really sent a letter which must have been responded to by the Russian Government, and only on that basis Netaji planned his escape to Russia in August, 1945. After some solicitious efforts made by the committed and determined followers of Netaji and research scholars, Russia did admit that a letter from Netaji was there and Yakob Malik, the Russian Ambassador in Tokyo, did receive the letter in November, 1944, but he returned it immediately without opening it.

The controversy of the above letter had been a discouraging point for Netaji's followers. It shattered all conscious efforts of those who were insisting that Netaji had gone to Russia where he might have been held as captive in Stalin's iron custody. But the absolute denial regarding any such correspondence from the Russian authorities was a big handicap, which made it very difficult to undertake any effort to trace Netaji's whereabouts. This deadlock created a state of inaction and helplessness and its advantage was encashed by those who were bent upon proving that Netaji had died in a plane crash.

This rather technical situation regarding the letter-controversy remained unchanged till 1993 when some new facts were discovered from the documents of the Russian archives. But these new facts could see the daylight in 1995 when these were noticed and verified by an Indian research team. The process of decipherment began when a project was undertaken by the Asiatic Society, Kolkata, to collect and compile those accessible materials pertaining to Indo-Russian relations. This project was prepared in pursuance of a cultural agreement signed between the Asiatic Society, Kolkata, and the Institute of Oriental Studies and Academy of Sciences, Moscow. Dr. Purabi Roy, a professor of International Affairs at Jadavpur University, was deputed in May-September, 1994, to collect the archival documents, after assessing the immense importance of the valuable materials available in the Russian archives which were virtually unknown to scholars till then. Extending the assignment further in May-August, 1995, the Asiatic Society deputed a team of three scholars which included Sobanlal Dutta Gupta and, Dr. Hari Vasudevan, along with Dr. Purabi Roy.

The team sent by the Society was only interested in search of those documents which were related to the period of 1917 to 1947. The team was also aware that after the October Revolution in 1917 the Soviet Union became a source of inspiration for the liberation movements especially in the countries of Asia. The relevant Russian archival documents were specifically required to confirm it. It was also a fact that many Indian revolutionaries who were in exile and had shifted their centre of activity to Russian cities during the period which was set by the Asiatic Society, Kolkata. The documents studied in different Russian archives revealed some unknown chapters of international communist movement and contradicted some hitherto known facts.

Although in this project the search for Netaji's whereabouts after August, 1945 was not the specific purpose for Dr. Roy's team, yet it became interesting for them to unearth such material which hinted that Netaji was in constant touch with the Soviet leaders. The team could guess that some documents relating to Netaji and the INA were available in former NKGB-KGB (the present FSB) Archives, President's Archive, Stalin's Archive, Archives of Far East Russian Federation, Archive of Omsk, Military Archive of St. Petersburg and Archive of Irkutsk. These archives were not accessible to the scholars and a special permission was required to scrutinize the files and documents kept in these archives. In their search the team had become full of conviction to get even such material which might eventually solve the mystery of Netaji's disappearance in August, 1945.

The team headed by Dr. Purabi Roy came to learn that the National Archives in India had received a few declassified files from Soviet Union in 1991 on Netaji under Ref. ACC No. 6757, S.C. Bose, Group IV, Serial No. 11, total six documents, with, number of pages 46. This information was neither known nor disclosed to Indian scholars.

The team had also learnt that during the period of *Glasnost* and *Perestroika* in Russia, many untold stories were publicly told by unravelling documents from the Russian archives. In November, 1990, an article was published titled as *'Subhas Chandra Bose and Soviet Russia'*, written by Professor A. Raikov, in the internationally famous journal '*Soviet Land*'. The writer emphasised further research to know the truth about Netaji's disappearance. In 1992 the Gorbachev Foundation released a few documents in the shape of a brochure which revealed the activities related to Netaji and Bhagat Ram Talwar during the period 1941-45 and the role played by German, Soviet and Italian embassies in Kabul, Afghanistan. According to this brochure, Bhagat Ram Talwar, who escorted Netaji during his 1941-escape, maintained close relations with a Soviet KGB agent Mikhael Andrevich Ailakherdov who was popularly known as *'Zaman'* in Kabul. The brochure mentioned a code word *'Silver Moon'* and the details about Bhagat Ram Talwar who was spying for at least four countries including Germany, British India, Soviet Union and Japan.

Dr. Purabi Roy stated in her affidavit submitted before the Mukherjee Commission that a former correspondent of Tass, the official Russian news agency, A. Vinogradov, had written an article in *'Echo Pleneti'* in its issue No. 22 (May/June 1992) about Netaji. This article was translated by Susmita Bhattacharya and was published in *'Netaji Subhas Chandra Bose Commemoration Volume as a tribute in his centenary year by Scottish Church College in 1998.'*

According to Dr. Purabi Roy, in 1993 an article titled as *'The Secret of Subhas Chandra Bose's Death'*, written by Professor A. Railkov, who was an ex-Soviet General, was published in *'Asia and Africa Today'* in its volume No. 8. This article was followed by a very important article in the same journal in its issue No. 9 and 10 by an Indologist, Victor B. Turadzhev. The theme of Turadzhev's article was *'Against Whom Subhas Chandra Bose Fought During the Years of the Second World War'.* In justifying his point of view, Turadzhev quoted verbatim the views of Netaji from his letter written by him from Tokyo. This was the same letter which the Russian authorities had denied till then inspite of the fact that it was received by her Ambassador Yakob Malik himself in Tokyo.

Without actually realising the value of Netaji's letter, Turadzhev cited it with all other related references to prove his article's authenticity. But the expert eyes of Dr. Purabi Roy could grasp and comprehend the real meaning of this letter. According to the details given by Turadzhev, this letter was written on the official pad of *'Arzi Hukumate Azad Hind'*, which was the Hindustani translation of the Provisional Government of Free India. The letter was drafted at the Imperial Hotel in Tokyo. It was dated November 20, 1944. **The most surprising fact mentioned by Turadzhev was that the Russian Ambassador Yakob Malik had met Netaji from whom he himself received the letter** which had been formally forwarded by A. Langfang, the Commissar of State Security (NKGB), to Colonel A. Otroshehenko, the Chief of the 5th Division of the First Command of NKVD, which was re-named as KGB and after breaking of the USSR the same intelligence body was again renamed as the Federal Security Bureau (FSB).

The Russian denial was finally negated by the discovery of this letter. Although still many more documents are required to conclude Netaji's presence in Russia after 1945, yet this discovery has been regarded as a good beginning in the right direction. It is a small step on the way which leads towards the real story of Netaji's last days. As a matter of fact the present democratic Russian Federation has declassified several files and documents of the past USSR in normal manner. It seems that the Russian Federation now has no prejudices and fears like that of the previous communist governments. Now its archives have been opened for scholars and other bonafide persons to pursue the documents. But they have not yet allowed access to classified papers and files and have made it mandatory to obtain a request letter from the related country's government and then only they would grant permission to witness the files or the documents. As the papers related to Netaji are directly concerned with the secret information service and the defence of the country, so in such cases cooperation has to be extended by Indian Government in particular and a more realistic approach has to be adopted by the Russian side.

As quoted by Turadzhev, the text of the letter speaks for itself about the mind of Netaji and about his circumstances. Netaji wrote this letter without any decorative and characteristic manner. He used a prosaic language and began it with simple words.

"I am seeking help of the Soviet Government through you to fulfil the task of our freedom struggle to free India ... I cannot deny the fact that at the moment we are closely associated with Axis Powers for a common struggle against the Anglo-American bloc. I am glad to inform you that the Axis Power is now having a clear idea about the main problems of India and they have accorded recognition to Azad Hind State (Free India) for which we are thankful to them. Besides, Japan's relations with the Soviet are strictly neutral, even Germany can understand fully well and evaluate the fact that we Indians are only fighting against England and America. The German Government has also understood and appreciated the fact that we are not interested in going against the Soviet Russia. Certainly, the activities of my organisation in Europe have generated an exclusive impression that we are only against the Anglo-American Bloc and not against the Soviet Russia. This was the understanding of cooperation between the Axis Powers and our organisation in Europe. In this connection, we have a clear policy and approval from the German Government, as well as the fascist Italian Government.

"I know that now there is an alliance between the Soviet Union, England and America. But I feel that I have clear perception about the prevailing international situation that if the Soviet Union extends its help to our freedom struggle, it will certainly not stand in your way. I am very much thankful to your Government and I do remember the help which was extended by the Soviet Government after I left India in

1941. I conveyed my thanks to His Excellency Minister for External Affairs Molotov in my letter I wrote from Berlin. I trust His Excellency had certainly received it.

"I have always been encouraged by the fact that Lenin in his time always from the core of his heart extended support to the countries which were struggling against colonial rule. So far as I understand, the Soviet attitude to the problems of the oppressed nations like India has not been changed after his death.

"As to my party' Forward Bloc, I can say that when the Soviet foreign policy had been condemned by almost all the political parties of India in 1939-40, ours was the only party which had openly supported the Soviet foreign policy in relation to Germany and Finland.

"My earnest desire is to pay a visit to your Excellency and find the way through which your Government can help us for the success of our struggle for freedom. The nature of help which the Soviet Government can extend to us depends on the decision of the Soviet Government in relation to the present situation of the war."

The discovery of the above noted letter in Russian archives had been regarded by the followers of Netaji as fool-proof documentary evidence which had exposed the Russians with whom Netaji had friendly relations even in the middle of the Great War II, inspite of the fact that he was with the Axis Powers. Actually, Netaji was well aware of his position but he was equally conscious and careful about his future strategies and actions. He always desired that the USSR's Government was the appropriate power which might exercise its influence in favour of India's independence struggle.

Victor B. Turadzhev gave hope that the story of the death of Netaji in a plane-crash could be challenged if some positive initiative is taken by the Indian Government, because the Russian archives are in possession of such documents which may throw new light about Netaji's life after August, 1945. Dr. Purabi Roy interviewed Turadzhev who was also positively hopeful that documents at the Military Archives of Paddolsk and Omsk would definitely open new chapters of Netaji's life. These Russian archives are particularly important because there were those papers in plenty which were related to the Japanese and East-Asian countries.

Dr. Purabi Roy has also stated that *"V. Turadzhev, Associate Editor of the journal 'Asia & Africa Today'* ***informed her that from the Indian Embassy, Moscow, he had been asked to discontinue any further enquiry related to this subject."*** Such pressure from Indian Embassy has been felt by many but there are a few who have openly expressed it. Any Indian Embassy cannot dare to go to this extent until it has been asked by the Indian Government.

Dr. Purabi Roy has narrated in her affidavit dated June 8, 2000 before the Mukherjee Commission such examples where some new facts had been unearthed and after a close examination she expressed her observations as follows:

"The general belief is that after the formation of the Provisional Government of Free India, it was recognised by the countries belonging to the Axis Powers. But records show that the USSR had also recognised the Provisional Government. Besides, Mr. Pramod Mehra of the National Archives of India, New Delhi, in March 1999, had presented a seminar paper at the Netaji Institute of Asian Studies, Kolkata. In his paper on "The Declassified Documents from the Ministry of Defence" on page 6 he mentions the recognition of the Provisional Government by the world powers, viz., Japan, Burma, Germany, Italy, Thailand, Philippines, Russia, declared the firm resolve of the Provisional Government to prosecute their struggle for India's freedom (File No. 265/INA National Archives of India)

"The records refer that the Provisional Government of Free India was having its representation at Omsk and the name of the representative consul was Kato-Kochu.

"Further records which are unravelled from the Russian and British archives indicate that Subhas Chandra Bose was all along trying to go to the Soviet Union and was seeking their help because he thought that the USSR will be the ideal place for arranging India's freedom struggle. On the other hand, the USSR has also all through maintained a positive attitude towards Netaji Subhas Chandra Bose and the Provisional Government of Free India.

"And finally, information obtained from reliable sources reveal that the classified documents on Netaji and the INA in the Russian archives confirm that Subhas Chandra Bose was in the Soviet Union upto October, 1946.

"That considering all these records, in 1996 I approached through Kolesnikov, the then Prime Minister of the Russian Federation, Chernomyrdir, who suggested to organise an Indo-Russian Commission in order to investigate the missing Indian nationals within the territory of the erstwhile USSR. Besides, I submitted my application to the Chief of FSB (Federal Security Services), Russian Federation, Mr. Trubnikov requesting him to permit me to get access to the relevant files but till now I have not received any reply."

—o—

8

Further Efforts: Mukherjee Commission Appointed

In the last decade of the last century there had been some abrupt incidents related to Netaji which revised again the mystery so as to keep it alive even if it might be accepted that physically Netaji was not alive. The revival of the issue actually began as chain-reactions when a leader absolutely committed to Netaji's cause, Professor Samar Guha, wrote letters in February 1991 to the then Deputy Prime Minister Devilal, and to some other senior leaders of the Congress Party as well as to the Russian leader Mikhail Gorbachev. But only one letter of Samar Guha was officially acknowledged and that too in a routine way, which replied on behalf of the Indian Ministry of External Affairs that his request had been forwarded and was awaiting results.

As a matter of fact, during the Janata Party rule in India, Professor Guha was instrumental in securing a statement from the then Prime Minister Morarji Desai on August 28, 1978. It was in a way a great success for the followers of Netaji. Commenting on this incident in his book *'Back from Dead'*, Anuj Dhar wrote: *"It was one landmark event that the media failed to break down and explain to the readers. That day Samar Guha forced the Government of India to reverse its stand on Bose's death and discard the accepted findings of the two panels it had constituted."* While replying to the motion moved in the Parliament by Samar Guha to reject the findings of the Khosla Commission and the Shah Nawaz Committee and to appoint a new panel to investigate the matter afresh, Morarji Desai said: *"The Shah Nawaz Committee and the Khosla Commission held the report of Netaji Subhas Chandra Bose's death following a plane-crash as true. Since then,* ***reasonable doubts have arisen on the correctness of the two reports and various important contradictions in the testimony of witnesses have been noticed.*** *Some further contemporary official documentary records have also become available.* ***In the light of these doubts and contradictions and those records, government find it difficult to accept that the earlier conclusions are decisive."*** Continuing his views, Desai concluded that *"at the same time, Government feels that no useful purpose would be served by having any further enquiry."* Prime Minister Desai also made a personal appeal to Samar Guha to withdraw his motion and said, *"I hope that in the light of this statement, my honourable friend will withdraw his motion."*

Samar Guha became emotional. Before giving his consent to withdraw his motion, he said, *"If I say Netaji was given burial out of political conspiracy, it would not be on exaggeration. Today, I express my gratitude to the Prime Minister because today ends a crusade that, in my humble way, I was trying to conduct, on behalf of the people of India, at least to see that officially and legally Netaji is not declared dead. Now, by undoing the findings of the two reports, at least this much we have achieved that today, Netaji is neither legally nor officially dead."*

Slightly changing his demand in February 1991 in his letter, Professor Guha desired for *"a high level investigation into the secret documents on the disappearnace of Netaji."* His request was sympathetically entertained by the then President of Indian

Republic, R. Venkatraman. But this was a time of fragile politics and therefore, no government was able to complete even one year of its tenure in power, till Narasimha Rao could form a Congress-led Government. Either Rao was aware of these developments related to Netaji or he himself planned to diffuse completely and also permanently the issue of Netaji, but it is yet a secret as to why Prime Minister Rao thought to award 'Bharat Ratna' to Netaji posthumously on January 22, 1992 on the eve of his 95th birth anniversary.

The declaration of this award to confer 'Bharat Ratna' on Netaji posthumously became an incident itself which revoked the issue and again provoked pro-Netaji followers and his family members against the malicious intentions of the Congress Government. Everyone was surprised that on whose demand and under which compulsion, Narasimha Rao had taken the decision to confer the highest award of the country to Netaji posthumously. The word 'posthumously' became the bone of contention. The contentious part was not the word but its ulterior motive which gave the suspicion that if the award would be conferred, the posthumous status would have meant that the death story of Netaji in a plane-crash was accepted by one and all as true. And perhaps then only his so-called ashes could be brought to India from Renkoji Temple, Tokyo, and thus once for all the mystery would be completely unwoven.

This incident of awarding the Bharat Ratna became further disputed when a young advocate Bijan Ghosh filed a writ of mandamus, on the basis of the press communique issued by the Government of India, before the Calcutta High Court. It was prayed in the writ to explain the rationale awarding the Bharat Ratna to Netaji posthumously. Ghosh requested the court to order the Union Government *"to declare full particulars of the whereabouts of Netaji Subhas Chandra Bose from August 18, 1945 till date on the basis of records and information"*, at the disposal of the Government of India. Calcutta High Court was also requested to pass such orders so that the Government of India might initiate proper investigations about Netaji and might *"furnish full particulars of his stay from August 18, 1945 onwards and his subsequent death and the place and the manner of disposal of his mortal remains."* Finally, the prayer of *"the Writ Petition was, inter alia, to issue a writ of mandamus commanding the respondents to recall resilient, cancel and revoke the 'Bharat Ratna' conferred on Netaji Subhas Chandra Bose posthumously and to notify each recalling — cancellation — withdrawal to the people at large, in proper manner."*

Considering the matter as of national importance and its direct concern with the Central Government, the writ petition filed before the High Court at Calcutta C.O. No. 6720(W) of 1993 by way of a Public Interest Litigation by Bijan Ghosh, a practising advocate of Supreme Court was forwarded to the Supreme Court. In spite of a favourable attitude of the Chief Justice of India, M.N. Venkatachaliah, the Government of India adopted a defensive and dilly-dallying policy. The writ petition was *"challenging, inter alia, the basis of the declaration of the term 'Posthumous' as there was no conclusive proof of the death of Netaji. Thus if an award is conferred upon him with the description 'posthumous' it would be tantamount to issuing a 'death certificate' in the veil of an award. It was further contended that conferring an award of 'Bharat Ratna' may be the highest civilian award, the Government of India had tried to belittle him and to rank him at par with the other recipients of 'Bharat Ratna'. He is much above any award. Conferring an award upon a person, that too after a long lapse of 45 years, who is one of the main architect in achieving independence of India, is an act of State-sponsored mockery."*

The Government expressed its inability to produce the related classified secret documents and other papers. On behalf of the

Government it was stated that the proposal had been dropped and the declaration to award Bharat Ratna to Netaji posthumously had already been withdrawn. Because of the delaying tactics of the Government, the Supreme Court could deliver its verdict on August 4, 1997 , which said that since the award had in fact not been conferred and the proposal had been dropped by the Government of India, it was not needed to *"go into the question whether the word 'posthumously' has been justifiably used in the press communique or the wider question whether there is enough material available for reaching the conclusion that Netaji Subhas Chandra Bose had died either in the air-crash of August 18, 1945 or at any time thereafter. This is a wider issue on which undoubtedly in future as in the past, there will be divergent views. The real controversy in these proceedings is related to the press communique. Since no further steps have been taken in pursuance to the press communique and the matter is treated as closed, we declare that the press communique should be treated as cancelled."*

The verdict against the decision of Narasimha Rao was an open defeat of the Government of India. By this time many political changes had occurred and now Indra Kumar Gujral was the Prime Minister. He along with his Defence Minister Mulayam Singh Yadav was under pressure to declassify all secret files related to Netaji and the INA. Perhaps without calculating the after effects and consequences, Mulayam Singh Yadav, who had always shown great respect for Netaji, got declassified about 900 documents on August 27, 1997, and decided to hand over the same to the National Archives. Simultaneously, he also hinted that he would like to use his good offices to bring Netaji's ashes from Japan.

There was a very sharp reaction from the All India Forward Bloc (AIFB). A senior leader of the AIFB, Debabrata Biswas challenged Mulayam Singh Yadav and said: *"It is ridiculous to assume that Netaji had died when there is no proof to establish that. The*

Government has to face the mirror and answer some questions. And that too in court. We will take them to court." Debabrata Biswas was irked because the issue of declassification of secret documents was being clubbed with the so-called ashes of Netaji still kept in Renkoji Temple, Tokyo.

Commenting on the reality of the declassified files, Debabrata Biswas charged that *"nothing has been declassified. What has been handed over to the National Archives consists only of speeches and sundry unimportant things. What purpose will these serve in unravelling Netaji's mystery? The INA held major discussions with foreign countries to establish diplomatic missions and contacts. Where are those papers? It is as if the history of the INA concerns only Netaji's speeches to Prisoners of Wars at various gatherings. These papers are a major eyewash."*

Further elaborating his arguments Debabrata Biswas vented that *"the real story is not there in those 900-odd documents. We want all documents on the INA and the alleged plane-crash. This Government and we have no qualms about saying so, is trying to suppress facts and that too at its own peril. A figure like Netaji cannot be played around by Mr. Gujral. Mr. Yadav and Mr. Bommai will have to do a lot of answering once they are asked to appear in court. They will not easily declassify the secret files. They won't do this for the simple reason that it will mean re-writing India's history.* ***Our history text books tell us that India's freedom was won through 'ahimsa' (non-violence). Now, is that true?*** *If the real story becomes public, then many leaders would be exposed and Indian history would become a 'farce'."*

As threatened, a writ petition was filed on August 29, 1997 by Asim Ganguly against the Government of India before the High Court at Kolkata. The petitioner stated that *"without there being a conclusive proof and or otherwise determined in accordance with the law, the Union of India cannot accept that Netaji Subhas Chandra Bose died in Taiwan."* There was no problem before the bench of

High Court at Kolkata consisting of Chief Justice Prabha Shanker Misra and Justice Barin Ghosh to decide the matter on April 7, 1998. Agreeing to the petitioner's prayer, the bench ordered that *"before accepting the ashes which are allegedly kept at the Renkoji Temple, Japan, as that of Netaji Subhas Chandra Bose, the Government shall obtain full particulars and evidence and satisfy itself about the genuineness of the claim that the ashes kept at the Renkoji Temple of Japan are that of Netaji Subhas Chandra Bose and take the people of India in confidence."*

Another incident which challenged the official stand was the discovery of declassified documents in Russian archives directly related to Netaji. In March 1995 a project was undertaken to compile accessible material available in the Russian archives pertaining to Indo-Russian relations. The project was to study and compile the missing links of the international communist movement in pursuance of a cultural agreement signed between the Asiatic Society, Kolkata, and the Institute of Oriental Studies and Academy of Sciences, Moscow. A three-member team including Sobhanlal Dutta Gupta and Hari Vasudevan of the Asiatic Society, led by Dr. Purabi Roy, was busy in collecting relevant documents from Russian archives, from which they would know about two most revealing documents already dug out from the archives from the files of the Russian Ministry of External Affairs covering a period from September 12 to October 28, 1946.

One of these documents disclosed that Joseph Stalin had a discussion with his Defence Minister Voroschilov, Foreign Affairs Minister Mikhailovich Molotov, and a most important member of the Politbureau, the apex body of the Communist Party of Soviet Union. The discussion was regarding the plans for the Communist movement in India. There was also a mention of Netaji's role in this connection. The meeting considered views/options to deal with Subhas Chandra Bose.

The second document had details indicating that just a few days before Stalin and his colleagues had discussed about Bose. Referring to this discussion, a Soviet agent named V.G. Sayadyants, based in Mumbai in 1946, reported to Russian authorities on August 28, 1946, through the then Soviet Ambassador in Tehran, T.V. Sadchkov, that *"Soviet Union cannot possibly work with either Nehru or Gandhi."* **Sayadyants expressed his opinion conclusively that the communist movement in India was in a disarray and Bose was the only hope for Soviet Russia. These documents clearly hinted that Netaji was alive in 1946** and was in Soviet Russia.

The episode of Bharat Ratna and the issue of bringing the alleged ashes of Netaji gained an importance more particularly in judicial circles because of its touchy and provocative sensitivity. There was yet another writ petition filed by Rudra Jyoti Bhattacharjee, a researcher on freedom-fighters, still pending for disposal at the High Court in Kolkata. He prayed the Hon'ble High Court to order specifically to the Government of India to institute afresh an investigating commission in the light of new facts which became known on the basis of the declassified documents of ex-Soviet Russin Government. The petitioner stated that although the statement of Prime Minister Morarji Desai in the Parliament on August 28, 1978 had already undone the findings of its previous investigations, yet the Government of India had taken for granted that Netaji had died in the plane-crash on August 18, 1945. It became evident when Narasimha Rao attempted to award Bharat Ratna to Netaji posthumously and Mulayam Singh Yadav thought to bring the alleged ashes of Netaji from Japan.

The writ petition of Bhattacharjee was well drafted and documented, so the unstable Governments at the Centre with their inherent shortcomings could not contest it forcefully. The Hon'ble High Court delivered its historical verdict on April 30, 1998. The statement of Prime Minister Morarji Desai in the Parliament on August 28, 1978 was not only admitted as a legal document but it was also accepted as the official stand of the Government of India. Relying on the statement the Court ordered: *"...two deviations/ aberrations, however, occurred, first when Government of India intended to honour Sri Subhas Chandra Bose by conferring 'Bharat Ratna' award ... and secondly, recount by Defence Minister of the country made a statement that Government of India intended to accept the factum of death of Subhas Chandra Bose and bring the ashes which are stacked and kept at Renkoji Temple in Japan."* The High Court order further said very specifically that *"the two aberrations are outside the Lok Sabha. True, one which carried the expression 'posthumously' was a communique of the Government of India which in deference to the popular feeling was withdrawn, but the other, that is to say, the statement of the Defence Minister in respect of the ashes of Netaji, was neither a statement in any of the Houses of Parliament nor a communique of the Government of India. That was out and out a statement most unwittingly made by the Defence Minister of the country."*

Thus responding favourably to the prayer of the writ petition the **Calcutta High Court ordered the Union Government to *"launch a vigorous inquiry as a special case for the purpose of giving an end to the controversy"* surrounding Netaji Subhas Chandra Bose's disappearance.** In its observation the High Court also said that *"no serious effort in this behalf (the disappearance) has been made by the Government."*

This order was neither further contested nor opposed by any political party. There was a widespread demand to close the chapter finally as it was necessary to enquire into the matter afresh. But there was no effort to implement the order of the High Court till

Atal Bihari Vajpayee became the Prime Minister of National Democratic Alliance's Government. After a series of meetings and demands from the leaders of the All India Forward Bloc and a careful perusal of High Court's order, the Government of India decided to appoint a commission. And thus **on April 14, 1999 a notification was issued by the Government of India to form a Commission for an *"in depth inquiry"* into this definitive matter of great public importance.** On the suggestion of the Chief Justice of India, a top and reputed criminologist, Justice Manoj Kumar Mukherjee, who was a former judge of the Supreme Court of India, was requested to lead the Commission.

The Government's notification, cited verbatim on the Court's order, outlined the following terms of references to be inquired into by the Commission:

(a) Whether Netaji Subhas Chandra Bose is dead or alive;

(b) If he is dead whether he died in the plane-crash, as alleged;

(c) Whether the ashes in the Japanese temple are ashes of Netaji;

(d) Whether he had died in any other manner at any other place and, if so, when and how? And

(e) If he is alive, in respect of his whereabouts.

—o—

9

Netaji's Religiosity: Gumnami Baba

Netaji in his adolescence was a serious-minded teenager and was deeply religious in the conventional sense. It was due to the religiosity, devotion and the regular Pujas performed by his mother Prabhabati, and also due to the literature of Swami Vivekanand that he read in the later part of his teenage. He had from his early childhood inherited devotion to Goddess Ma Durga and Lord Shiva from his mother who used to make her children sit and join her at Puja in a daily routine and on religious occasions.

The above views regarding Netaji have never been disputed. But these might be disputed if these are endorsed by Gumnami Baba alias Bhagwanji. The firebrand revolutionary Leela Roy who became the second editor of the weekly *'Forward Bloc'*, after Netaji had published in her most reputed magazine *'Jayshree'* **a number of write-ups written by *'Mahakal'*, a name alleged as a pseudonym of Gumnami Baba.** These write-ups had been compiled in a book titled *'Oye Mahamanav Ashe'*. Mahakal confirmed the above views in a very appropriate manner as under:

"To understand a man you have to understand the bedrock on which he stands and he works. My most and only beloved mother was a direct initiated disciple of Paramhansa Deva. By every suck of her breast, through every kiss of her, by the channels of her caresses, touches, tender looks and words, the Tattwa-Shakties (phenomenal powers) of the Divine Mother flowed in and filled me. My father gave unto me thoroughness and strength in service to others and fighting activeness. My first tutor-guardian gave me missionary sacrificing zeal and all-fighting, all-over coming stamina."

Netaji started the journey of his religious and spiritual life at an early age. In his later teenage, after reading the writings of Swami Vivekanand, he became eager to search for a Guru who could enlighten him with truth about religion and spirituality. The write-ups of Mahakal endorsed that *"I inherited mysticism from Mother, Paramhansa and Vivekanand. Throughout I have been constant, even during most hectic times the deepest hours of night afforded a bit of time for that."* From the writings of Swami Vivekanand he learned that *'self-realisation and spiritual truth are to be attained through service to humanity.'* Thus his temperament for social service in the form of humanitarian service took root and developed steadily in him.

One more endorsement of Mahakal is cited as under:

"From my childhood I began hearing and perusing scriptures. As I grew up, my mystic hunger also grew. I went through all scriptures and philosophies again and again. In college and university years I used to seek out, hunt for the so-called — great seers and wise men of our days and questioned-questioned-questioned them on mysticism. None satisfied me, I even left everything in search of true mystic 'Satguru' and searched far and wide in the country and high and low in the Himalayas. None could satisfy me. It was bitter winter. I remembered my own mother, dear darling adored mother and came back to her lap and feet."

With the philanthropic blood of his father Janaki Nath Bose in his body and the spiritual light received from the writings of Swami Vivekanand, Netaji started going among the poor, needy, ailing and neglected people in nearby villages and suburbs of the city. After personally seeing the actual miserable conditions prevailing in contemporary India which was groaning under foreign exploitation, he realised that neither spiritual advancement nor peace and prosperity could be possible in a country suffering under the problems of penury and pestilence, along with illiteracy and ignorance. He thought that all such problems had to be combated as top priority. Later on as he grew and learnt more about the miserable condition of India due to foreign rule and exploitation, Netaji changed his priority and advocated that freedom of India from foreign exploitation had to be achieved as top priority. In the absence of freedom, no progress in removing poverty, eradicating illiteracy and checking pestilence and other ailments could be possible.

Netaji's religious bent of mind and his spiritual queries were gradually sublimated to a certain extent with his interest developing into his philosophical and psychic advancement. His logical approach was based on practical experiences and reasoning. After seeing the huge amount of money being spent on sumptuous pomp and show exhibited during Durga Puja, Netaji frankly expressed his disapproval to his mother. In one of his letters written to her on the occasion of Durga Puja being celebrated at his ancestral village, in which he could not be present as he was away in the service of the poor villagers in an epidemic calamity, he as an adolescent of 15-17 years of age wrote: ***"Devotion does not demand pomp and show but sincerity."*** In this regard he made himself bold, in view of his age, to express a mild caveat against the waste of money in the name of Puja in a country where the people starved due to poverty. At the same time, he showed his appreciation of the elaborate and awe-inspiring ceremonials of the Puja that required devotion though he did derive spiritual satisfaction from the rituals of the Puja.

Although Netaji had no inkling of the scientific ground of the Buddhist concept of religion in his adolescence, he developed a scientific outlook and approach, right from his teenage in his religious and spiritual pursuits as propounded by Lord Buddha in his precept *"Appa Deepo Bhava"* (Be Your Own Light). He led himself to his own faith based on his own experiences of spiritual practices. Despite the influence of Swami Vivekanand on his mental and spiritual development and his interaction in the religious and social functions, he could never be a blind follower of any great man or religions preacher.

In his early age, Netaji started searching for the *'Truth'* within himself by meditation and humanitarian services. He failed in his search for a Satguru in outside world by having obtained light from the writings of Swami Vivekanand. He became his own Guru through contemplation, meditation and selfless service to humanity. He developed a great spiritual force in himself and maintained the same trend in his political life also. We know that he could not become a blind follower of the then great political leaders like Mahatma Gandhi, Chittaranjan Das or even Vitthal Bhai Patel, whose views were common to his own views, not withstanding that he deeply admired and revered all of them.

From Mandalay jail he wrote on May 2, 1925 to his bosom and spiritual friend Dilip Kumar Roy, living in Pondichery Ashram of Sri Aurobindo, telling him that *"the forced solitude in his long term jail life had given him an opportunity to think deeply into his ultimate problems of life that would make him a spiritual gainer."* He made the best use of his imprisonment period, far away from his home, by meditating regularly and persistently while he kept himself busy in reading, writing, learning and teaching as well. Thus he could make himself mentally and spiritually more mature in that period of incarceration. There in jail he even fought for funds and facilities to perform Durga Puja and did *'Shakti Sadhana'* by worshipping the Goddess Durga according to his family tradition.

He used to take a keen interest in his childhood in Durga Puja, Kali Puja and Saraswati Puja, ritually and collectively performed by the Bengali community during a fixed time every year. But later after coming under the influence of Swami Vivekanand's writings, Netaji was led to change his religious sentiments and had turned to the service of the suffering humanity. During epidemics coinciding with the Puja-days, his young mind refused to participate in the Durga Puja organised, as usual, by his father in their ancestral village, Kodalia, because he with his logical thinking, considered that the service to the suffering poor children of Ma Durga, who loved all her children, rich or poor alike, was more important. For him service to the suffering humanity was a better form of worshipping the Goddess than eulogising her with pomp and show in the formal performances of the Puja that often promotes ego of being a good devotee of the Mother.

In due course as Netaji became intensively busy in his studies at Cambridge and later on in national service through the Indian National Congress and then in his incarcerations, detentions and exiles to Europe, his Puja or worshipping Hindu Gods and Goddesses took the form of private prayers and meditations in seclusion when he retired at night after his hectic work-schedule of the day.

An interesting instance of Netaji's rational approach to a collective Puja was narrated by Abid Hasan to Lt. Manwati Arya. Netaji had come to Singapore along with him after the proclamation of his Provincial Government of Azad Hind. The Chettiers, the rich banker community of South India living in Singapore, desired to organise a Puja festival. They kept very intimate relations with the INA and had very generously and lavishly donated huge amounts to the INA fund to support Netaji's movement. In a delegation they came to meet and invite Netaji to attend their Puja as Chief Guest. Netaji was well aware of the caste disparity being observed between the upper castes of South Indians with the low caste Pariahs who were considered to be untouchables. Netaji flatly refused even to meet them saying, *"I will not attend any Puja which is not open to all the people belonging to any caste, community or faith."* So the delegates had to go back in sheer disappointment.

It was a phase of the time when all the Indians of South East Asia revered Netaji considering him to be a person next only to God. The Chettiers felt that their Puja would not be complete without the presence of Netaji. They discussed among themselves about Netaji's all inclusive approach to Puja considering that all human beings were the sons and daughters of the same God and Devi Ma, the Goddess. They jointly reflected very deeply on Netaji's broad views of considering all human beings as equals before God and decided to open the Puja Pandal for all members of the Indian community without any distinction. They again ventured to come and sent a message to Netaji that *'The South Indians seek a few minutes audience with Netaji to extend respectfully their most cordial invitation to honour "All Caste, All Religion Puja Assembly" on the occasion of Dussehra Puja. Netaji allowed the collective interview and gladly accepted the invitation.'*

As Netaji reached the Puja Pandal full of Indians belonging to different castes, communities, and religious faiths, he was welcomed by the head priest. He was accompanied by Abid Hasan, who, later on, said, *"First of all Netaji accompanied by me was ushered reverentially into the temple. I felt hesitation to approach further, knowing that being a Muslim, I would not be allowed upto the pedestal on which the idol of a Hindu deity was placed. When the priest requested me to come along with Netaji, I was hesitant what to do before the deity and remained a step behind Netaji and tried to ape him in performing the Puja rituals as directed by the priest.*

"After the Puja was performed inside the temple, both of us came out to the pandal where Netaji was to address the huge gathering assembled on the occasion. Customarily both of us were applied with 'Tilak' on the sacred spot of forehead by the priest. Netaji was conscious that I would feel embarrassed to appear before the audience with a 'Tilak' mark on my forehead and therefore he abruptly wiped off his forehead with his handkerchief soon after leaving the temple so that I also would feel free to do so."

One more instance regarding a proposed performance of an exceptionally sumptuous Yajna by some Hindu sadhus, would further bring to light the rational religious outlook of Netaji. While working in Rangoon headquarters of the Provisional Government of Azad Hind, Lt. Manwati Arya happened to catch hold of a hand-bill in Hindi appealing to the Hindu populace of Burma to contribute generously to their committee which was going to perform a very big Yajna of burning in Holi fire about 1.25 lakh worth *'Havan'* material consisting of ghee, gur, honey, dry fruits, sandalwood and many other expensive items in their prayer to God for the success of Azad Hind Fauj in winning India's independence.

On reading and pondering over the hand-bill of an unusual appeal Lt. Manwati Arya personally felt it to be illogical and improper to waste so much money which could better be utilized to provide for the patriotic army for their necessities that would help them to fight. So she rushed with that hand-bill to Netaji's office and handed it over to him. She boldly expressed her opinion and sought his judgement. Netaji appreciated her rational view and said that considering the religious sentiments of the organisers and their projected patriotic appeal he would summon the leading persons and would ask them to pray for India's freedom and perform the symbolic Yajna on a small scale. He issued a circular directing all the Indians, through the branches of the Indian Independence League (IIL) not to donate any money or material to any other organization.

The conventional religiosity, awareness of moral and ethical values that took root in young Netaji as a material process, during his childhood and adolescence, later developed into an unostentatious broad outlook on religion and spirituality. This broad outlook he sustained with him all along his tempestuous life of triumphs and tragedies. Religion was strictly the personal and private aspect of his life which had no access to his political life. As a matter of fact, he was against the use of religious idioms in political talks. Despite his secular approach in politics, his personal belief in God did not find an expression in the formal inauguration of the re-organised Indian National Army, which was re-named as Azad Hind Fauz on July 5, 1943 in Singapore and also in his proclamation of the Provisional Government of Azad Hind on October 21, 1943.

However, there was no hint of any particular religion or God as mentioned in any religious scripture. It was a reference to the all-pervading God, common to all religions that he referred to in his historical speeches on those occasions. Never in his life Netaji was seen making a show of his Hinduism, though the Indian philosophy-pregnant Hinduism had been prevalent in his personal conduct. While in Singapore where Ramkrishna Mission existed, Netaji used to visit there frequently and quietly in the nights, when he could find time, dressed in an ochre *dhoti* and *chaddar*, to meditate quietly for hours in the serene and peaceful Meditation Hall of the Mission. There he would find solace after the whole day's hectic and worrisome life. By this he would get inspiration for further work for the following day.

Netaji grew more and more religious imperceptively as the days passed but it always remained strictly his personal matter without any outward show. Though he was born and brought up in a family of idol-worshipper community in which every home had its own *'Thakur Ghar'*, an exclusive place of worship, his religious outlook being very broad, he could establish communion with the Omnipresent God anywhere, quietly in his bed before sleeping, be it even late after midnight. Spending most of his life-time away from his home he had confined his religious practices to reading of scriptures, silent prayer and meditation at the end of his day's work.

By his own practice Netaji had set an example and proved that one need not shun the society to develop one's spirituality. Spiritual strength could be developed by contemplation and meditation done while remaining tremendously busy with selfless work for the benefit of one's nation in particular and entire humanity in general. He considered spirituality to be one of India's characteristic feature. That is why he could not envisage the Marxist type of socialism in India as it is devoid of spirituality and religion.

It was his firm conviction that a person with spiritual power gains moral strength and his inner transformation that empowers him or her to overcome cupidity for wealth and power for mere personal benefits and also such weaknesses that lead to sexual corruption. Netaji believed that only spiritual citizens could reconstruct the society and could mould it in the right shape with their selfless service, renunciation, sacrifice and personal interest for others. He emphasized Sri Ramkrishana's synthesis of different religions in India and considered religious harmony and tolerance to be the foundation for nationalism in India.

In his Indian National Army, Netaji gave equal importance to spiritual and military training because a spiritually strengthened person lives wholly from within and derives energy, zeal and inner strength which is as much necessary for a soldier as his training in warfare. By spiritual training in the Indian National Army he did not mean to indoctrinate the soldiers in any sort of religious belief or practice of religiosity or meditation. Imparting spiritual lectures to the soldiers was a process that involved promoting his mental power, enthusiastic feelings, courage, fortitude, determination and loyalty. Spiritual motivation in a nutshell was meant to develop intellectual power and promote physical energy.

Once when the INA Officers Training School (OTS) under the able command of Lt. Col. Thimaiya was functioning at Bauktaw, a suburb of Rangoon, Netaji ordered Lt. Manwati Arya to prepare and deliver a *'spiritual lecture'* after two days. She was nonplussed on getting such an assignment on the subject about which she had no idea at all. Observing her perplexity Netaji smiled and said, *"Pandey (the surname of Manwati Arya before marriage), you are always bubbling with enthusiasm and are prepared to take challenges. I expcet you to embolden yourself in this new task also."* As he had realised her ignorance of the subject, he explained to her what was meant by a *'spiritual lecture'*. He gave her a few hints and said, *"I want you to enthuse the cadets by relating the instances of patriotic and heroic deeds of our great historical ideals to boost up the morals of a would be officer of the INA so that they may face the war hazards bravely with fortitude and ever remain high-spirited while fighting the battles on the war front."*

Netaji provided more time to Lt. Manwati Arya to prepare her lecture and told her to accompany Major A.D. Jehangir to the OTS the next day and observe the spiritual lecture which he was going to deliver. It was only to familiarize her in advance with the classes of the OTS and the cadets. This was an example as Netaji used to apply to train his young and less experienced personnel to prepare the various units functioning in his movement for the independence of India from foreign yoke.

It was his hard earned spiritual power that made Netaji a 'Sthitaprajna', a state of equanimity in all circumstances of pain and pleasure. It was also his secret of calmness and equanimity for all his triumphs and tribulations that came his way. He remained a warrior and a sanyasi at the same time. For him it was actually one coin which had two faces.

Addressing the INA soldiers on July 5, 1943 Netaji said: *"A true soldier needs both military and spiritual training. You must, all of you, train yourself and your comrades that every soldier of the INA will have unbounded confidence in himself, will be conscious of being immensely superior to his enemy, will be fearless of death, and will have sufficient initiatives to act on his own in any critical situation, should the need arise."*

—o—

10

Baba Alias Bhagwanji Alias...

Inspite of the negative opinion on account of technical grounds in the findings of the Justice Mukherjee Commission of Inquiry (JMCI) report, the controversy over the real identity of the unnamed saint Gumnami Baba of Faizabad alias Bhagwanji alias Anam Saint, alias Swamiji, alias Srivijay, etc., has still been raging. There were too many common points between him and Netaji Subhas Chandra Bose. **He looked like Netaji in his outer gestures, postures and physical body. He was as tall and robust as Netaji. His age was similar. Like Netaji, he had gaps between his teeth. The scalpel mark on the abdomen was similar.** While speaking, Gumnami Baba sounded like Netaji. With identical reading habits, including the habit of scrawling in style and manner on left, right, top and bottom corners on the pages of the books, was similar. Both were interested in common subjects. **Both had the habit of chain-smoking for which Gumnami Baba used to say that *"Mussolini gave me this bad habit."*** Even Justice M.K. Mukherjee could not answer as to why some rare and familial letters, documents, photographs, books and souvenirs personally and directly related to Netaji were recovered from the collections of Gumnami Baba.

It was also strange that both had liked to wear round-rimmed spectacles and round gold wrist watch which in case of Netaji was gifted to him by his father and in case of Gumnami Baba it was a prized possession. Some original photos of Netaji's parents, his family members and friends included a distinctive umbrella which was said to be owned by Netaji's father. The original summons served by the Khosla Commission on Suresh Chandra Bose, the elder brother whom Netaji used to call *'Mejda',* was listed among 2673 items of Gumnami Baba. Some notes of Mejda found in original in Ram Bhawan, Faizabad, where Gumnami Baba lived for three years.

Politically speaking, it was general experience that both were staunch Indians with an international perspective. Whoever met them had concluded that both were equally talented and well versed in world history and international affairs. Both were Bengali and both were multilingual, thoroughly proficient in English and Hindustani. Both had used occasionally a spattering in Sanskrit and German in their conversation and sometimes had spoken the words of other foreign languages including Japanese, Vietnamese and Burmese. Both had Kolkatan accent in their vernacular, indicating that they had lived for a sufficiently long time in Kolkata.

It was very clear from the diaries found in trunks that this apparent mystic **Gumnami Baba took great pains to keep himself well informed about the affairs of Netaji and particularly the proceedings of the Khosla Commission.** While speaking, he named strange places in countries like Russia, China, Tibet, Japan and Burma, etc., as if he had been to those places. He used to describe the name of roads and specialities of those cities as if he had been there in his normal routine and these cities included Kolkata, Berlin, Omsk, Stuttgart, Tokyo, London, Kabul, Saigon, Singapore and many more like these.

Talking from behind a curtain Gumnami Baba sometimes spoke on international politics and described details about some most important personalities of the first-half of the last century. And among them Mahatma Gandhi, Joseph Stalin, Mao Tse-Tung, Ho Chi Minh, M.A. Jinnah, Jawaharlal Nehru, Mussolini, Hitler, Maulana Abul Kalam Azad, etc., were such names whom he knew personally and intimately. In his long and endless discussions with visitors Gumnami Baba used to mention that *'this body'* — which was his pet phrase to refer to himself — **had travelled for months under the seas in a submarine and in the same breadth he used to say, *"Do you know Churchill could not pronounce 'S'? I am alive to tell you this."***

According to the President of Subhas Chandra Bose Rashtriya Vichar Kendra, Faizabad, and the son of the landlord of Ram Bhawan, Shakti Singh, *"Gumnami Baba had indirectly confessed himself to be Netaji."* He further said that since Baba was living in a four-room suite of Ram Bhawan *"we were in close touch with him. His daily chores, likes and dislikes and his views were openly known to everyone living there. Once when we told him that people know him as Netaji Subhas Chandra Bose, he replied very calmly to stop thinking about his identity. 'Reign of India in Indian hands was our mission' and now he has taken up the path of 'ADHYATMA' and that is why he was staying in Ram Bhawan."*

Gumnami Baba had been residing in the pilgrim city Ayodhya for about two decades before he died in Ram Bhawan in the morning at 9.45 a.m. on September 16, 1985. After his cremation ceremony, which took place on September 19, 1985, the shanty apartment was locked by three devotees Dr. Raghunath Prasad Mishra, the Civil Surgeon of Faizabad, Dr. Priyabrat Banerjee, a renowned homoeopath of Faizabad, and the maid

Saraswati Devi Shukla, who remained in the service of Gumnami Baba from 1953-54 since his stay in Shringar Nagar, Lucknow, till he breathed his last.

Due to public pressure generated by representations and agitations before the local administration of Faizabad, Police Inspector Harish Chandra Singh was deputed by the Senior Superintendent of Police Karma Vir Singh to enlist the articles of Baba on October 31, 1985. After the enlistment the place was locked and was regularly guarded by the police. Suddenly, one of the closest members of Netaji's family' Miss Lalita Bose, the daughter of Suresh Chandra Bose, appeared on the scene. She had paid frequent visits to Ram Bhawan and had expressed her feelings that she believed firmly that Gumnami Baba was none else but her uncle Netaji. Lalita Bose asked the local administration to investigate the matter, but she could not get success. On February 6, 1986 she personally brought the matter to the knowledge of the then Prime Minister Rajiv Gandhi, and later on immediately to the notice of Vir Bahadur Singh, the then Chief Minister of Uttar Pradesh. But again no suitable action was initiated.

Meanwhile, on February 10, 1986, Lalita Bose along with two social workers, Dr. M.A. Haleem, All India Vice-President of the Socialist Party, and Vishwa Bandhu Tewari, Vice-President of Subhas Mukti Vahini, got success in obtaining an interim order from the Lucknow Bench of Allahabad High Court. The order on their Writ Petition No. 929/1986 directed the District Magistrate, Faizabad, that *"(i) An inventory of the articles left by the nameless saint at Ram Bhawan, Faizabad, shall be prepared or get prepared, through an Adovcate Commissioner who may be appointed either by the District Magistrate himself or he may get such an Advocate Commissioner appointed by the District Judge, Faizabad;* and *(ii) after the inventory has been prepared the articles shall be shifted from Ram Bhawan, Faizabad, to the Treasury to be kept in safe custody under own lock and seal. This arrangement shall continue until further orders of the Court."*

Complying with the orders of the High Court, Indra Kumar Pandey, the District Magistrate, Faizabad, nominated an advocate Satya Narain Singh 'Satya' to prepare the inventory as ordered by the Court. Satya Narain Singh was to be assisted by Ashok Tandon who was well acquainted with this subject as a journalist as he had written several articles and investigated the matter himself. Ashok Tandon was also a registered advocate. The process of cataloging began on March 23, 1986 and continued till April 23, 1987. During the preparation of the inventory, Lalita Bose and Netaji's sister's son Jitendra Nath were present along with many others who were curious among locals and journalists.

Before coming to Ayodhya, Gumnami Baba had lived in Lucknow for two years. At Naimisharanya he lived for six years. He had been in Basti for nine years. The author of the book *'Gumnami Subhas'* Ashok Tandon writes that in Basti, Baba was living in the house of Nawal Kishore Srivastava in Mohalla Pathan Tola before shifting to the house of Raja Saheb of Basti.

According to the common story published in various newspapers and periodicals, **Gumnami Baba never appeared before anyone including his personal staff.** He was reported to have reached Ayodhya sometime in the year 1974 and lived in Lal Kothi temple at Swargadwar for one year. Later on, a house in Urdu Bazar locality of the pilgrim city was hired for him by Surendra Chaudhary, a former inhabitant of Etawah, Uttar Pradesh. After a few months, a house at a lonely place was engaged for him at Brahmakund. In 1978 Gumnami Baba was shifted to an abandoned palatial temple known as *'Lucknow Kothi'* at Mohalla Deokali **where he lived till 1983 when he was shifted to Ram Bhawan.**

As per the description published in the second instalment of a report published in *'The Hindustan Times'* on April 26, 2002, *"Ram Bhawan was carefully chosen so that Bhagwanji could lead his reclusive life."* Dr. Raghunath Prasad Mishra, who was Baba's follower since 1975, approached Gurbasant Singh, the landlord of Ram Bhawan, and said that the rooms were required for his grandfather who *"stays in his room and worships all the time. He never appears before anyone."* Dr. Mishra also told him that Baba would be accompanied by his caretakers Saraswati Devi Shukla and her son Raj Kumar Shukla. While deposing before the JMCI Gurbasant Singh said that *"I heard him speaking.* ***His voice was heavy and crisp, like that of a Military General."***

The report published by *The Hindustan Times* gave two incidents to highlight the mystery of Gumnami Baba. The first incident was related to Dr. Priyabrat, whose father Dr. Taradas Banerjee was requested one fine morning in 1975 by Saraswati Devi Shukla to accompany her to attend Gumnami Baba. Dr. Priyabrata narrated before the JMCI that *"my father was a changed man when he returned ...he was perplexed and excited."* According to the hints of the report, the reason of his excitement was that Dr. Banerjee had seen Netaji in the 1930s and Gumani Baba was the same person.

The second incident was related to Ramji Pandey, the masseur of Gumnami Baba. The report said that ***"Bhagwanji used to cover his face with a monkey cap*** *but the cuts on his abdomen did not escape Pandey's attention."*

Narrating the story of shifting to Ram Bhawan *Northern India Patrika* wrote on January 4, 1986 that *"Once again the shifting was executed with precision ... all precautionary measures were observed."*

At this point of time, it is said that Gumnami Baba was incapacitated and physically immobilized due to a fall at Lucknow Kothi. He was now completely dependent on his protege Dr. Mishra and his family who were *"now in command of the situation and for all intents and purposes ... even food and breakfast were being provided by Mishra's family."*

The other family which was already in close touch with Gumnami Baba and having access to him was that of Dr. Taradas Banerjee, the reputed homeopath of Faizabad.

According to another report filed by Udayan Namboodiri and published by *'The Pioneer'* on March 25, 2005, *"Bhagwanji or Gumnami Baba, the mysterious ascetic of Faizabad ...* ***is believed to have entered India through China sometimes in 1953.*** *Until his death in 1985 this enigmatic character lived on the margins of life, but commanded respect from people high and low."*

The Pioneer's report said: *"The Commission* (the JMCI) *had evidence that successive Indian governments were aware of his movements....Important leaders like Charan Singh, Sampoornanand, Guru Golwalkar, Samar Guha and others kept in touch with him ...* ***the Nehru Government had tried to prop up an 'alternative' guru to confuse people who saw striking similarities between Bhagwanji and Netaji. That was the famous 'Shoulmari Baba'*** *who lived under tight security in an Ashram in Alipurduar, a sub-division of Jalpaiguri in Cooh Behar district in West Bengal.... ."*

The report further wrote: *"Bhagwanji was a thorough recluse who seldom exposed himself physically. With the exception of a couple of doctors and a few personal attendants, few ever got a glimpse of him."*

In its investigation, the report said: *"Bhagwanji was no ordinary 'Baba'. There were hints in many letters that the* ***governments of Indira***

Gandhi and Rajiv Gandhi not only knew all about him but also backed him in a strange way. *The district administration of Faizabad, under orders from an unknown source, also ensured that his privacy was guarded. There were also hints that the Government bore some of his expenses."*

V.N. Arora, a correspondent of *Times of India* had reported with an interrogative introduction on January 23, 2004 that *"Was Bhagwanji, the Sadhu who lived incognito for about two decades in this pilgrim city and died on September 16, 1985, none other than Netaji Subhas Chandra Bose?"*

Commenting on a technical matter related to Gumnami Baba, Arora said, *"Well, reviving the decades old controversy a noted forensic expert has found characteristic similarities in their writings strongly suggesting common authorship of specimens."*

Detailing about the experts' views Arora wrote: *"Reputed forensic expert B. Lal, a former Additional Director of National Institute of Criminology and Forensic Science, Government of India, after examining certain documents belonging to the nameless saint, has summed up that it was a result of detailed examination and comparison of questioned and submitted writings of Sri Subhas Chandra Bose (based on scientific principles), it is found that there are characteristic similarities in general and individual writing habits, strongly suggesting common authorship of relevant questioned writings and admitted writings of Sri Subhas Chandra Bose."*

Arora wrote further in the same report that *"the Baba whom nobody had ever seen but only heard behind an ochre curtain maintained strict secrecy about his movements to evade prying eyes of those believing him to be Netaji Subhas Chandra Bose."*

Lalita Bose had always desired that the mystery sprang due to belongings of Gumnami Baba should be solved. She expressed her surprise in The *Hindustan Times* on October 24, 1989 that *"why the Government was not serious to find out whether Gumnami Baba of Faizabad was Netaji?"* She told her personal opinion that there were *"considerable evidences to prove that Netaji did not die in an air crash"* and Gumnami Baba *"was of the same age, size and colour of Netaji"*. According to her, the room of Gumnami Baba as seen by her, had not only the pictures of Goddess Kali, Ramkrishna Paramhans, Sarda Devi, Vivekanand, but also pictures of Janaki Nath and Prabhabati Bose, the parents of Netaji. Based on press-reports and the statements of Lalita Bose a question was raised in the Legislative Assembly of Uttar Pradesh by Krishna Pal Singh and Nityanand Swami of Bhartiya Janata Party and it was supported by Jagdambika Pal, a Congress Party member. The then Finance Minister of Uttar Pradesh, Baldev Singh Arya, replied conclusively that the inquiry had already been conducted and it revealed that Gumnami Baba was not Netaji. But any such report by the Government of Uttar Pradesh had never been made public.

By the end of 1997 Vishwa Bandhav Tewari had again tried in vain to raise the issue through his letters to high dignitaries of the country including Prime Minister, Home Minister, Speaker of Lok Sabha, Governor and the Chief Minister of Uttar Pradesh.

After the appointment of the JMCI an application was moved by an advocate before the Lucknow Bench of Allahabad High Court seeking to allow the inspection of articles of Gumnami Baba. On July 30, 2001, Justice D.K. Tewari and Justice M.A. Khan ordered that *"it is contended by Sri Umesh Chandra that in view of the order dated 10.2.1986, passed by this Court in Writ Petition No. 929 (M/B) of 1986 the Commissioner appointed by Government of India will not be able to inspect the articles. We find no such obstacle in the way of Commissioner appointed by the Government of India."*

The High Court order had further explained: *"However, the opposite parties are permitted to get the articles inspected by the Commissioner if appointed by Government of India (Hon. M.K. Mukherjee) former Judge of the Supreme Court appointed by the Government of India as Commissioner of Enquiry."*

The belongings of Gumnami Baba, kept in 28 boxes preserved in the Treasury of Faizabad, were unlocked on November 26, 2001 for examination by the team of the JMCI. Thus the articles possessed by Gumnami Baba could see the light after 15 years and could tell us more about the life-style of their possessor. The articles disclosed that Gumnami Baba was a regular reader of *'Time'* and *'Readers' Digest'* magazines of international standard. The *Indian Express, Statesman, The Pioneer, Times of India* and *Hindustan Standard* were his choice of English dailies. He liked *Dainik Jagaran* and *Dharmayuga* in Hindi and *Jugantar, Anand Bazar Patrika* and *Bartman* in Bangla.

The huge collection of books in the belongings of Gumnami Baba had included complete works of Rabindra Nath Tagore, Sarat Chandra Chattopadhyay, William Shakespeare and Charles Dickens. Homer's *Odyssey* and *Illiad* were not so surprising in the collection of a saint as Berlitz's book *'The Bermuda Triangle'* and Von Daniken's *'Miracles of God'.* Famous Irish author Jonathan Swift's *'Gulliver's Travels',* American writer Henry Miller's *'Tropic of Cancer',* Leslie and George Adamski's *'Flying Saucers Have Landed'* and Swami Abhedananda's *'Life Beyond Death'* were books of international fame whereas Maulana Abul Kalam Azad's *'India Wins Freedom',* Kuldeep Nayar's *'Between the Lines'* and *'India: Critical Years',* Brigadier John Dalvi's *'Himalayan Blunder',* Neville Maxwell's *'India's China War',* Leonard Mosley's *'The Last Days of the British Raj'* and all the three volumes of the great Indian historian Dr. R.C. Majumdar's *'The*

History of Freedom Movement in India' were descriptive books on Indian affairs.

Among other worth mentioning books found in the collection of Gumnami Baba included *'Jap Sutram'* by Swami Pratyagatmanand, *'Mrichchhakatikam'* by Shudrak, *'Subhas Chandra Bose'* by Nanda Mukherjee, *'Netaji at Nehru's Funeral'* by Swami Nirvananand, who claimed that Gumnami Baba visited Shoulmari Ashram while entering into India via Nepal. Swami Nirvananand had also written that Netaji adopted the name *'Saardanand'* when he undertook his adventurous and secret journey of Himalayas at the age of 17 years in search of a spiritual Guru.

Gumnami Baba also possessed books like *'A Tale of Two Cities'*, *'Great Expectations'*, *'Christmas Stories'*, *'American Notes for General Circulation'*, *'A Child's History of England'*, *'The Sacred Rome'*, *'David Copperfield'*, *'The Old Curiosity Shop'*, *'The Winter's Tale'* and *'Rubaiyat of Omar Khayyam.'*

The mystery-linked scrawlings on the pages of books were denoting that all books had been read intensively and seriously. In the collection of Gumnami Baba, some books which attracted the attention of many, were *'Celebrated Crimes'* translated by I.G. Burnhum, Victor Hugo's *'The Hunch/back of Notre Dame'*, and Lewis Carroll's *'Alice in Wonderland'*. These were such inspiring and motivating books which were rarely thought to be possessed by a Sadhu. Justice Mukherjee could not conceal his inquisitiveness and excitement when he expressed his personal desire to read a book of Baba's collection titled as *'International Military Tribunal For The Far-East: Dissentient Judgement of Justice'* by Radha Binode Pal. Gumnami Baba had not only underlined its many paragraphs expressing his approval for Justice Pal's courageous pro-Japan stand but had also written such comments which clearly indicated that Baba himself was aware of those incidents.

All the ten volumes of *'The Story of Civilization'* by Will Durant were marked by critical lopsided remarks of the Baba. According to Gumnami Baba, almost all western writers had always been prejudicial in their treatment and leaning against the genuine achievements of Eastern civilizations. In the collection of books Peter Sengar's *'Moscow's Hand in India'* and Rani Mukherjee's *'Moscow's Shadow over West Bengal'* hinted that Gumnami Baba like Netaji was not a blind follower of the USSR. This view was further supported by his scrawlings on the pages of *'The Gulag Archipelago'* by Alexander Solzhenitsin. Sita Ram Goyal's book *'Nehru's Fatal Friendship'* was marked as if Baba's thinking was similar to that of the author, to a great extent.

Besides numerous religious books like Mahabharat, Durga Saptasati, treatises on Islam, Sikhism, Judaism, Christianity, etc., and books on Shakti and Shakta philosophies, *'The Charter of United Nations'* disclosed Baba's frame of mind. He could have lived the graceful, holy and containable life of a spiritual preceptor like Aurobindo Ghosh and Pester John and would have contributed a new philosophy in theological sense, but Gumnami Baba opted to remain concealed even when he was well aware of his surroundings, his past and those, of his limitations which were never disclosed to his intimates and followers.

The letters and documents which attracted the attention of everyone included a photocopy of a letter dated September 23, 1923, written by Netaji from Mandalay jail which was duly stamped as *'censored'* by D.I. Police. Another photocopy of a letter dated February 23, 1934 written to Netaji's mother was sentimentally eye catching. A copy of *'Jugantar'* dated January 23, 1979 was a very historical collection as it had published the photograph, claiming as the latest photo of Netaji, released to press by Prof. Samar Guha on January 22, 1979 during his press conference in Kolkata. There were press-cuttings of *Weekend Telegraph* and a long article under the heading *'The Netaji-Mahatma Letters'*. Gumnami Baba had in his collections several magazines which had material on Netaji.

Letters received by Gumnami Baba indicated that he had meticulously tracked those incidents which were related to Netaji. One such letter dated October 1, 1980 in Bangla had an information about Nanda Mukherjee, the author of the famous book *'Netaji through German Lens'* that the documents from the museum and intelligence reports of German archives had been photocopied.

In the collection of Gumnami Baba, a letter written to Netaji by Rashtriya Swayamsewak Chief Guru Golwalkar was a curious item. Likewise, several letters of Dr. Pabitra Mohan Roy and a copy of his houseplan attracted the attention of the gathering. Dr. Roy's letters were very informative and sentimental. A veteran leader of Anushilan Samiti and an old asssociate of Netaji, Aushutosh Kali's letters were written in a most expressive manner exposing the mystery of Gumnami Baba as in these letters Baba was addressed as Netaji.

—o—

11

Scrawlings in Baba's Books

The JMCI managed to secure the reports of three handwriting experts. Among these experts the first were Amar Singh and M.L. Sharma who were in active service of the Government of India. They stated in their report that the handwritings of Gumnami Baba did not match with Netaji Subhas Chandra Bose as there were *"distinct individual features."* The other handwriting expert was N.K. Nag, officially serving the West Bengal Government. Nag wrote in his report that *"There were similarities in the handwritings of Netaji and Gumnami Baba. Despite the time gap there are fundamental similarities between the two handwritings in English. There are characteristic similarities. There is no evidence of imitation. In Bengali there were fundamental differences as well as dissimilarities in size and spacing, but some of them were written by the same person."*

The third handwriting expert was Dr. B. Lal Kapoor, popularly known as B. Lal. He was an ex-Government Examiner of Questioned Documents and had also served as Additional Director at the National Institute of Criminology. B. Lal was awarded Life-Time Achievement Award at the Indian Science Congress in 2000. His services were obtained in the famous St. Kitt's case and he had received appreciation for his expertise by international agencies including the United Nations.

In the case of Gumnami Baba in his report B. Lal wrote very firmly that *"He is the same man. The writer of documents brought from the National Archives and writer of Faizabad documents is the same... My 44 years of experience tells me that all these are written by one person."*

B. Lal continued in his report that *"the documents of this case have been carefully, thoroughly and scientifically examined... there is a gap of a few decades between the questioned and admitted handwritings... A question arises whether there is an attempt to disguise?"*

The query raised had been well answered by B. Lal himself. He wrote in the report that *"It may be stated that disguise is adopted in order to conceal the identity... the writer has tried to hide his identity but has failed to do so... It is not possible for a writer to change his writing habits completely. Even in an effort to hide his identity, the writer is not able to leave his individual characteristics and other peculiarities found in his handwriting. There is such a faithful reproduction of some peculiarities that even a gap of time to the extent of decades cannot hide them."*

In the opinion of B. Lal, *"Similar habits of overwriting the letter or lines or brackets — a sort of emphasis or trait to make the strokes more clearly and more prominent to be seen are found in both the questioned and admitted."*

Commenting on scrawlings, B. Lal submitted that *"The habit of underlining words is also found in both sets of writings that is questioned and admitted. Similar habits of making certain abbreviations and giving a mark over the figure representing year is also found in both the questioned and admitted."*

B. Lal also considered the handwritings from various angles and opined that *"in addition there are similarities in the manner of execution of various letters and their combinations and also the manner of execution of figures."*

Concluding his report, B. Lal said that *"It has been found that there was no evidence to show... that the questioned writing has been made by a writer other than Sri Subhas Chandra Bose... it is found that there are characteristic similarities in general and individual writing habit strongly suggesting common authorship of relevant questioned writings and admitted writings."*

The JMCI said in its findings that the opinions of different handwriting experts were not similar and the major problem was related to the admitted handwritings of Netaji. There was no evidence from any person conversant with the handwriting of Netaji. The documents procured from the archives could not become evidence until these were endorsed or confirmed by reliable supporting evidence. The same sort of legal problem was also in regard to the handwritings of Gumnami Baba. There was no evidence to confirm that the questioned handwritings had really belonged to Gumnami Baba.

Thus in the absence of any clinching evidence for the satisfaction of the JMCI, the claim had no legal merit.

—o—

12

Pardewale Baba in Naimisharanya

The other important aspect of the story related to Gumnami Baba is equally mysterious and surprising. An old acquaintance of Netaji and ex-Member of Legislative Assembly of West Bengal, Professor Atul Sen, visited Naimisharanya, Sitapur, in Uttar Pradesh, in April 1962. Without any serious planning and desire he could get an opportunity to meet a saint popularly called there as *'Pardewale Baba'*. He was residing in a ruined Shiva temple. After a little discourse with Pardewale Baba, Atul Sen could guess with firmness that the Baba was none else but Netaji in disguise. This feeling overwhelmed him and he could not control his emotions which burst out before the Baba. *Pardewale Baba* had not only denied but also asked Atul Sen to contain his emotions. Baba had forbidden him not to repeat his sentiments and his guess about Netaji.

Atul Sen was discouraged and told by Baba that he had to stop discussions about his guess. But defying Baba's instructions Atul Sen communicated his feelings and his guess to Dr. R.C. Majumdar, a great Indian historian, and a few of his friends of former revolutionary organisation famous in Bengal as *'Anushilan Samiti'*. He also wrote a letter to Jawaharlal Nehru keeping the location of Baba as secret. His letter was replied by Nehru. It is said that **Atul Sen's reaction had disqualified him and he could never meet Baba in the future.**

On receiving the information that Netaji was alive and was living in disguise, an associate of Netaji during INA's offensive against the British, Dr. Pabitra Mohan Roy, traced the person who had originated the news. He could search out Atul Sen and his information about Netaji. Dr. Pabitra Mohan Roy himself was a renowned revolutionary and had joined the INA as a fearless and undaunted secret agent after he fled to South-East Asia from India. Dr. Roy was assigned by the INA to mobilise and seek support of the Indian revolutionaries against the British. In 1943 he along with Amrik Singh Gill, Tuhin Mukherjee and Mohinder Singh were dropped somewhere at Puri on India's Eastern Coast by a Japanese submarine. Mohinder Singh was a bomb specialist and Amrik Singh an expert in creating D.G. Cells to collect special information on army, navy and airforce activities of the British centres for supplying to INA. Dr. Roy could instal a transmitter on the roof of Jyotish Bose's house near Deshpriya Park on Bipin Pal Road in Kolkata with the help of Haridas Mitra. They could get success in establishing the contact with Netaji and thus the messages were regularly sent for the consumption of the INA for a few months, till it was shifted to Behala, where very soon it came to the notice of the police and Mohinder Singh was arrested. The police applied inhuman and third degree torturing methods on Mohinder Singh and extracted from him the names of his colleagues before he died of injuries inflicted due to torturing. Thus in their initial planning Tuhin Mukherjee betrayed and accepted to become approver due to torturing of the police. All of them were arrested and tortured by the British. After a summary trial Amrik Singh Gill and Dr. Roy were ordered to be hanged. While Gill escaped with handcuffs on from the jail, Dr. Roy's death sentence was commuted into transportation of life on November 4, 1945.

Dr. Roy desired first to verify the news about Netaji and he himself ventured to visit Naimisharanya, Sitapur. After collecting the preliminary information he managed to meet Pardewale Baba and convinced himself that Baba was none else but Netaji. In the beginning of January 1963 Dr. Roy passed this information to Leela Roy, who was better known amongst the revolutionaries as 'Didi' and who *"was one of the greatest freedom fighters of this country,"* according to the statement of Krishna Kant, ex-Vice President of India, at a function in Kolkata to mark her birth anniversary in 1997. The firebrand Leela Roy had herself attempted in 1931 on the life of the District Magistrate, Comilla, now in Bangladesh. After her arrest in 1931 she remained in prison until 1937. With her revolutionary husband Anil Roy she joined the Forward Bloc since its inception and after Netaji left the country in 1941, she became the editor of the weekly *'Forward Bloc'*. Besides her active and inspiring revolutionary involvement' Leela Roy's relief efforts were praised by Mahatma Gandhi during the riots at his short stay in Noakhali.

Leela Roy, though sick in those days, was almost of the same age group as Netaji. Even then she proceeded from Kolkata on March 23, 1963 to meet Pardewale Baba with her confidants who included Anil Das, Sailo Sen, and Professor Samar Guha. All who accompanied her and others like Sunil Das, Bijoy Nag, Ajit Nag, Helena Dutta, Santosh Bhattacharya, Sagarika Ghosh, Basant Guha, R.S. Ruikar, H.V. Kamath, Dr. Atindra Nath Bose, etc., had undertaken an oath to maintain strict secrecy about the Baba. After reaching Naimishranya, Leela Roy had to wait for a long time and she could meet Pardewale Baba only when she assured them to obey completely the terms dictated by Baba. She remained in Naimisharanya until April 30, 1963.

On her return to Kolkata, Leela Roy suitably abided by the instructions of Pardewale Baba and the information about him was passed on to a few members of Netaji's family and to Trailokya Nath Chakravarty of Anushilan Samiti. Trailokya Nath was known in his group of revolutionaries as *'Maharaj'.* He had been in Mandalay jail with Netaji in 1924. According to a revolutionary belonging to Hindustan Socialist Republican Army, and the author of *'Bharat Ki Krantikari Partiyan'*, Shiv Kumar Misra, the whole group of Anushilan Samiti led by Maharaj was active supporter of Netaji's *'Anti-Compromise Movement'* launched at the Ramgarh Conference in 1940 and they firmly supported Netaji in taking advantage of the World War II for India's freedom struggle. They resolved to join Netaji in his efforts to launch a militant struggle if needed, to hasten the freedom of the country. The Britishers arrested Maharaj several times and kept him behind the bars for about 30 years which included over a decade in the deadly concentration camp in Port Blair in Andaman Islands.

Maharaj was very close to Netaji. His letters were found in Ram Bhawan, Faizabad. In one of his letters, he reminded Gumnami Baba treating him as Netaji, that both had stayed in Shankerlal's residence in 1940 and had *"toured United Provinces (now Uttar Pradesh) on a chilling winter night in the Agra ground where hundreds of people waited for him till nine at night."* After the partition of the country in 1947, Maharaj decided that he would not live in India and would stay in the then East Pakistan (now Bangladesh).

The written documents recovered from the collections of Gumnami Baba had the letters of Ashutosh Kali, a veteran of Anushilan Samiti. Kali was older than Netaji. In his long letter dated May 9, 1963, Kali addressed Baba, as if he was very sure that he was Netaji. He wrote, "*...ever since we got news of you, we all, I mean the entire Anushilan group, have been yearning to gain from your guidance and work under your instructions ... you and Maharaj do know everything. He is in East Pakistan...*"

The other important persons who used to visit Baba were Jyotish Chandra Bose, a very senior sympathiser and helper of revolutionaries, Nandlal Chakravarty, who accompanied the JMCI to Russia on his own expenses, Kamlakant Ghosh, a famous practitioner of alternative medicines, and Dr. Madhusudan Pal.

As per the evidence recorded by the JMCI Suresh Chandra Bose, the elder brother of Netaji had also received information about Gumnami Baba through Leela Roy and Dr. Pabitra Mohan Roy. He deputed Sukrit alias Sunil Krishna Gupta to inquire about the fact. Later on Sukrit became a devoted and dedicated follower of Gumnami Baba and he was always very emphatic in saying that *'Netaji did not die in 1945 and had disappeared'*. Sukrit deposed before the JMCI and said that on the instructions of Gumnami Baba he had followed the proceedings of the Khosla Commission. Sukrit had always addressed Gumnami Baba as *'Bhagwanji'*. For a very long time he pursued the matters related to Netaji and had reported the progress step by step to Bhagwanji. Sukrit was a regular visitor to Gumnami Baba and he managed all personal and financial matters of Bhagwanji with his full commitment and submission only next to Leela Roy who died in 1968 and Dr. Pabitra Mohan Roy who became sick in the 80s of the last century. In this connection the self-committed support of a few locals including Saraswati Devi Shukla and her son Raj Kumar Shukla, Dr. R.P. Mishra, Dr. Taradas

Banerjee and his son Dr. Priyabrat, Ramkishore Panda of Swargadwar, Ayodhya, hinted that their belief about Gumnami Baba was sacred and their services to him were without prejudice. Maharaj alias Trailokya Nath Chakravarty needed special attention because, like Leela Roy his interest Gumnami Baba could be taken as authentic. All these Kolkatan dignitaries visited Gumnami Baba wheresoever he lived particularly on and around January 23 and Durga Puja festival.

Lt. Manwati Arya herself has her ancestral house in Bikapur Tehsil in the village Bardanda; which is about 20 kilometres away from Faizabad on Rae Bareli Road. During her visits to Faizabad she could not meet Gumnami Baba but was privileged to listen to a very interesting incident narrated by Mrs. Pushpa Banerjee about a discussion between Gumnami Baba and her husband Dr. Taradas Banerjee. Mrs. Banerjee said that once Dr. Taradas told *"Gumnami Baba that he had seen Netaji Subhas Chandra Bose in 1938 when he had gone to Lucknow at the house of Sen Dada at A.P. Sen Road. On hearing the statement Gumnami Baba corrected him that it was not 1938, but 1939."*

—o—

13

Mukherjee Commission Rejects Plane-Crash Theory

'I, ...(name) will tell the truth, whole truth, nothing but truth, and will not conceal anything' — were the beginning words of those who deposed before the Justice Mukherjee Commission of Inquiry (JMCI). After its formation on April 14, 1999, the JMCI was required to complete its task within six months. But during this period it lived without an office, without funds and without a Secretary. Due to the cold and depressing treatment of senior bureaucrats, responsible for the purpose, almost another six months till April 2000 passed when the JMCI could get its basic requirements to start its functioning officially.

At this point of time Atal Bihari Vajpayee was the Prime Minister with his National Democratic Alliance's team yet the experiences of Justice Manoj Kumar Mukherjee and his Secretary, Pradyot Kumar Sengupta, a former judge, were humiliating and disgusting. The high-handedness and trickery employed by the bureaucrats were generally speaking frustrating and nothing else than killing precious time. On the excuse of classified documents treated as *'Top Secret'*, *'Secret'* and *'Confidential'* the JMCI's functioning was made further difficult. The JMCI was required to invest its expertise in dealing with the comments such as that the *"information contained is 'Top Secret', papers may be made use of by the Commission in camera, since these are classified as 'Top Secret' they may kindly be considered not to be published."*

On the other side, the government's officials were shaky to forward the required documents and to share information, which, if presented, had to be presented before the JMCI along with a supporting *'affidavit'* of an officer not below the rank of Joint Secretary. Such judicial procedure was tedious and time-consuming. A junior officer in his administrative capacity and performance could never dare swearing in writing even regarding petty and simple matters related to his establishment without seeking prior permission of the competent authority. In this background, how would an officer be expected to cooperate with a judicial commission? Quite often taking advantage of such administrative and judicial complexities, many live truths had been buried in India.

Perhaps it is what is called the *'Rule of Law'* which, according to experts, governs and administers all equally and commands respect of all and in all the 'cracies' but the best in a democracy. It is always against the arbitrary and discretionary functioning of any authority. But this merit part of the *'Rule of Law'* has no remedy for its demerits which include lengthy procedures, red-tapism, shouldering of responsibilities and never-quick-to-response even at the time of a severe crisis or an emergency. Generally, the power is administered hierarchically, but if a needbound top bureaucrat desires all subordinate ranks and file become unitary and within no time and all formalities and requirements are completed to obtain the desired results. But the JMCI was going to become the victim of the demerits of the *'Rule of Law'* in coming years more seriously inspite of its judicial immunity and declared sincerity.

Anuj Dhar appropriately commented on the basis of the JMCI's proceedings dated August 31, 2000 that *"The Centre and the West Bengal governments showed paradoxical unease in parting with the documents required by the Commission to get the basic inquiry started. There was no way Justice Mukherjee could have moved an inch without the aid of the official papers on the mystery now that almost all the witnesses had departed. West Bengal Home Department became too possessive about certain Index Books concerned with Bose. The Union Ministry of Home Affairs was finding it impossible to trace even the complete original records of the proceedings of Justice Khosla Commission of Inquiry, including the evidences recorded by and documents produced before the said Commission. The Ministry of External Affairs was clueless where in the world the records of the proceedings of Shah Nawaz Committee had disappeared. Both Intelligence Bureau and Research and Analysis Wing were shying away from filing affidavits before the JMCI over an issue that most journalists felt, was dead as dodo."*

On June 20, 2000 the Director of Internal Security in the Ministry of Home Affairs narrated in an affidavit that only two files on Netaji were available with them and *"those files do not have any bearing on the ongoing inquiry."* Thus denying to submit the files before the JMCI was simply a routine bureaucratic gesture. Justice Mukherjee reacted unsusceptibly and ordered to *"submit those files before the Commission immediately."* On their turn the Ministry of Home Affairs opted to file a supplementary affidavit on January 1, 2001 regarding the claim for certain files on Netaji under the signature of the its Home Secretary, Kamal Pandey. The ten-page affidavit filed by Pandey negated the orders passed by the JMCI. Its few lines are quoted hereunder:

"I have carefully examined the documents and I am bonafidely satisfied that the disclosure of the documents would cause injury to the public interest and the public interest would suffer thereby.

"I believe that disclosure of the nature and contents of these documents would also hurt the sentiments of the people at large and may evoke widespread reactions as these documents if disclosed may lower the image of Netaji Subhas Chandra Bose.

"These are unpublished official records relating to the affairs of State, and contain communications made to public officers in official confidence. The disclosure of the records would cause injury to the public interest.

"The records ordered to be produced also belong to the classes of documents which it is the practice to keep secret for ensuring the proper functioning of the public service.

"Diplomatic relations with friendly countries may also be adversely affected if the said documents are disclosed."

During the seventh hearing of the JMCI in his affidavit, the Home Secretary claimed his privilege under Section 123 and 124 of the Evidence Act and Article 74(1) of the Constitution of India. In another affidavit filed **on April 27, 2001 Home Secretary Pandey stated that he would not *"produce the said records or disclose their contents or give any evidence derived therefrom."*** Pandey very clearly conveyed to the JMCI the decision of the Government which itself appointed the Commission and assigned its job in its notification along with the terms of reference. **The same government asked to conduct an inquiry and the same government was not prepared to open files and divulge the details about Netaji.** Now it was a priority with the government to safeguard a secret in order to avoid the trouble of the people, the trouble of the government and the trouble in our ties with friendly countries.

Discussing the Home Secretary's affidavit, Government Counsel Tarakeshwar Pal claimed that the JMCI should not press for the publication of the documents considering public interest. The Forward Bloc Counsel Shaktinath Mukherjee said that greater public interest would be served if the documents were made public. It was argued that the JMCI could overrule the government's objections but the government could always appeal to any High Court or the Supreme Court against the JMCI's decision. The implications of such as situation would be that the legal battle might stretch on for much longer period than expected.

Relating to the statement of Prime Minister Morarji Desai in the Parliament on August 28, 1978, an affidavit was filed on December 18, 2001 by the PMO's Joint Secretary Jarnail Singh before the JMCI, in which he very plainly admitted: *"Due searches were made in this office to trace any contemporary official documentary records based on which the then Prime Minister had made the statement on the floor of the Parliament on August 28, 1978... But no such records could be found in this office. The PMO is not in a position to provide any classification/explanation regarding the circumstances under which Late Morarji Desai, then Prime Minister, had made such statement on the floor of the Parliament."*

It was also ridiculous that the then Home Minister, Shivraj Patil, with his political vendetta expressed his inability to provide those documents on which basis the then Prime Minister Desai made a statement. Although Morarji Desai was well known for his truthfulness and strictness in following the Gandhian principles, yet Shivraj Patil had tried to twist the matter to suit his political prejudices. The Home Minister commented, *"I respect Shri Morarji Desai very much. He is not with us today. But then, political facts also had to be borne in the mind when he made the statement. It is said that he had doubted the reliability in view of the documents available in the office of the Government. No dates, no names, no numbers to identify the said files were given, which could help to find out the documents mentioned by the Prime Minister. They could not be found out in the offices, if particulars about them were not provided. The fact that the then Prime Minister had formed the Government by defeating the Government which was in power when the two inquiries were conducted, cannot be brushed aside, to come to the conclusion that his statement could have been motivated not by reasons of law, but by reasons of politics."*

If documents and details about Netaji would be kept secret, how the complete picture would come out? In the absence of related information our common sense would start speculating. It is natural to speculate as to what were those details which Government of India did not want to disclose even after the gap of such a long period of about seven decades. The furtive attitude of the Government of India was exposed before the Calcutta High Court when it failed to produce those reports and comments which conduced to take a decision to award Bharat Ratna to Netaji posthumously and to bring his alleged ashes from Japan. Likewise, there had been an open involvement of Ministeries of Home Affairs and External Affairs along with the Director of Intelligence Bureau when some new facts were unearthed from Russian archives and published in a magazine *'Asia and Africa Today'* in its volumes Nos. 8, 9 and 10 in 1993, but **no disclosure was made and a mischievous silence was maintained by the Government.**

Anuj Dhar describes in his book '*Back from Dead*' that *"despite their public posturing of disinterest, the Government was quick to take note of the news breaking in Russia. V.K, Jain, Special Secretary, MHA, wrote to Foreign Secretary K. Srinivasan and the RAW on March 18, 1994 "regarding disclosure made in a series of articles based on classified*

KGB records." RAW prepared a report (No. 11/1/94-1c-2829) on March 25, 1994, and around a month later Home Secretary N.N. Vohra (of 'Mission Kashmir' fame) wrote to K. Srinivasan. Simultaneously, Vohra wrote to A.N. Verma, Principal Secretary to the Prime Minister, regarding the controversy regarding Netaji's death and bringing his ashes to India from Japan."

In spite of these consciously created hurdles by the Government, a lot of evidence had come from public for consideration during the proceedings of the JMCI. There were 131 witnesses examined and 730 files and documents were exhibited though the **Government of India had not produced even a single witness of its own.** The JMCI also received 105 books, which included 47 in English, one in Russian and 57 including 14 journals in vernacular from different deponents and sources. The JMCI had in its consideration many tape-recorded versions, photographs and compact discs to go ahead in its cause.

Under the Terms of Reference, the JMCI issued the public notification. As a result five versions relating to Netaji's death were placed before the JMCI as under:

(A) Netaji was murdered at Red Fort in Delhi on August 15, 1945, (as claimed by Usha Ranjan Bhattacharji);

(B) Netaji died at Dehradun in 1977 in the name of Shoulmari Baba;

(C) Netaji died at Sheopurkalan, Madhya Pradesh, on May 21, 1977; (Deposed by Jagannath Prasad Gupta);

(D) Netaji died at Faizabad, Uttar Pradesh, on September 16, 1985, identified as Gumnami Baba;

(E) Netaji died in an air crash at Taihoku on August 18, 1945, as propagated by the Government of India.

Before discussing various claims regarding the death of Netaji, the story of air-crash had to be given priority as it had been published very widely and also because it had a close connection with the historical date of August 18, 1945 when Netaji either died or disappeared.

We would like to begin and examine the JMCI report regarding the contention that the story of the plane-crash was contrived in pursuance of a well laid out plan and to which the Japanese military authorities were a party to ensure safe passage to Netaji. The JMCI report submitted that *"a stratagem including the manner of its execution ingenuously and meticulously hatched in secret cannot, owing to its very nature, be proved by direct evidence... It can, therefore, be proved by circumstantial evidences and individual and detached acts or omissions of the planner including their dialogue inter se, written correspondence and contemporaneous documents prepared by them or at their instance including entries made therein relative to the main design."*

Analysing the circumstances and facts as on August 16, 1945, while in Bangkok Netaji had a meeting with General Isoda, the Head of Hikari Kikan, a unit of the Japanese Armed Forces to liaise between the Japanese Government and the Japanese Army on the one hand and a combined group of the Indian Independence League (IIL), Indian National Army (INA) and the Provisional Government of Free India (PGI) on the other. Relating to the planning of Netaji to go to Russia, Isoda's testimony before the JMCI was as under:

"Commission: When Netaji came on 16th to Bangkok, he came by his personal plane?

Isoda: I think so.

Commission: At Bangkok, the future plans were decided between you and Netaji as to where Netaji should go?

Isoda: It was decided immediately in talks between myself and Mr. Bose where Mr. Bose would go?

Commission: So, it was decided that Mr. Bose will be going to Russia via Manchuria and Diren?

Isoda: Yes."

When Isoda was cross-examined before the JMCI he said that he had strongly suggested to Netaji that he had to leave hurriedly to a safe place to hide from the Allied Forces. He specifically said that these plans of Netaji going from Bangkok to Russia were kept secret. Isoda further said, *"The purpose of his flight was to go to the Soviet Union and with the help of the Soviet Union he was to continue his independence movement. That was the aim of his mission. After reaching Diren, if time allowed he had intended to go to Tokyo to express his gratitude for the Japanese help and also to collect some supplies from Tokyo. I thought no such time would be available to him going to Tokyo. The main purpose of Mr. Bose was to go to the Soviet Union and his desire to go to Tokyo was only secondary."*

Isoda's statement got ample support from the other colleagues of Netaji, including Col. Pritam Singh, Netaji's confidential Secretary E. Bhaskaran, Watanabe Kinji and others. Watanabe was a civilian interpreter attached to the military branch of the Hikari Kikan and he was called on August 17, 1945 to interpret the conversations between Lt. General Isoda, and Col. Kagawa on one side and Netaji, Major General Bhonsle and Col. Habibur Rehman on the other side.

The PGI's Propaganda and Publicity Minister S.A. Ayer stated before Shah Nawaj Committee that it was a practice that in taking any important decision Netaji had an opportunity to consult the Head of Hikari Kikan Lt. General Isoda, who had also acted as a liaison man between Netaji and Field Marshall

Hisaichi Terauchi, who was Japan's Supreme Commander for South East Asia.

Thus the JMCI found that there was a secret plan which was to be implemented with active participation of the Japanese military authorities. In its report the JMCI concluded that *"It is thus seen that besides his colleagues, the Japanese army officers who were liaisoning with Netaji and his organisation, were parties to his escape plan and the Japanese officers took all possible steps to ensure his safe escape by providing accommodation in a plane and other logistic support."*

Further examining the entire story of the plane-crash, the death of Netaji in the hospital and his cremation, the JMCI considered firstly the seating order or positions of the passengers including Netaji in the plane. As per the statement of Col. Habibur Rehman, the plane had no seats and seat-belts and all the passengers were squatting on the floor, the inevitable result immediately following the nosedive would have been rolling of all the passengers with luggage inside the plane down the floor to the cockpit. In that event half of the passengers could not have survived or come out of the plane either unhurt or with some minor injuries as claimed by the survivors. Further it is worth noting that Habibur Rehman had testified that *"the plane nosedived from a fairly high altitude possibly over 12000-14000 feet."* The JMCI had observed that *"If the evidence of Habibur Rehman is to be believed then none of the 12/13 passengers — not to speak of the crew members could have survived."* Commenting on the position of Netaji, the JMCI had remarked that *"as Netaji was sitting by the side of the petrol tank, gasoline flashed all over his body resulting in his sustaining third degree burns cannot also be believed, for Netaji could not have been in his original position on the floor immediately following the plane's nosediving."*

Habibur Rehman's statement before Shah Nawaz Committee on April 9, 1956 regarding his injuries was *"As for myself, my both hands were very badly burnt. As I came through the fire, right side of my face was burnt and I noticed I had received a cut in the forehead which was bleeding and the right side of my right knee was also bleeding profusely as it had hit some hard substance. The head cut was caused by hitting the floor as the planecrashed. My clothes did not catch fire. My hands were burnt very badly in the attempt to take off Netaji's clothes. Both my hands upto the wrist show marks of deep burning even after a lapse of more than ten years."*

The injuries on the palms of Habibur Rehman and other parts of his body required continued medical treatment. According to his version, he was treated for injuries at Nanmon Hospital (the Army Hospital) and Hokuto Hospital for a number of days. But the JMCI observed, *"...no documentary evidence in support of the injuries sustained by him or the treatment he received in the hospitals were produced. On the contrary, his evidence in this respect stands belied by the evidence of Captain B. Karmkar, an ex-INA member, who had stated that in the last part of August 1945 (that is, within a few days after the plane-crash) he met Habibur Rehman in Tokyo when he showed him some burn spots on the back of his both hands and white patches behind his ears and the above. Evidence of Captain B. Karmkar is corroborated by the evidence of two other witnesses, viz., Captain Bipul Kumar Sarkar, also of the INA, and Shri Swadhin Sanyal."* Relying on the witnesses the JMCI concluded that *"...therefore there cannot be any manner of doubt that the version of Habibur Rehman about the nature of injuries sustained by him in the plane-crash is suspect."*

The JMCI also pointed out the unusual conduct of Habibur Rehman as evinced by his non-communication of the news relating to the death of his Supreme Commander to his superiors in the INA and his colleagues in Bangkok, Singapore, Saigon and Tokyo.

The JMCI observed that *"his such conspicuous silence cannot be explained in any way except that he was playing a very vital role along with the Japanese army authorities in formulation and execution of Netaji's escape plan."*

Further non-availability of any document supporting the air-crash of August 18, 1945 made the accident more suspicious. Although before the Chinese takeover on October 25, 1945, the Japanese were continuing their control over Taipei for more than two months when the said plane-crash took place, yet they ignored to launch an official investigation of such an important incident. In the meantime, on September 13, 1945 a team of the British Intelligence headed by Mr. Finney conducted its inquiry and did not believe in the air crash story and also doubted the death of Netaji. After the formation of Shah Nawaz Committee, the Japanese stand was again confirmed when a Japanese official Hisaji Hattori, Chief of the 4th Section, Asian Affairs Bureau, informed on June 4, 1956 A.K, Dar, First Secretary, Embassy of India in Tokyo, that no official inquiry commission to determine the causes of accident was held till then.

Commenting on a message from the Chief of Staff, Southern Army to O.C., Hikari Kikan, on August 20, 1945, that *'T'* (code name of Netaji) had been flown to Tokyo, the JMCI report said that it interpreted it as a support to the escape plan.

The JMCI report quoted a passage from page 86 of S.A. Ayer's book *'Unto Him A Witness'*. In this passage Ayer recorded his memories while he was preparing for his journey from Saigon airport to Tokyo and when he came across with one of his previous acquintances, Rear Admiral Chuda of the Japanese Navy, who divulged to him the news of Netaji's death. Ayer had written:

"I had no chance to ask him for any detailed information because in the next few moments I was aboard the bomber bound for Japan.

On the flight I was escorted by Col. Tada, Staff Officer of Field Marshal Terauchi's Command, and Capt. Aoki. When we reached Canton at about 5 p.m. and halted for refuelling, Col. Tada through Capt. Aoki told me for the first time that Netaji's plane had crashed over Taihoku (Formosa, now called Taiwan) on August 18 and that Netaji was seriously injured and succumbed to his injuries the same night, and Col. Habibur Rehman who was not so seriously injured, was still alive and lying in a hospital at Taihoku. I told Col. Tada bluntly that neither Indians in East Asia nor Indians in India would be prepared to believe the story of the air crash unless positive proof was forthcoming, and I pressed him to see that the plane takes me to Taihoku so that I may have a chance of seeing Netaji's body with my own eyes and be of some service to Col. Habib in his then condition. I also told him that it was necessary as thereby at last one more Indian beside Habib could claim to have gone to Taihoku and satisfy himself about the truth of the air-crash story. Col. Tada promised that I would be taken to Taihoku, but later we actually landed at what I learnt was Taichu aerodrome. (So far as I know Taihoku was the Japanese name of Taipei). I expressed my bitter disappointment particularly when I was told that from Taichu we were to fly direct to Japan without touching Taihoku."

It had been contended by the JMCI that *"such reluctance on the part of the Japanese military authorities to take Shri Ayer to Taihoku or show him the dead body of Netaji falsifies the story of the plane-crash and for that matter Netaji's death therein."*

The JMCI assumed a new dimension in its investigation when the Commission acknowledged an E-mail in September 2003 from the Taiwanese Ministry of Transport and Communications and the Mayor of Taipei who had negated the happening of any air-crash in Taihoku Air Base between August 14 and September 20, 1945. In this connection the JMCI had already received the documents sent by the U.S. National Archives and Records Administration.

Commenting on this great achievement the Secretary of the JMCI, Pradyot Kumar Sengupta said: *"The problem is not with the taking cognisance of the documents on Netaji coming via E-mail. It is admissibility of these documents which is important. E-mail can be taken as evidence in certain conditions but there is always a possibility of the evidence being tempered with."*

During their visit in January 2004 to Taipei, the JMCI requested the Taipei City Government to furnish the records on which basis an E-mail was sent to them for the denial of any air crash in Taihoku Air Base between August and October, 1945. The JMCI was told that the information was based solely on contemporary newspaper accounts kept in their archives. During his four days stay in Taipei in his visit to the Institute of Taiwanese History and after perusal of the microfilmed daily newspapers Justice Mukherjee had himself confirmed that there was no report of any plane-crash on August 18, 1945. The JMCI report analysed that *"it can be legitimately inferred that if really there was a plane-crash resulting in the death of quite a number of persons including Netaji, a prominent and recognised Head of a State and Mr. Shidei, a military officer of the rank of General of the Japanese army, the news about the same would have been published in the local daily 'Central Daily News'. It is of course true that this circumstance by itself does not negate the story of plane-crash but it certainly lends assurance to the finding already arrived at in this regard on the basis of other facts and circumstances appearing on record."*

The JMCI report also mentioned that *'news of lesser importance but relating to Netaji's family was published in the same daily (Central Daily News) in its issue dated September 14, 1945.'* The relevant portion of the said news item translated in to English reads as under:

"September 14, 1945. The Indian Government decided today to release the younger brother(s) and family of Bose who were detained

since the beginning of the Japanese war. The members belonging to the Bose family (clan) who opposed the Government of India will also be set free. The official announcement states, 'in view of the Japanese surrender, there is no need for detaining these people for a long time.' According to the assessment of the JMCI report it *"indicates that Subhas Chandra Bose was well-known to the people and press there."*

This necessitated that the plane-crash news could not be withheld from the people of the town, which had been actually done and therefore raised doubts.

—o—

14

The Cremation Story also Falls

As an epilogue of the plane-crash theory another disputed issue examined by the JMCI was the cremation of Netaji's body at Taipei crematorium. There had been glaring contradictions in the versions of Col. Habibur Rehman. He told SA Ayer on September 8, 1945 in Tokyo and Shah Nawaz Committee on April 9, 1956 that Netaji's dead body was cremated on August 20, 1945. In his written statement earlier in Japan on August 24, 1945 and while deposing before the Counter Intelligence Corps (CIC) on September 29, 1945, he had mentioned August 22, 1945 as the date of cremation.

Incidentally, no other corroborative and contemporaneous official records related to death or cremation were available. The JMCI in its search for relevant records of Taihoku airport, Nanmon Military Hospital, Hokuto Hospital, Taipei Bureau of Health and Hygiene and Taipei City Crematorium had done the best efforts before and during their visits between September 20 to 23, 2002 in order to test the veracity of witnesses's assertions.

In his book *'Gallant End of Netaji'*, a trade union activist Harin Shah, who had been the editor of a well known journal *Indian*

Worker, published by the Indian National Trade Union Congress, described the details of his visit to Taipei. Harin Shah was successful in obtaining three documents allegedly related to Netaji's death and cremation. These were the doctor's report, the police report and the certificate issued by the Bureau permitting cremation. Harin Shah had appeared before Shah Nawaz Committee and submitted these documents.

According to Harin Shah, the certificate of death was given in the name of *'Ichiro Okura'* as the death certificate of Netaji. *'Sickness and heart failure'* were mentioned as the reasons of death. The time of death was 4.00 p.m. on August 19, 1945. Harin Shah clarified that on being asked about the false particulars, the issuing clerk replied that they were directed by their senior officers that the particulars of the person had to be kept confidential.

When the question of the false particulars was raised by the JMCI, the Taipei Municipal Bureau of Health and Hygiene informed them that in those days the first requirement for cremating a dead body was a doctor's report. Then in order to obtain permission for cremation a prescribed form was required to be duly filled by a family member of the deceased giving full particulars regarding the date of birth, nature of illness, date and time of death, etc. Besides this the dead body was also required to be brought before the officials of the Bureau to enable the authorities to verify the particulars provided in the application. After such strict and essential formalities a permit for cremation of a dead body was issued. And after cremation an entry was made in the cremation register.

The JMCI inferred that if Netaji was to be and in fact cremated, his body would have been brought to the Bureau and on the basis of the application all other formalities would have been fulfilled. Dr. Yoshimi Yani yoshi, better known as Dr. Yoshimi, had deposed as well as confirmed in the cross examination before the Shah Nawaz

Committee that *"on 18th August, I had issued a medical certificate of death in respect of the deceased person writing his name in Japanese 'Katakana' as 'Chandra Bose' and giving the cause of death as 'burns of the third degree'."* As per the statement of Dr. Yoshimi, it could be said that an application as per procedure for seeking a permit for cremation was filed on the same day, i.e., August 18, 1945. The JMCI presumed that the permit would have been obtained and after the cremation, the required entry in the cremation register would have been made.

The JMCI requested the Government of Taiwan vide letter dated February 1, 2005, to send the records for the period from August 18 to August 24, 1945, including all entries in the cremation register of the old crematorium of Taipei city. The documents of cremation sent by the Ministry of Foreign Affairs of Taiwan had no entry either in the name of Netaji Subhas Chandra Bose/Chandra Bose, or in the name of other co-passangers in the plane, Asst. Pilot Major Takizawa, Pilot Aoyagi, and General Shidei during the period from August 17 to August 27, 1945. But surprisingly, in the inquiry report submitted by the Department of Health of the Formosan Government, it had been stated that in the register of cremation there was an entry in the name of 'Ichiro Okura' who was cremated on August 22, 1945.

Following the appointment of the Shah Nawaz Committee the Government of India on April 5, 1956 sought the help of the then High Commissioner for United Kingdom in India in the absence of diplomatic relations with Formosan Government, to get a copy of the cremation certificate of Netaji. In its request the Government of India had also requested to procure the signed statements of some or all of those witnesses or to persuade them to appear before the Shah Nawaz Committee in Hongkong, for which the Government of India assured to pay travel and accommodation expenses.

The then Formosan Government's Department of Health had conducted an inquiry and its report was sent along with a copy of an extract from the cremation register then kept by the Welfare Section of the Taipei Municipal Government. The report was duly authenticated by the Consul of United Kingdom and was handed over to the Indian Ministry of External Affairs by the High Commissioner, United Kingdom, in India on August 10, 1956, just one month before presenting the Shah Nawaz Committee report in the Parliament. **It is noteworthy that this document was not provided to the JMCI by the Government of India and the JMCI could collect this report from the United Kingdom National Archives on its own initiative.**

In a similar move the Government of India had requested the Japanese Government to make available the doctor's report on Netaji's death and cremation permit. The Japanese Ministry of Foreign Affairs had forwarded a copy of an entry under serial number 2641 of the cremation register in the name of 'Ichiro Okura' with a forwarding letter dated July 20, 1956, addressed to the First Secretary, Embassy of India in Tokyo.

It was irritating that the contents of none of these documents, i.e., the death certificate, the permit to cremate the dead body and the connected entry number 2641 in the cremation register had any relation with Netaji. According to the JMCI, a mere discovery of these documents by Harin Shah relating to Taiwanese soldier Ichiro Okura did not and could not have a bearing whatsoever on Netaji's death or cremation. Any such attempt to base the findings on the oral evidences of eye witnesses, would be over simplification of the extremely complex issue and would look like a superficial approach, as had been done by the Shah Nawaz Committee and the Khosla Commission in the past.

The JMCI report said: *"Culling the evidence or record both oral and documentary (some of which have already been referred to and relied upon in arriving at the conclusion that Netaji's death has not been proved) — it is seen that Ichiro Okura who was a member of the Taiwan Government Army, died of heart failure on August 19, 1945 in the Army Hospital. After his death, Mr. Yoshimi, a member of the Japanese Army (Unit No. 21123) obtained a death certificate from the Army Hospital on August, 21, 1945 issued by Dr. (Toyoshi) Tsuruta, whose name in the Formosan dialect is "Chhuluta" (vide page 90-91 of Shri Harin Shah's book Ext., 295 para 8-9 of Khosla Commission's report, and Anglo-Japanese translator Shri Sandeep Kumar Sett's report, dated April 5, 2005 Ext. 305 collectively) and with that certificate he went to the Bureau to obtain the necessary permit for cremation."*

After the required procedure was complied with a cremation permit, in the prescribed form, was issued to him on that day of August 21, 1945 fixing the date and time of cremation on August 22, 1945 at 6.00 p.m.

Narrating further the story of cremation Tan Ti-Ti, who at the time was in charge of issuing cremation permits in the Bureau and who narrated the procedure for issuance of permit, stated before the Formosan Inquiry Officer that *"On the following day (August 22, 1945) the army officer who had obtained the permit for cremation of Ichiro Okura the day before, came in a car in the company of an Indian* (the discussion to follow will prove that the said Indian was none other than Habibur Rehman) *followed by a military truck carrying a boxlike coffin. Some army officers who were present there, unloaded the coffin and after depositing the same in the auditorium closed the door. The body was then put inside the furnace of the crematorium. Therefore, the furnace was locked and the key was given to the Indian for custody. The Indian was told to come back at 8 a.m. on the following day to collect the ashes."*

The JMCI report observed that the statement of Tan Ti-Ti who was the most competent person to testify the cremation, coupled with the death certificate issued in respect of Ichiro Okura dated August, 21, 1945, the application by Mr. Yoshimi on the same day for obtaining the cremation permit, cremation of the body on the following day and entry in the cremation register against serial number 2641. In the views of the JMCI *"On this point it needs to be mentioned that Mr. Yoshimi, the applicant, is not to be confused with Dr. Yoshimi of the Army Hospital:*

"Firstly, because the unit number of the applicant (21123) tallies not only with the entry in the cremation register but also with the application filed for seeking cremation permit;

"Secondly, because Dr. Yoshimi had all along been asserting that he issued the death certificate and applied for the cremation permit in the name of 'Chandra Bose';

"Thirdly, because he deposed before this Commission that he did not know any person by the name of Ichiro Okura;

"Fourthly, because he never claimed that he visited the Bureau for receiving the permit and was present at the time of cremation; and

"Lastly, because even in the copy of the death certificate which he claimed to have issued as late as in 1988 he gave the name Chandra Bose as the deceased."

The JMCI report confidently said that the supporting documents had unerringly lead to the conclusion that the death of Ichiro Okura owing to heart failure on August 19, 1945 and his cremation on August 22, 1945 on the basis of a permit on the previous day were pressed on as those of Netaji.

The other five facts and circumstances to make out an untrue story of Netaji's death and cremation with the connivance of Habibur Rehman and to execute their plan successfully were also considered in the JMCI report:

(i) In course of the inquiry by the Japanese Government on December 13, 1955, Dr. Toyashi Tsuruta said that *"the Army Headquarters had requested him to write a death certificate for the purpose of cremation."* They had informed him that *"the change in circumstances do not allow us to send the body to Tokyo. A decision was taken suddenly to cremate the body at Taipei."* Dr. Tsuruta had also said that *"It is absolutely not true that the body was cremated on the following day of his death. Several days after the death of Mr. Bose, at the* ***Army Headquarters' sudden request to write a death certificate I issued it in my name .... the Army Headquarters told me not to write Mr. Bose's name in the death certificate.*** *I gave a false Japanese name of 'Hachiro Okhura' after 'Kihachiro Okhura'."*

The JMCI report pointed out that Dr. Tsuruta had used the above Japanese name obviously because he had earlier given a genuine death certificate for the death of Ichiro Okura. The Ministry of Foreign Affairs of Japan had also given a similar explanation in their letter dated July 24, 1956 to A.K. Dar, the First Secretary of Indian Embassy in Tokyo. Combined with these references in the absence of any entry in the cremation register relating to the cremation of the dead body of any of the passengers of the ill-fated plane, the JMCI report concluded that *"It is obvious that reference to the name of Ichiro Okura and reliance upon the entries in the cremation record against the name which did not and could not by any stretch of imagination relate to Netaji clearly indicate* ***that the story of Netaji's death in plane-crash is untrue. The reason for resorting to such a camouflage by the army authorities is not far to seek."***

(ii) Regarding the message dated April 20, 1945 that *'Netaji's dead body had already been flown to Tokyo'* the JMCI believed that it was sent at the instance of the Japanese army authorities.

(iii) As the Japanese army officers had resorted to various precautionary measures at the time when the dead body of Ichiro Okura was brought to the Bureau for regulatory inspection, the JMCI report presumed that the Bureau people were not likely to be party to the escape plan. In this connection the JMCI quoted the statements of Li Chin Qui and Tan Chi Ch from Harin Shah's book *'Gallant End of Netaji'* (page 87-89). Li Chin Qui and Tan Chi Ch being employees in the Bureau during the Japanese rule were allowed to remain in employment. They were on duty on August 21, 1945 when the body of Chandra Bose was brought to the Bureau. They had not seen any Indian in the team. They heard the accompanying Japanese officer telling the then Director of the Bureau that the body was of a distinguished Indian leader Chandra Bose. They stated that normally they themselves would have checked up the body but in this case they were not allowed to follow the routine by the Japanese officers and they could only notice that the body was very big and wrapped in cloth.

(iv) As the permit to cremate Ichiro Okura was issued to an army officer Yoshimi on August 21, 1945, with fixing the date of cremation on August 22, 1945, Habibur Rehman was required to accompany him on both the days so that the Bureau people could be misled to believe that cremation was being done of the body of Netaji. Deposing before the Khosla Commission, Bureau's employee Chang Chuen said, *"When the coffin was taken out of the truck, the keeper of the crematorium came and said the coffin was too big to enter the furnace. So, we opened the box which was filled with calcium oxide. The Japanese ordered to pull the dead body from the coffin and it was wrapped in a cloth and a Japanese army blanket."*

Likewise, Habibur Rehman had earlier said before the Shah Nawaz Committee that *"I was present when the body was put in the coffin. The body was fully dressed and no part of it was visible."*

Both the above statements confirmed that the body including the face was fully covered, and thus according to the JMCI report there was no room for doubt that all possible precautions were taken for hiding the identity of the deceased till cremation.

The JMCI also observed that Habibur Rehman had ensured that the photographs would cover only the dead body minus the face. He told Shah Nawaz Committee that *"The photo of his body (excluding the face) was taken at my request. Since the face was not in good condition..."* The JMCI report concluded that *"The only plausible inference that can be drawn therefrom is that as Ichiro Okura had died of heart attack and, as such, could not have any injury on his body, not to speak of face, Habibur Rehman decided to have the photographs taken of the dead body without the face to avoid discovery of the identity of the deceased, namely, Ichiro Okura."*

(v) Harin Shah had remarked before the Shah Nawaz Committee that the Japanese Buddhist custom had required preservation of the dead body for three days before cremation. It was exactly adhered to in Ichio Okura's case: death being on 19th and his cremation three days after on 22nd and picking up the bones from every portion of the body after cremation and keeping the same with ashes. The JMCI derived its conclusion that it was *"another circumstance which indicates that the body cremated and the mortal remains taken there/from were of Ichiro Okura and not of Netaji."*

After consideration of the relevant records and circumstances on the point of death and cremation, the JMCI report reached to the conclusion that *"It stands established that emplaning at Saigon on*

August 17, 1945 Netaji succeeded in evading the Allied Forces and escaping out of their reach and as a camouflage there of ***the entire make-belief story of the air-crash, Netaji's death therein and his cremation was engineered by the Japanese army authorities including the two doctors and Habibur Rehman, and then aired on August 23, 1945 through a statement prepared by S.A. Ayer at the dictation of aforesaid authorities."***

In its report the JMCI also observed that *"In cooking up the story of Netaji's death in the plane-crash and giving it a modicum of truth (the Japanese military authorities and Habibur Rehman) had no alternative than resorting to suppression of facts and in so doing they not only invited material contradictions in their evidence... but also left latent loopholes which have now been discovered."*

—o—

15

Whose Ashes?

Regarding the issue of the ashes kept in an urn inside a glass chamber in Renkoji Temple, Tokyo, the then Chief Priest Nichiko Mochizushi[1] was requested by the Chairman JMCI to open the urn. The purpose of the JMCI was to ascertain whether there were any bones in the ashes which could be subjected to the DNA test. In the absence of a competent mechanic, it could not be opened on Saturday September 14, 2002 at the time of Justice Mukherjee's visit to Renkoji Temple. The Indian Ambassador in Japan was assigned to make all arrangements and to obtain samples of the bones. The casket could be opened on October 24, 2002 in the presence of the Chief Priest and his wife and the required samples were obtained. The JMCI approached the Director, Centre for Cellular and Molecular Biology (CCMB), and the Director, Centre for DNA Finger-printing and Diagnostics at Hyderabad, for conducting tests on the bone-samples received from Japan. The Director CCMB expressed his inability to carry

1. His father Kyoi Mochizushi was the Chief Priest in 1945 when the ashes were reverently deposited on September 9, 1945 in the Renkoji Temple, Tokyo. Now 35 years old, his son Kyojen Mochizushi has taken over as the Chief Priest.

on the proposed DNA tests as the necessary facilities were not available with them.

The JMCI then contacted Prof. Dr. Svante Paabo, the Director, Department of Genetics, Max Planck Institute for Evolutionary Anthropology, Liepzig, Germany, but they recommended to approach Prof. Sir Alec Jeffreys, Department of Genetics, University of Leicester (UK), who also expressed his inability to do the needful. Another centre, the Forensic DNA Experts of Nagoya University, Japan's Prof. Saiton Naruya and Dr. Yamamoto advised that since all the bones and teeth had received high heat, there was almost no possibility of obtaining the DNA from the bone material.

The CCMB, Hyderabad, was again approached by the JMCI, as there was new information that their ancient DNA facility had been updated. The response of the CCMB was again negative as they had required the less charred bones to be brought in a plastic bag at room temperature. Fresh efforts were undertaken by the JMCI but the Chief Priest of Renkoji Temple had not replied. Thus the JMCI could not get the appropriate samples of the mortal remains for the DNA test and the venture was lost due to circumstances beyond the control of the JMCI.

On the basis of facts, circumstances and statements of witnesses the JMCI report emphatically concluded that *"Since ashes collected were of Ichiro Okura — not of Netaji —* ***the only inference that can be drawn is that the ashes lying in that temple cannot be of Netaji."***

—o—

16

Other Death Stories

Of the other four versions of Netaji's death, *'whether Netaji Subhas Chandra Bose is dead or alive?'* was the first agendum to be discussed and decided by the JMCI, but its all other four agenda were very closely interrelated and therefore, the question of priority for agenda was not important. Before taking up this agendum the JMCI considered the fact that the average life span of Indians could be 70-75 years and only in exceptional cases it is about 100 years. As Netaji was born on January 23, 1897 and if he would have survived he would have been 108 years in the year 2005, when the JMCI report was submitted. This was such an age when there was no possibility of his being alive. Thus, abandoning all hopes and expectations to search for Netaji alive, the JMCI's aim was to find out as to how, where and when Netaji died?

As stated earlier, in order to consider all sorts of probabilities the JMCI issued a notification in accordance with Rule 5(2)(b) of the Commissions of Inquiry (Central) Rules -- 1972 for general public and asked to furnish any related information along with an affidavit before the JMCI. After processing and analysing such claims the JMCI rejected outright the claim of Usha Ranjan Bhattacharjee of Kolkata that Netaji was deliberately murdered in the Red Fort on August 15, 1945 at zero hour. There was no documentry support or evidence in support of this contention. According to the report of the JMCI, the story was based on such assumptions and presumptions which were self-contradictory and poor in merit for a judicial trial.

The notification of the JMCI was responded to by Jagannath Prasad Gupta, a resident of village Nagda in the district of Sheopur Kalan in the State of Madhya Pradesh. Gupta claimed that Netaji died on May 21, 1977 in Sheopur Kalan as a sadhu who had survived along with Hitler and Col. Habibur Rehman in a plane-crash in 1945 in his neighbouring village of Pandola. In favour of Gupta, four more affidavits were submitted before the JMCI by Ram Bharose Sharma and Mrs. Dulari Bai of village Nagda, Kartar Singh of village Raipura and Gurdayal Singh of village Mohana. All the five claimants told the JMCI that the sadhu was known by the name Jyotirdev but he was none other than Netaji. As all the witnesses had neither seen Netaji earlier before August, 1945 nor documents filed by them had any relevance to the issue, the JMCI had no hesitation in rejecting their claim outright, being patently absurd on the face of it and need not be delved into.

The versions claiming that Netaji had died at Dehradun in Uttar Pradesh, now in Uttarakhand State, had stemmed from the setting up of an Ashram named and styled as *'Shoulmari Ashram'* at a place called Falakata in the district of Cooch Behar in West Bengal. Shoulmari Ashram was set up in or about 1959 by a sadhu known as Sharadanand. As per the report of the JMCI, *"at it inception nobody took notice of the Ashram and of sadhu Sharadanand, but when it extended its geographical area to over 100 acres of land and its inhabitants rose to about 1500 where armed guards were posted, outsiders living in and around the place became inquisitive about the real identity of the sadhu as well as the goings-on at the Ashram. Within a few months thereafter rumours spread in the district of Cooch Behar that Netaji had been living in the Ashram in the guise of the sadhu."*

By the year 1961, the rumour had spread throughout the country. In February 1962 an ardent follower of Netaji, Major Satya Gupta, had a meeting with Sharadanand and after coming back to Kolkata he called a press conference on February 13, 1962 to assert that sadhu Shardanand was none but Netaji. The matter was electrified so quickly that questions were raised in the Indian Parliament and pro-Netaji discussions became hot all over the country.

According to File No. 2(64) 56-66 PM Volume II letters 1039-PM H/63, Nehru had written a letter to the editor of 'India Reformer' on April 18, 1963 that *"we have inquired into this matter and we are quite sure that the story about his (Shardanand's) being Netaji is completely without basis."*

On August 23, 1963 Atal Bihari Vajpayee had also raised in the Rajya Sabha that some self appointed persons and organisations were propagating that Shoulmari Ashrams' sadhu Shardanand *'is none but Netaji Subhas Chandra Bose'*. Has any enquiry been made in this connection? Nehru replied that *"We are aware of such propaganda which was carried on. It has faded now more or less. But such enquiries we have made and the Government of West Bengal have conclusively established that Swami Sharadanand is not Netaji Subhas Chandra Bose, and he himself denies it absolutely."*

In this case the JMCI examined eleven witnesses who were broadly divided into two groups. On this score the group of eight witnesses had put forward vehemently that the sadhu was Netaji in disguise. This group of witnesses was represented by Sudhansu Kumar Poddar, Sudhir Kumar Poddar, Lalit Mohan Chowdhury,

Bikas Chandra Guha, Surjit Kumar Biswas, Subhas Ranjan Daspupta, S.S. Padhye and Viswajit Dutta. The group of other three witnesses were Rajat Kanti Bhadra, Dinabandhu Dutta and Nikhil Chandra Ghatak who disputed the claim. After hearing both the groups and ignoring the majority opinion of the witnesses the JMCI rejected their claim on the following grounds:

(i) The witnesses claimed that the sadhu was Netaji were occasional visitors to the Ashram and had not produced any reliable document in support of their claim, except that Bikas Chandra Guha had presented a letter which according to him was handed over by Sharadanand on October 15, 1967, authorising him to collect/raise donations on behalf of the Ashram. At the instance of the JMCI the handwriting of the letter was examined by experts, with the admitted handwriting of Netaji, and the opinion was not favourable.

(ii) Rajat Kanti Bhadra used to look after the stores of the Ashram during 1961-1967, Dinabandhu Dutta was connected with the Ashram since it was established in 1959 and was continuing with it, and Nikhil Chandra Ghatak was a senior practising Advocate in Jalpaiguri courts and also a lecturer in Jalpaiguri Law College, who was looking after the litigations concerning and/or related to Ashram. All three had categorically stated that Swami Sharadanand denied in no uncertain terms that he was Netaji born in wedlock of Janaki Nath Bose and Bivabati Bose. They asserted that Sharadanand was born in a Brahmin family of East Bengal (now Bangladesh). They reiterated Swami Sharadanand's denials/assertions in various meetings held in the Ashram as also in meetings outside. This statement was corroborated by

another witness S.S. Padhye. According to the JMCI, it was an admitted fact that Netaji was born in a Kayastha family of Cuttack in the State of Orissa.

The JMCI report mentioned the statements of Dr. Pabitra Mohan Roy and Surendra Mohan Ghosh who told the Khosla Commission that Swami Sharadanand had himself stated to them that he was not Netaji and that he was not the son of Janaki Nath Bose. On the same issue Niharendu Dutta Majumdar had specifically distinguished before the Khosla Commission that Sharadanand's appearance, accent and his manner of speaking was totally different from that of Netaji and as regards resemblence it did not match with Netaji and so his dialect. The dialect of Sylhet border in East Bengal was the language of Sharadanand whereas Netaji belonged to Cuttack (Orissa) and his ancestral house was in 24 Pargana district of West Bengal.

—o—

17

The Sadhu of Faizabad

The most important among all such claims was filed by Dr. Alokesh Bagchi of Gorakhpur and Ashok Tandon, Shakti Singh and Kailash Nath Jaiswal of Faizabad. A common case was made out from the statements of claimants that after the death of Joseph Stalin in March 1953, Netaji escaped from the Soviet Union. After coming to India he lived at different places in Uttar Pradesh and lastly arrived at *Ram Bhawan* in Faizabad where he was generally known as *'Gumnami Baba'* but for some he was *'Bhagwanji'.* Some people believe that he did not die on September 16, 1985, but some time in September 1985 he left Ram Bhawan for an unknown destination, leaving behind a large number of household articles, including family photos, books, letters and other documents. The custody of his belongings was taken over by the District Magistrate and had been deposited in the Faizabad treasury after the direction given in a Writ Petition No. 929 of 1986 filed by Netaji's niece Lalita Bose and two others.

There were 31 witnesses who deposed before the JMCI, which categorised them in its reports in eight categories according to their statements and beliefs, and in order to examine their versions to arrive at a correct decision. The first category was of those whose statements were based on either hearsay or their own beliefs without any substantial document in their support. This category included Dr. Alokesh Bagchi, Viswabandhu Tewari, I.B. Saxena, Dr. Ramendra Pal and Kailash Nath Jaiswal.

The next set of witnesses were journalists as their claim was based on the results of their investigations into the mystery that surrounded Gumnami Baba. This category included Ashok Tandon, Dr. Viswambhar Nath Arora and Sayed Kausar Hussain. All of them wrote several articles in their respective newspapers, magazines and books, relying upon the statements made before them by several persons knowing Gumnami Baba directly or indirectly.

The third category consisted of those who admitted that they had not seen Gumnami Baba. The witnesses of this category were not genuine and could be entertained as they were only repeating the unauthentic statements of others. Among these witnesses were Gur Basant Singh, Shakti Singh, Nirupam Misra, Rabindra Nath Shukla. Prof. Nandalal Chakravorty and Dulal Nandi.

The fourth category of witnesses included Raghuraj Singh Rathore, Baba Bhandari alias Sheo Bhagwan, Shyam Narain Bind, and INA's Col. A.B. Singh. Among these none except Col. A.B. Singh had seen Netaji before August 1945 and he had claimed that Netaji was living as *'Mauni Baba'* who was also known as Sant Samrat Yogi and who used to live in an Ashram in Sitapur district, Uttar Pradesh. Col. A.B. Singh testified before the JMCI that he went to Sitapur on February 19, 1966 and saw Mauni Baba who resembled Netaji in his appearance. But since it had been found that the photograph of Mauni Baba had no similarity whatsoever with Netaji, the evidence of these witnesses were not acceptable to the JMCI.

In the fifth category there were three witnesses: Dr. Priyabrat Banerjee, his wife Smt. Rita Banerjee, and his mother-in-law Smt. Bithi Chatterjee. In the year 1975 Dr. Banerjee had gone to the residence of a saint at Brahmakund in Ayodhya and he was given to understand by his father that the saint was none else but Netaji. In the beginning, he and his family members were not allowed to see the saint as he used to sit behind a curtain. But after their persuasion the saint talked to them face to face. In his evidence Dr. Banerjee himself did not assert that the saint was Netaji and thus his evidence in this regard for the JMCI was nothing else than hearsay. The other two members of his family averred that they had seen Gumnami Baba but Smt. Rita Banerjee based her claim on her belief, and Smt. Bithi Chatterjee stated that though she had seen Netaji in Lucknow in or about the year 1943, she found it difficult to say whether Gumnami Baba was Netaji. The evidences of this category therefore, did not assist the JMCI in answering the issue.

In the JMCI report the next category was represented by Raj Kumar Shukla, whose late mother Smt. Saraswati Devi Shukla had been the attendant of Bhagwanji since 1955-1956 when she had come in contact with him at Sringar Nagar in Lucknow. Smt. Shukla served Bhagwanji till his death on September 16, 1985 at Ram Bhawan, Faizabad. Raj Kumar Shukla's evidence disclosed that almost on every January 23, the birthday of Netaji, and during Durga Puja festival, eminent persons from Kolkata like Smt. Leela Roy, Prof. Samar Guha, Dr. Pabitra Mohan Roy and Amal Roy used to come and talk to Bhagwanji from behind a curtain. According to the JMCI report, *"As regards the identity of Bhagwanji his (Raj Kumar Shukla's) evidence is that he heard from his mother that he was Netaji and since then he shared the same belief. Though his evidence does not in any way prove that Bhagwanji was Netaji, it at least proves that quite a number of eminent persons from Kolkata used to visit Bhagwanji."*

The seventh category was of those people of Kolkata who had not seen Netaji before August 1945 and who frequently visited Bhagwanji/Gumnami Baba wheresoever he lived during the period from 1963 to 1983. A staunch supporter of Netaji and a friend of his family, Sunil Krishna Gupta alias Sukrit, told various things about Gumnami Baba to support his claim that he was none else but Netaji. Surajit Dasgupta, Jagatjit Dasgupta, Tarun Kumar Mukhopadhyay and Bijoy Kumar Nag were also in witnesses of this category. Sunil Krishna Gupta told the JMCI that in or about 1963, the elder brother of Netaji, Suresh Chandra Bose, had asked him that Netaji was reportedly staying in Naimisharanya, an ancient pilgrimage centre near Sitapur, Uttar Pradesh. Further, he said that on coming to Naimisharanya he met a sadhu in a temple and had stayed there for ten days to have an opportunity to interact with him. Since then he and almost all other witnesses of this category and some others used to visit him, particularly every year on January 23 and during Durga Puja. He had liked to address the sadhu as Bhagwanji. He also confirmed that the other frequent visitors were Dr. R.P. Misra, INA's secret service personnel Dr. Pabitra Mohan Roy, Sheo Prasad Nag and others. Gupta also admitted before the JMCI that *"he had not seen Netaji before August 18, 1945 but averred that after seeing and interacting with Bhagwanji he was convinced that he was none else than Netaji. He next stated that at the instance of Bhagwanji, he went to Taihoku to watch the proceedings of the Khosla Commission and on return, apprised him of all the details thereof."*

Bijoy Kumar Nag in his testimony before the JMCI added that *"Bhagwanji used to talk about various events of his earlier life, including his days in the INA from which he was convinced that*

Bhagwanji was none else but Netaji. He also produced before this commission a book titled 'Oye Mahamanab Ashey' (in two volumes) wherein he has incorporated what Bhagwanji told him. He also referred to a monthly journal 'Jayashree' of which he was editor, where also the same issue was written about." Bijoy Kumar Nag was adopted by Leela Roy as her son. He always accompanied Leela Roy in her visits to Naimisharanya and other places in Uttar Pradesh where Gumnami Baba lived. Nag became the editor of the journal *'Jayashree'* after the death of Leela Roy in 1968.

The last category of witnesses before the JMCI were those who had seen Netaji before 1945 and had meetings with Gumnami Baba at different places in Uttar Pradesh. They included Durga Prasad Pandey, Shrikant Sharma and Apurva Kumar Ghosh. Pandey met Gumnami Baba first in 1967 when he was living in Basti and his meetings continued for about nine years almost every night. Sharma had seen him in Naimisharanya in 1963. Ghosh's first meeting with Netaji was in 1939 in Dacca and after that he met him several times in Kolkata before 1945 and again in Basti, Uttar Pradesh in 1965 as a saint. Ghosh told the JMCI that *"in the course of his conversation Bhagwanji enquired of him (Ghosh) about 'Bahadur' who was a durban in his (Netaji's) Elgin Road residence and also asked him whether he had seen a calender with a picture of Goddess Kali in the room."*

According to the JMCI report *"Apparently, there is no reason for not relying upon the evidence of the last two categories of witnesses ...there are other formidable facts and circumstances or records which stand in the way of this Commission in arriving at a conclusive finding that Bhagwanji/Gumnami Baba was none else than Netaji."* The JMCI opined in its report if photographs of Bhanwanji/ Gumnami Baba were taken by those who had an opportunity to interact with him face to face, then a reliable piece of documentary evidence in support of the ocular version of the witness could have been compared with the admitted photographs of Netaji.

In the record of the JMCI there was a joint affidavit filed by Sunil Krishna Gupta, Surjit Dasgupta, Jagatjit Dasgupta and Tarun Kumar Mukhopadhyay that *"Netaji did not die in a plane-crash on August 18, 1945 but they were conspicuously silent about the entire episode of Netaji living in disguise as a saint long thereafter, even though they could have furnished proof in support of their assertions."*

Sunil Krishna Gupta could not defend his version while replying to a question to ascertain why he had not divulged the truth before the Khosla Commission during its hearings which he had attended in Delhi, Taihoku and other places. The JMCI was not satisfied by *"the explanation offered for his such unusual stance that he was under oath of secrecy against its disclosure, but it is extremely difficult to rely on that explanation, more so when he has now divulged that fact inspite of that oath."*

In its visit to Faizabad the JMCI scrutinised more than 2673 items left by Gumnami Baba at Ram Bhawan, Faizabad, and felt that about 700 of them might be relevant for its purpose. Selected items were brought by the JMCI to its Kolkata office. The JMCI agreed to send to experts for comparison with the admitted handwriting of Netaji, the writings in some books and journals by Gumnami Baba/Bhagwanji as found at Ram Bhawan, Faizabad. Besides, of the nine teeth collected from Ram Bhawan, five were sent to ascertain whether those dentures belonged to Netaji's lineage.

Regarding the comparison of handwriting the expert report of Shri B. Lal, Ex-Government Examiner of Questioned Documents, New Delhi, had *"given a firm opinion that those (both Bengali and English) handwritings were of Netaji."* But Shri Amar Singh and Shri M.L. Sharma of the office of the Government Examiner of

Questioned Documents, Government of India, Simla, had filed a joint report and Dr. S.K. Mondal of Forensic Science Laboratory, Government of West Bengal, Kolkata, gave contrary opinions.

The report of the DNA profiling test to fix the identity of the person was conducted by Dr. V.K. Kashyap, the DNA expert. The report concluded that *"the forwarded teeth belong to a single human aged male individual (alleged Gumnami Baba). The individual source of teeth does not belong to either maternal or paternal DNA lineage of Netaji Subhas Chandra Bose, therefore, cannot be of Netaji Subhas Chandra Bose."* At the same time, on cross-examination it became clear that *"all the teeth belong to a single human aged male individual and since except Gumnami Baba, the only other aged member who stayed with him all along was Smt. Saraswati Devi Shukla, the negative findings recorded by Dr. Kashyap quoted earlier militates against the eyewitnesses' account."* And thus the JMCI could not agree that Netaji died in Faizabad on September 16, 1985.

—o—

18

Government's Role: Visit to Russia

The Government of India led by the United Progressive Alliance (UPA) had been overtly hostile towards the JMCI. There were attempts to reduce the JMCI to a lower position even for the officials of the PMO, the Ministry of Home Affairs (MHA), and the Ministry of External Affairs (MEA). **Not only legally required documents/files were denied to the JMCI but also the denial was communicated after consuming a good amount of time.** This policy became more evident when the JMCI proposed and insisted to visit Taiwan and Russia. Although the proposal for the visits was made as early as in February 2001, yet the JMCI could get permission to undertake visits to Japan and Taiwan in September 2002. The JMCI's direct interaction with Taiwanese Government had yielded the disclosure that there was no evidence related to air crash in or around Taipei between August and October, 1945. In this connection the JMCI could also get a similar report originating from the US State Department, supporting the claim of the Taiwanese Government and confirming that there had been no air crash during that frame of time which the Government of India was propagating. The JMCI could also collect clinching and direct evidences to finally conclude that Netaji and other victims of the alleged air crash of August 18, 1945 were not cremated in Taipei.

Time and again the JMCI asked the Government of India to make arrangements for their visit to Russia to access and testify the evidences hinted to be available in Russian archives, but the delay and dallying policy of the Government was acted playfully and it was played with the desire to avoid the visit proposal to the extent of non-implementation or to discourage Justice Mukherjee emotionally for the withdrawal of the proposal by himself. The animosity and rancor in the attitudes of the bureaucrats were so intense with ill-will that the **JMCI was threatened by the MHA vide a curt letter No. 11034/18/98-NCB-11 dated November 19, 2004, which asked Justice Mukherjee to submit the final report of his inquiry before May 14, 2005,** as it has been decided that *"no further extension will be allowed"* and it was a Cabinet decision. It was an irony of fate that the same officials who were manipulating that Justice Mukherjee gave up his desire to travel, Russia and to testify documents in different archives, were also arbitrating whether an extension would be required by him.

Actually the Government had never been interested in allowing any official effort to unravel the mystery related to Netaji. The decision to order the two earlier probes — one, headed by Shah Nawaz Khan and the second, led by the Justice G.D. Khosla — were taken on account of public pressure and political circumstances. This time, Government was compelled to form the JMCI, when the High court of Calcutta ordered to launch a fresh probe considering the new facts which were dug out from Russian archives and other supporting incidents. **In such circumstances, the JMCI was actually thrust upon the Government, and therefore, there was lack of cooperation and goodwill in the Government circles.**

Justice M.K. Mukherjee, whose name was sponsored by the Supreme Court, was bearing his pains calmly and without complaint. He had realised that the Government was bent upon hiding something tangible and substantial in relation to Netaji. While performing his duties religiously as an experienced jurist and a mature citizen, Justice Mukherjee manifested several times forbearance under provocations and strains. He was neither hasty nor impetuous and could maintain his patience to carry on his job peacefully and without further complicating the matter despite opposition, difficulties and adversities created by senior bureaucrats representing the side of the Government. He was fully aware that his report would be incomplete if he was not permitted to go Russia and once he would submit his report, however incomplete, it would become all the more convenient for the Government to wriggle out of it. **With his own voluntary service at the rate of Rupee one per month as fee, Justice Mukherjee was functioning with a skeletal staff at his disposal and free accommodation for his office provided by the West Bengal Government in Kolkata.**

Only after coming under severe pressure from Netaji's followers, the Government allowed the JMCI to visit Russia in September 2005, with the condition that it had to submit its final report by November 2005.

Replying to a question related to the above in Rajya Sabha on December 8, 2005, the then Minister of State in the Ministry of External Affairs, Rao Indrajit Singh, said, *"The Justice Mukherjee Commission of Inquiry into the alleged disappearance of Netaji Subhas Chandra Bose, during its visit to the Russian Federation from 20 to 30 September, 2005 visited the following archives:*

"(i) *Russian State Archive for Social and Political History, Moscow;*

(ii) *Russian State Archive for Audio Documents, Moscow;*

(iii) *Russian State Naval Archive, St. Petersburg;*

(iv) *Central State Archive, St. Petersburg;*

(v) *State Archive, Irkutsk Region; and*

(vi) *Private Archives of Prof. Eva Ya Luisternik at the Institute of Oriental Studies, Moscow."*

Singh said, *"According to the Russian Legislation (Archives Law of 2004) which is applicable not only to the representatives of foreign countries but also to the Russian citizens, access to classified archives, without any exception, is given only to strictly defined categories of officials."*

He further informed that *"despite the above law, taking into consideration the interest of the Indian side, the Russian Government had competent authorities to conduct a detailed study of these archives and copies of all documents found with the name of S.C. Bose, had been handed over to the Indian side. These, in turn, have been given to Justice Mukherjee Commission."*

In fact the JMCI was looking for certain classified documents concerning Netaji, preserved in the Russian archives related to the Federal Security Bureau (FSB), the successor of the USSR's KGB. But as per the provisions of the Russian Archives Law of 2004, foreign nationals might be permitted to study the archival documents only when their requests were accompained with consent letters provided by their concerned governments. The recently implemented Russian Law was legislated only after adverse reactions by the governments including the Indian Government, which diplomatically conveyed its protest about the ongoing researches by a few Indians like Dr. Purabi Roy and some Russian Indologists like Voctor B. Turadzhev and Alexander Kolesnikov on Netaji based on the archival documents. As the JMCI was not provided with any official request/consent letter by the Government of India to the Government of Russian Federation, the Russian archival authorities did not allow access to the FSB archives.

Justice Mukherjee said to the Press Trust of India (PTI) in Moscow on September 21, 2005 that *"he had come to speak to those witnesses who were named by Dr. Purabi Roy in her affidavit."* Without disclosing his identity Justice Mukherjee said that *"One of the witnesses clearly said that he never told Dr. Roy anything like that. Another witness is an author of a book and we have asked the embassy (Indian Embassy, Moscow) to translate the related chapter from the Russian into English."* But none of these documents were found relevant by the JMCI. It was also surprising that a very important witness, A. Kolesnikov, could not be traced in Russia during the visit of the JMCI.

Justice Mukherjee also told PTI that the Presidential Archives, earlier known as the CPSU General Secretary's Archives, and the Archives of Federalnaya Sluzhba Bezopastnosti, where documents significant to this case were earlier discovered, would remain out of reach as the Indian Government had not asked the Russian Federation to allow study of those documents. Justice Mukherjee further told PTI that the FSB informed the JMCI that there were no relevant documents in these archives and therefore, there was no reason to visit these archives.

At the Russian State Archives for Social and Political History, Moscow, Justice Mukherjee could get a file on Netaji and another relating to famous firebrand revolutionary Rash Behari Bose, who lived in Japan after his escape from India in 1915, and who was the founder President of Indian Independence League. These documents were nothing but only newspaper clippings which were irrelevant to the JMCI. At the Russian State Archives for Audio Documents, Moscow, the JMCI checked some tapes of speeches of Dr. Radhakrishnan, Krishna Menon and Jawaharlal Nehru, but there was nothing on Netaji.

The authorities belonging to the Central Archive of the KGB, the Central State Archive, Russian Federation, the Russian State Military Historical Archive, the State Archive of Russian Federation, and the Archives of the Far-East of Russian Federation had separately written to the JMCI that there were no documents relevant to its terms of inquiry. The Institute of Oriental Studies, Moscow, also informed that it did not have any document needed by the JMCI. The directors of archives at Irkutsk and St. Petersburg also gave similar replies to the JMCI. During his visit to Omsk, Justice Mukherjee was told by the Director, State Archive, Omsk Region, that since all visiting foreigners were required to register themselves to study the documents no permission could be granted to him.

Dr. Purabi Roy had already raised a very important point in this connection before the JMCI that *"if Netaji had used a pseudonym, any document relating to him at Omsk would never be traced. If he was arresed, such documents would be available with KGB,"* but it denied possessing any such material. The importance of Omsk's document was highlighted by Dr. Roy as according to her *"Netaji went to Manchurian border near the Siberian city of Omsk from Singapore and was received at Omsk on August 23-24, 1945, by the Azad Hind Government's Consul, Kato Kachu,"* who was possibly an Indian with a name resembling a Japanese name. Dr. Roy also disclosed that there were a lot of material on Netaji in the Military Archive in Omsk. Explaining her point of view she said that Omsk was the shifted administrative capital of the USSR during Second World

War and had an office of Consulate General of the Provisional Government of Free India.

In this connection it was Alexander Kolesnikov who disclosed to Dr. Purabi Roy about Kato Kachu, who was the Indian Consulate in Russia. Anuj Dhar described that this information was supported with evidence in March 1999 when Pramod Mehra of the National Archives in Delhi presented a seminar paper, *The Declassified Documents from the Ministry of Defence, in Kolkata ... he revealed that like Germany, Japan, Italy and Ireland, the USSR had recognised the Provisional Government of Free India."* It is also surprising that the claim of Pramod Mehra was based on documents vide page 6 File No. 265/INA which were handed over by the Russian Government to the Department of Culture, Government of India, through the Embassy of India in Moscow on May 15, 1991. This disclosure was also made by the National Archives of India in a letter dated October 24, 2000, to the JMCI. Under Ref.: Acc No. 6757 S.C. Bose Group IV Serial No. 11, total six documents — these documents on Netaji consisted 46 xerox pages which were also referred to in the reply to a question of R.K. Anand in Rajya Sabha on December 8, 2005, replied by Rao Inderjit Singh, the Minister of State in the Ministry of External Affairs.

There were other stories with the JMCI about Netaji that he was seen in Russia after August 1945, but those were not confirmed by the JMCI due to lack of evidence. One such story was narrated to Khosla Commission by Dr. Satyanarayan Sinha, that **he was told by Georgy Mukherjee, son of the founder of Communist Party of India, Abani Mukherjee, that his father and Netaji were prisoners in adjacent cells in Siberia.** Sinha told the Khosla Commission that according to Georgy's information, Netaji had assumed his name there as *'Khilasi Malang'*. Here it is important to keep in mind that Abani Mukherjee and his companion Virendranath Chattopadhyay, who was the brother of freedom-fighter Sarojini Naidu, were detained in 1937 in Russia and later on both were killed on the orders of Stalin.

Supporting the above story Dr. Purbai Roy also mentioned in her affidavit that *"During the period of 'Glasnost' and 'Perestroika' many untold stories were told mainly by unravelling documents from the NKGB-KGB archives. Russian Indologist Mitrokhin remarks, 'Glasmost is removing many blank spaces in Soviet history ... Indian revolutionaries like Virendranath Chattopadhyay and Abani Mukherjee had disappeared from the Soviet society without leaving any traces.' In 1989 an article was published in 'Soviet Land' journal which informs the destinies of two above-named revolutionaries."*

According to the report C-4, Part IV, dated April 8, 1946, National Archives, Delhi, the Intelligence Bureau, discussed a Russian report which said that *"The Governor of the Afghan province of Khost had been informed by the Russian Ambassador in Kabul that there were many Congress refugees in Moscow and Bose was included in their number. There is little reason for such persons to bring Bose into fabricated stories. At the same time the view that Russian officials were disclosing or alleging that Bose is in Moscow is supplied in a report received from Tehran. This states that Moradoff, the Russian Vice Consul General, disclosed in March that Bose was in Russia."*

Another story connecting Netaji with Russia after August 1945 had been circulated through researches based on the documents discovered in the Russian archives. In August 1946 a Soviet agent V.G. Sayadyants left India for Moscow via Tehran. According to Dr. Purabi Roy's affidavit, in Tehran he submitted a brief report dated August 28, 1946 to T.V. Sadchkov, the then Soviet Ambassador in Tehran. Mumbai-based Sayadyants wrote in his report that *"The Soviet Union cannot possibly work with either Nehru or Gandhi and that the Communist movement in India is in a disarray ... Bose is the only hope for Soviet Russia."* This report hinted that Netaji was alive by that time in the USSR.

Before the Khosla Commission there was a witness named Shyamlal Jain, whose statement on oath was narrating almost the same story as the British Intelligence team had affirmed in their report to their Government vide File No. 273/INA, Document C-4, Part IV, National Archives, Delhi, that **Jawaharlal Nehru had received a secret communication from Netaji saying *"he was in Russia and that he wanted to escape to India. He would come via Chitral where one of Sarat Bose's son should meet him"*** and had asked Nehru to make arrangements for his comeback. The background of Shyamlal Jain was that he was working as a confidential steno with Asaf Ali, who was Secretary to the INA Defence Committee headed by Bhulabhai Desai as Chairman, and Nehru as one of its prominent members.

Shyamlal Jain told the Khosla Commission that *"One evening, the date may be December 26 or 27, 1945, I was called by Shri Jawaharlal Nehru on telephone to come to the residence of Shri Asaf Ali with a typewriter as he had a lot of work to be typed by me, to which I complied. After getting some papers typed by me Shri Jawaharlal Nehru drew out a paper from the pocket of his Achkan and asked me to make four copies of it for him. The said paper was a handwritten matter and was somewhat difficult to read. Now, what was written on that paper, I am typing to reproduce from my memory:*

"Netaji Subhas Chandra Bose proceeding by aeroplane from Saigon arrived today, August 23, 1945 in Diren, Manchuria, at 1:30 afternoon. The said plane was a Japanese bomber plane. It was full of gold in the shape of bars, ornaments and jewellery. Netaji carried two attache cases,

one in each hand. On alighting from the plane, Netaji took tea with bananas. When Netaji finished tea, he along with four others, out of which one was a Japanese named General Shidei, and others have lapsed from memory, took their seats in a jeep standing nearby. The said jeep proceeded towards Russian territory. After about three hours the said jeep returned and informed the pilot of the plane who flew back to Tokyo.

"After handing over the said paper to me for typing, Shri Jawaharlal Nehru went to Mr. Asaf Ali and remained busy in conversation with him for 10 or 15 minutes ... I could not complete the work, because the name of the writer on that letter was not readable, and I kept waiting for Shri Jawaharlal to come and tell me the name. In the meantime, I went through the letter several times, and that is all that I could remember to the present day. Shri Jawaharlal could not discern the name of the writer and asked me to pull out the papers and hand them over as they were.

"I solemnly affirm and state on oath that thereafter Shri Jawaharlal Nehru gave me four papers from his writing pad to make four copies of a letter, which he would dictate to me on typewriter, which I also complied. The contents of the letter, as far as I could remember, were as follows:

Dear Mr. Attlee,

I understand from a reliable source that Subhas Chandra Bose, your war criminal has been allowed to enter Russian territory by Stalin. This is a clear treachery and betrayal of faith by the Russians. As Russia had been an ally of the British-Americans, it should not have been done.

Please take note of it and do what you consider proper and fit.

Yours sincerely,

Jawaharlal Nehru"

It is astonishing that the statement of Shyamlal Jain was not challenged at any stage either by the Government counsel or any other witness appearing before the Khosla Commission. The veracity of Jain's testimony was also not refuted by Justice Khosla in his final report.

Considering the other factors which connected Netaji and Russia, it is also a naked fact that after becoming the Prime Minister of India, **Jawaharlal Nehru must have known all the secret reports submitted by various intelligence agencies from time to time to the British Indian Government, including all those reports which communicated that Netaji had reached Russia or that his death story was doubtful,** but as Prime Minister, Nehru neither spoke publicly about these reports nor himself initiated any inquiry on the matter; rather he had been consistently declining the demand for a full-fledged judicial inquiry about Netaji's disappearance. Although the Shah Nawaz Committee was appointed by him due to public pressure, its total functioning was cunningly maneuvered to hide the facts concerning Netaji's mystery.

There is another angle of assumption which Dr. Purabi Roy told the JMCI, that during her research she pursued a wartime Major of M15 who had snooped around Netaji. She could meet the agent in Oxford and he told her that a huge amount of the 'INA Money' was collected by Netaji for freedom struggle at a big rally organised by the Indian Independence League in Singapore. This rally had been often referred to because in the rally, after thanking the gathering, Netaji announced that he would like to auction the garlands that had been put around his neck. **The bid started with one lakh and the first garland was auctioned for Rupees one crore and three lakh. It was purchased by a Muslim industrialist of Malaya, named Habibur Rehman, who later on had also**

volunteered his services to join the INA movement. According to Lt. Manwati Arya, this incident was named as *'Habib Mixture'* by Netaji who used to refer to it most often when he was motivating the people to sacrifice all their belongings for the sake of motherland's freedom. In the rally many women offered their valuables and gold ornaments. **The total collections at this auction were about Rupees 25 crore.** The collected amount was deposited in Azad Hind Bank.

After the Japanese surrender on September 2, 1945, the Supreme Allied Commander for South-East Asia, Admiral Louis Mountbatten, took over Singapore. He could also learn about huge money deposits of the INA in Azad Hind Bank. **It was alleged that Mountbatten managed to acquire the entire *'INA Money'* which was co-shared with him by a senior Congress leader.** This huge *'INA Money'* was a disgrace, which, if disclosed, would have harmed the great reputation of both the leaders, and to avoid such happenings there was no inquiry undertaken related to Netaji.

It is also a fact that Lord Mountbatten had always evaded answering questions related to Netaji's mystery. After perusing the wartime records of Mountbatten, the JMCI concluded that he did not believe in the death of Netaji. Prof. Samar Guha in his booklet *'Country Must Know What Happened to Netaji'* mentioned that during the Janata Party rule in India in 1978 an acutely sensitive letter was written by N.G. Goray, the then Indian High Commissioner in United Kingdom, to Lord Mountbatten, the first Governo-General of India.

Goray wrote: *"As you took over from Lord Wavell it will not be wrong to presume that you must have come to know every detail about the incident... Will it be possible that, we at this late hour at least shall know what happened to that intrepid, great and beloved leader of ours?"*

Explaining his purpose Goray further submitted that *"You would say: 'Why rake up the past?' My answer would be: Because there* ***is deep suspicion in India that Sri Bose took asylum in the USSR and all this was known to you, to Nehru and the Soviet Government. But all of you preferred to observe silence, an intriguing silence. I would say, because the British did not want to pick up a quarrel with their erstwhile ally and Nehru did not want to have a rival."***

On March 10, 1978, in his reply Mountbatten had expressed something conforming to a general pattern and an over-simplified information that *"there was no official record of Subhas Chandra Bose's death in his archives."* It was again a prudent forethought to minimise risk with a play of words in answering the question while killing its interrogative spirit.

Considering all the facts and views connecting Netaji's logical presence in Russia after August, 1945 in its final report the JMCI concluded particularly referring the minutes of the Russian Cabinet meeting on October 25, 1945 that ***"No doubt it seems to suggest that Netaji was alive on that day,*** *but an inference on the basis of the above minutes can and may be drawn at an appropriate stage if sufficient reliable materials are found in support thereof."*

—o—

19

Was He A War Criminal?

There had always been confusion and uncertainty in answering the question whether the name of Netaji Subhas Chandra Bose was borne in the list of war criminals prepared just after the World War II. There was a long gap of about one decade since August 1945 and no one liked to discuss the issue of war criminals. Mrs. Muthurama Ingan Thever was the first to raise the issue publicly on April 9, 1956. Mrs. Thever proposed that perhaps the Government of India should disassociate itself from *"the declaration made by the Allies in regard to war criminals"*. She further demanded that *"It is necessary on the part of the Government to make it known categorically to public whether Netaji's name is still in the list of war criminals and if not, when it was removed and how?"* Till today it is an apprehension whether Mrs. Thever was reacting **against a rumour that a few days before the then Home Minister Govind Vallabh Pant had officially agreed and signed a secret pact with the British Government to hand over Netaji to them if he returned to India in the next ten years.** Now it is also alleged that this so-called secret pact was further renewed secretly in 1966 by the Government of Indira Gandhi.

Actually, a few days earlier to Mrs. Muthurama Ingan's statement the issue of war criminal was directly raised before the Prime Minister Jawaharlal Nehru by Suresh Chandra Bose, the elder brother of Netaji. At that moment of time preparations were on to activate the functioning of the Netaji Inquiry Committee which was being headed by Shah Nawaz Khan and was prominently being represented as a member by Suresh Chandra Bose. Though Suresh Chandra Bose himself had direct access to Nehru, he opted to write a letter dated April 2, 1956 to seek clarifications from the Prime Minister on some points including the issue of war criminal. He wrote in his letter: "*...whether the name of Netaji Subhash Chandra Bose was and still is in the list of war criminals drawn up by America and her allies. If his name still exists and if they request the Government of India to hand him over to them, if he be found on Indian soil, for being tried as a war criminal, whether this Government will have the option of handing or not handing him over to them for the aforesaid purpose.*"

In this connection a note in the File No. 2(64)56-P.M. I Volume, disclosed that Nehru with a long face, discussed the issue of war criminal with Suresh Chandra Bose on the next morning and told him that "*the question of war criminal does not arise and we are not going to ask USA or any other country as to whether Netaji is in the list of their war criminals.*"

The mystery of the disappearance had thickened only because Netaji was being considered as an Enemy No. 1 of the Allied Forces in general and of the British Indian Government in particular. Consequent upon their efforts his name might have been included in the list of "*war criminals*" just after the end of the World War II. In this context it was an admitted fact that Netaji fought against the British, and therefore, like others who fought against the Allied Forces and belonged to the Axis Powers, his name also would have been included in the list of *"war criminals"* for all purposes. Anuj Dhar, the author of *'Back from Dead'* has claimed that he had seen a list of *"war criminals"* among the INA personnel which *"had the names of Mohan Singh, M.Z. Kiani, A.C. Chatterjee, S.C. Alagappan, Mahboob Ahmed, G.R. Nagar, Gulzara Singh and Gurbaksh Singh Dhillon ... There is no reason why the British shouldn't have clubbed Bose in the same league as his men. Even his doctor was categorized as a war criminal, and Dr. Taneyoshi Yoshimi, who had treated Bose in Taipei, was interrogated by War Crimes Section in 1946. Propaganda had it that Bose's men had tortured Allied military personnel and that they had extracted money from Indian expatriates."*

While deposing before the Khosla Commission on April 14, 1971, Netaji's physician Dr. S. Vasava Menon told it that in Bangkok on August 17, 1945, it was also a point of discussion that *"the Japanese did not want him (Netaji) to be caught as a war criminal."* According to some new facts now disclosed, Indian Viceroy Wavell was seriously considering as to how Netaji would be brought to India after the Japanese surrender and Wavell's Private Secretary Evan Meredith Jenkins had viewed Netaji as *"one of the bigger war criminal"*. Jenkins charged Netaji that he had *"offended against His Majesty's Government quite as much as against India."* Keeping in mind the Indian political situation Wavell opined about Netaji and his associates in a secret communication that *"it might be better to have them dealt with as war criminals outside India."* This communication was made perhaps after ascertaining the expert opinion on the matter from his Home Department in the shape of a note prepared by R.F. Mudie, the Home Member of the Viceroy's Executive Council.

It is now a confirmed fact that the British Cabinet had also discussed this matter on October 25, 1945 and recorded in its minutes that *"it was generally agreed that the only civilian renegade of importance was Subhas Chandra Bose."*

After Independence, in Indian Parliament whenever the *"war criminal"* issue was raised, the Government's replies were stereotype with the words that *'to the best of their knowledge Netaji's name was not borne on any list of war criminals'*. In 1961 there was a statement issued by the British High Commission in Delhi that Netaji's name did not appear in any *"British list"*. Although it is now much late but in December 1999, the then British Prime Minister Tony Blair wrote to an Oslo-based economist Amalendu Guha that the matter related to the war criminals had a description in the correspondence published in the *'Transfer of Power'* series which was indicative that in 1945 the then Government of British India had viewed Netaji as a *"war criminal"*. And a similar reply was also received by the JMCI.

When Gumnami Baba was residing in Naimisharanya near Sitapur in Uttar Pradesh, adopting the name *'Pardewale Baba'*, in April 1962 Prof. Atul Sen, Member of Legislative Assembly, West Bengal, could meet him. Believing firmly that Baba was none other but Netaji in disguise, Prof. Sen asked him, *'Why was he hiding away from his own people?'* Disagreeing about his identity as to be Netaji, Baba had carefully warned Prof. Sen to keep his whereabouts secret, but Prof. Sen insisted that he reply to his question. **Baba replied plainly: *"I have been declared an international war criminal."*** Prof. Sen could not digest the answer given by Baba. After reaching Kolkata Prof. Sen leaked the information to some persons and decided to write to Prime Minister Jawaharlal Nehru.

In his letter dated August 28, 1962 Prof. Sen wrote: *"I take the liberty of addressing these few lines to you in the matter of the widely prevalent belief that Netaji Subhas Chandra Bose is not dead. Mine is not mere belief but actual knowledge that Netaji is alive and is engaged in spiritual practice somewhere in India. Not the Sadhu of Shoulmari, Cooch-Behar, in West Bengal, about whom some Calcutta politicians are making a fuss at this moment. I deliberately make the location a little vague because from the talks I had with him for months together, not very long ago, I could understand that he is yet regarded as an Enemy No. 1 of the Allied Powers and that there is a secret protocol that binds the Government of India to deliver him to Allied 'justice' if found alive. If you can persuade yourself to assure me that his information is not correct, or even if it is correct, your Government shall resist any action by any of the said powers against the Great Patriot. I may try to persuade him to return to open life."*

Nehru had replied to the letter and wrote: *"I have never heard of any secret protocol about Netaji Subhas Chandra Bose. Certainly the Government of India have not bound themselves to any such thing. Even if any country asks the Government of India to hand him over, it is not going to be agreed to."*

As a matter of fact, the issue of *"war criminal"* had never been solved satisfactorily and finally. There were denials based on *'the best of knowledge'* from the Government of India, the Indian Embassy, Japan, the Japan Foreign Office, the British High Commission in India, the Permanent Mission of India to the United Nations in New York, the Secretary-General, United Nations, the United Nations War Crimes Commission, etc., but there was no authoritative statement or declaration which gave a clean chit.

On February 15, 1997 the chairman of *'Netaji Forum'*, Air Vice Marshal S. Goyal wrote a letter to Kofi Annan, the then Secretary-General, United Nations. Goyal wrote that *"The worthy 'Patriot of patriots'*[1] *as Mahatma Gandhi called the great Indian freedom-fighter Netaji Subhas Chandra Bose, deserves the World Body's highest consideration to relieve him, dead or alive, from the dishonourable reference of 'War Criminal' unjustly and hastily dubbed by the Super Powers of the U.K. and U.S.A. after Hiroshima and Nagasaki destruction by the Allies. Bose, like any other patriotic fighter, deserves a patriotic award and not a punishment of witch-hunting imposed arbitrarily by world powers of vested geopolitical interests."*

The then Executive Assistant to the Secretary-General, United Nations, and the present Minister of State, Ministry of External Affairs, Shashi Tharoor, replied on May 1, 1997 that *"The Secretary-General is aware of the great regard in which Netaji is held, but he is powerless to undo references that may have been made in the past. He is confident that no United Nations agency or publication would use the term 'war criminal' in reference to Netaji in the future."*

In this context there had been discussions referring to the issue of *'war criminal'* in relation to Netaji almost in all official inquiry panels and in their reports, the matter remained inconclusive. On December 24, 1970, a very poor show was demonstrated when Justice G.D. Khosla himself passed a pooh-pooh comment and emphatically remarked that *"he was authorised to state that Netaji's name had never figured in any 'war criminals' list."* Immediately, Justice Khosla was cornered by an M.P. and a former IFS officer, M.L. Sondhi, who pressed him to reveal the source of his information. Ridiculously, Justice Khosla replied, *"I am making the statement on my own authority."*

Later on, in order to maintain his dignity he had posed five questions before the Ministry of Home Affairs (MHA) as under:

1. *Was Netaji's name borne on the list of war criminals prepared at the conclusion of World War II?*
2. *If so, is there such a list which is still in force, and is Netaji Bose's name on that list?*
3. *Should Netaji Bose be proved to be alive, is the Government of India under any obligation to hand him over to an international body for being tried upon the charges of committing war crimes?*

4. *What will be the Government's attitude towards the freedom of Netaji Bose, should he be found and appear in person?*
5. *Was any list of war criminals maintained apart from the list which was placed before the International Court which held its sittings in Japan?*

Justice Khosla had included in its report the reply received from the MHA. According to Justice Khosla *"The Home Minister has consulted the Ministry of External Affairs, the Ministry of Information and Broadcasting, and the Ministry of Defence, and all the three Ministries had stated that no such information was available with them. This reply however, did not deal with five questions which I had referred to the Ministry, and so a fresh reference was made."*

According to the report of the Khosla Commission, this time a more detailed reply was received and it stated that *"Enquiries made from the Indian Missions, The Hague, New York and-Tokyo had revealed that the name of Netaji was never borne on any list of war criminals, and therefore, questions (3) and (4) which I had posed in my first letter did not arise."* And thus he could justify his earlier pooh-pooh comment.

Chief Justice Prabha Shanker Mishra and Justice B. Bhattacharya of the Calcutta High Court had also questioned that *"Who will call Netaji a war criminal? Any Indian except a traitor, a person who does not have the defence and love for the country and its heros, alone can do so. We do not have any hesitation in concluding that the statements in the documents which are lying in archives which are to the effect that Netaji is a war criminal and all persons who have been saying such a thing are relic of the British raj... The people of India, and the Government of India, can never even in dreams think of Netaji as a war criminal..."*

—o—

20

Clandestine Files

Netaji's friend since his boyhood, Dilip Kumar Roy, wrote in his reminiscences that *"All who have known his lovable self, limpid like morning star; who have even once come under him affectionate glance of silence; who have worked with him even for a few days on a footing of simple comraderie, must have realised he could never impose his will on the free choice of those whom he would have given much to win over."* It was because *"his faith in the liberal moral values was too luminous, his heart of affection too pure, his mental sympathy too genuine to suffer him to break others on the wheel of ruthless dictatorship."*

The above comments of Netaji's bosom friend proved justified when on the eve of the 61st year of Indian independence a reputed weekly journal, *'India Today'*, conducted a survey between March and April, 2008 through e-mail and SMS to name the greatest sons of India in the last century. Sardar Bhagat Singh, the greatest martyr of India was voted first with 37 per cent votes, followed by Netaji Subhas Chandra Bose with 27 per cent votes. Both together had secured nearly two-third of the total votes. According to this survey, published in 'India Today' on April 23, 2008, the top ten included

Mahatma Gandhi with 13 per cent votes, Sardar Patel 8 per cent, JRD Tata 4 per cent, Indira Gandhi and Rabindranath Tagore each 3 per cent, Jawaharlal Nehru and Homi Bhabha each 2 per cent and in the tenth position was Jayaprakash Narayan securing one per cent of total votes.

Appreciating Netaji's contributions the veteran journalist Chandan Mitra wrote: *"India's freedom struggle is not replete with the tales of daredevilry or romance, the odd militant nationalist like Bhagat Singh being the exception rather than the rule. But this variant of nationalism operated through secret societies with little or no mass participation. Subhas Bose fired the imagination of many Indians, particularly the youth, because his brand of militant nationalism had a mass component...Most historians find fatal flaws in his inconsistencies, his simultaneous flirtation with communism and fascism and his attempt to emerge as an alternate pole to Gandhism...At the same time, it is undeniable that he was a patriot to the core who firmly believed in 'My Country, right or wrong'."*

Chandan Mitra further wrote in his article published in 'The Pioneer' that *"For more than half-a-century people were made to assume that Netaji died in an air crash, that we now know never happened. What was the reason for this cover up? I believe this fundamental lapse casts a shadow on many subsequent actions of various Congress Governments at the Centre."*

According to Chandan Mitra, *"The issue is no longer whether Netaji is dead or alive ...However, the questions — (1) where did he go after World War II ended, and (2) how did he die — remain unanswered."* The same questions are better expressed when Anuj Dhar, the author of *'Back from Dead'* says that *"People may or may not like Netaji, but they have a right to know what happened to him — how he died and where?"*

Thus the mystery related to Netaji is still equally hot and curious and marked by the desire to investigate and learn. Considering Netaji's active and positive activities during the Indian freedom movement, his career later after August 1945 is shrouded in a series of ifs and buts. A bonafide question is raised by Chandan Mitra: *"Had the Gandhi-backed CWC (Congress Working Committee), not compelled Netaji to resign by declaring non-cooperation with the elected party Chief, he might not have embarked on an eventually self-destructive path, beginning with a daredevil escapade from his Kolkata residence and ending in his alleged death in an air accident in 1945."*

The above question cannot be accepted because it is imaginary and absolutely against the spirit of Netaji's life and his style. In his mind, Netaji was very clear that the most important political party or organisation in India was the Indian National Congress. He was also sure that the aim of the Congress was the *'attainment of complete freedom by peaceful and legitimate means'*. He was also well aware that the President of Congress was not the real leader and the real leader of the Congress (in the thirties of the last century) was Mahatma Gandhi whom Netaji regarded as a virtual dictator because no one could find a place in the CWC if he was not thoroughly submissive to him and his policy.

The Congress Party was regarded by Netaji as an organisation which represented the whole country and all communities with the exception of the communal parties. In those days all the other organisations and political parties in India were on the whole friendly towards the Congress and worked in closecooperation with it. But within the Congress there were several groups, including a powerful radical left wing to which Netaji belonged. It was also an open fact that Gandhiji was maintaining a middle position among all the groups within the Congress or he was always ready for a more compromising position.

The attitude of Mahatma Gandhi was very keenly observed and well recorded in the book *'The Indian Struggle'* written by Netaji as an exile in Europe. The book was published by Lawrence and Wishart in London on January 17, 1935 and its entry into India was banned, however, the British political circles and its press had welcomed the book.

Describing the Lahore Congress held in 1929, Netaji said that this Congress Session was presided over by Jawaharlal Nehru, but he *'was a figurehead and the entire proceedings were dominated by Mahatma Gandhi.'* In this session Netaji had presented a resolution on behalf of the left wing that *'the Congress should aim at setting up a parallel Government in the country, and to that end, should take in hand the task of organising the workers, peasants and youths.'* The resolution was defeated.

Reacting against the left wing in the Lahore Congress, when the time came for electing the CWC for the coming year, Gandhi came forward with a list of fifteen names, from which the names of Srinivasa Iyenger, Netaji and other left wingers had been deliberately omitted. There was a great hue and cry to include both the names — Iyenger and Netaji's — but Gandhi did not listen.

According to the observations of Netaji, the Lahore Congress was a personal victory for Gandhi. He could henceforth proceed with his own plans for India's freedom movement without fear of opposition within his cabinet, and whenever any opposition was raised outside the cabinet, he could always coerce the public by threatening to retire from the Congress or to fast unto death. Politically commenting on this situation, Netaji wrote that *"from his point of view, it was the cleverest move."*

Netaji was also conscious that for the general public, unacquainted with the intricacies of politics or with differences in the inner council of the Congress, Gandhi became a father figure. But the effect of the Lahore Congress was bad on Srinivasa Iyenger who decided to retire from public life. Netaji felt that Srinivasa Iyenger had been treated shabbily by the President 'Jawaharlal Nehru' and also by Gandhi who was instrumental in excluding him from the CWC. Netaji wrote in his book that *'This insult he (Srinivasa Iyenger) had taken to heart so much that he vowed, he would have nothing to do with the Congress so long as Mahatma Gandhi remained the leader.'*

This incident was important for Netaji as Srinivasa Iyenger was not an ordinary person. He was a former Advocate-General of Madras Presidency and the leader of Madras Bar. His status with the great reputation and prestige in the then Madras Presidency as Advocate-General would correspond to the position of the Solicitor-General in England. Iyenger was elected in December 1926 the President of the Indian National Congress in the Gauhati (now Guwahati) Session.

In such background Netaji tried his best to negotiate his stand with Gandhi in 1939 but when he found it impossible, he ventured to remain within the Congress while floating his group titled as *'Forward Bloc'*. He also tolerated the *'disciplinary actions'* initiated by the CWC against some members of the Forward Bloc. But lastly, inspite of a successful propaganda campaign launched by the Forward Bloc against the compromising policy of the CWC when Gandhi openly and Jawaharlal Nehru secretly opted to help the British Indian Government in their war-efforts indirectly, Netaji and his team consciously decided to part with the Congress.

It is also not a relevant question — *'Had Netaji returned to India after the Second World War, he would have prevented partition of the country?'* Although in the history of Indian freedom struggle, there were several occasions when Netaji repeated his warning that the Congress would pay dearly for adopting the policy of compromising in all situations, on the pretext of Gandhian non-violence and for accepting berths in provincial governments under the Government of India Act, 1935. Certainly to imagine the presence of Netaji in free India is a supercilious idea to speculate many solutions for existing problems, and certainly Netaji was not a tired politician ready to accept office even under damaging terms.

On this question the INA's Major General M.Z. Kiani of Rawalpindi wrote in his book *'The Great INA' (1944)* that Netaji *"was known to be an upright man and had a solid political standing in India."* According to him, a majority of the officers in the INA were Muslims and the three regiments raised initially, two were commanded by Major Aziz Ahmed and I.J. Kiani. Major General Kiani described Netaji like Caesar, because **after Netaji's arrival and the reorganisation of the INA among the six major formations, five were commanded by Muslims,** with the army itself being under his authority. Such ready acceptance of Netaji by the Muslims in the British Indian Army raises an interesting question. As described by Major General Kiani, Netaji *"could speak for hours, not in chaste but effective Urdu."* **Kiani had speculated that if Netaji would have been the Congress leader instead of Gandhi or Nehru, the partition could have been averted and perhaps Netaji would have overshaodwed Jinnah in the eyes of the Muslims.**

As per the assessment of Major General Kiani, Gandhi's speeches and writings were replete with statements that show that he was prepared to go to any length to placate the Muslims. In Kiani's words *"appeasement evokes neither appreciation nor deference".* Kiani wrote that Jawaharlal Nehru was averse to dealing with assertive Muslims and, sub-consciously favoured the partition of the country.

Kiani further examines what could Netaji have done to draw Muslims away from Jinnah, the Muslim League, and the idea of Pakistan? According to him, Netaji had courage, imagination and articulation. With their deployment, he could have made them realise the disadvantages of the partition to the community, especially those left behind in Hindustan. Kiani further wrote that Maulana Abul Kalam Azad knew this but his community did not lend him an ear nor was he sufficiently forthright in his articulation.

Coming back to the issue of the secret files and documents, it is clear inspite of three inquiry panels there is still no success in declassifying those secret files which hide the secret of the mystery. At this stage the governments of Russian Federation and United Kingdom cannot be blamed when the incredible and shocking conspiracy in this regard is forcefully maintained by the Indian Prime Minister's Office (PMO) itself. These secret files are still hiding the circumstances and conditions surrounding Netaji's disappearance and subsequent rumours that he lived his later life in disguise in India as a Sadhu or he was killed either in Russia or in Baluchistan.

It should not be treated simply as a question about a single person or personality, who has been adored in India and abroad for his love and dedication for his motherland, but it is a matter of paying our debts to that great soul who sacrificed his entire ambitions for human posterity, and **whose contribution has given birth to many free and independent countries in the world of a chain of freedom struggles against the most powerful imperialist powers of the world**. The conscience of the Indian people demands that the Indian Government must show the courage and fortitude by overcoming its political compulsions by revealing the facts related to Netaji's mystery. The classified and secret files possessed by the PMO should be declassified as early as possible, otherwise there will be ramifications of various types of rumours and hatred towards the suspicious persons and agencies.

Under the provisions of the Right to Information Act, 2005 (RTI), the PMO was requested to furnish the details of the secret files related to Netaji and the INA, but in vain. In this matter an appeal was filed before the Chief Information Commissioner (CIC) with a request to intervene as the PMO was adamant on its stand and refused to declassify Netajis related files. The PMO declined to produce even the list of the classified files with arguments that their contents may effect India's sovereignty and its relation with foreign countries. Wajahat Habibullah, the CIC could prevail upon the PMO's officials and thus he personally examined in camera 33 files in reference and ordered that only four files had references to foreign countries, and therefore, the remaining 29 files could be declassified. Out of these 29 files related to Netaji and the INA, seven were marked as *'Top Secret'*, three as *'Confidential'* and nineteen as *'Secret'*.

On the pretext of transparency, in November 2007, the 'Mission Netaji', a voluntary organisation seeking truth behind Netaji's death, could get a landmark judgement. The CIC had recommended that the Ministry of Home Affairs (MHA) unveil the secret and controversial documents related to Netaji. An activist of *'Mission Netaji'* S. Dasgupta requested the MHA for copies of all the documents exhibited before the Netaji Inquiry Committee, headed by Shah Nawaz Khan in 1956 and the Khosla Commission in 1970-74. These documents were not provided by the MHA, repeating almost the same arguments that *"the documents sought under the RTI Act, 2005 are voluminious — 70,000 pages — and top secret in nature and may lead to chaos in the country, if disclosed."*

The above case was put forward to the CIC in July 2006. In the beginning the Information Commissioner A.N. Tewari was not convinced regarding getting copies of all the papers, and advised to seek some specific documents as the MHA's officials had strategically denied the knowledge of the exhibited documents. After about one year of persuasion when A.N. Tewari was convinced, the MHA officials turned up in March 2007 with a letter that the required documents could not be declassified because the disclosure would cause trouble in the country, specially in West Bengal, where according to their supposition, Netaji was not liked by the Communists who were ruling the State for more than three decades.

The logic tendered by the MHA officials was not merely an assumption, because although Indian Communists had opposed Netaji, the officials had ignored the altered stand and persuaded the present leadership of the Communist Party of India (Marxist) to amend their policy. On the eve of Netaji's 105th anniversary on January 23, 2003, the Chief Minister of West Bengal, Buddhadev Bhattacharya, apologised and said that the Communists had made a *'great mistake'* in wrongly evaluating Netaji Subhas Chandra Bose's role during the freedom movement. He said in simple words that *"I am apologising for our mistaken assessment of Netaji."* The Chief Minister not only saluted the statue of Netaji at the Maidan in Kolkata and further said that *"It is unfortunate that we, the Communists, doubted Netaji's fiery patriotism and selfless sacrifice."*

Further regarding the secret files related to Netaji, the JMCI was informed that in April 1957 a file was opened in the Prime Minister's Secretariat (now PMO) related to Netaji and the same was destroyed in March 1972 on the pretext that *"during routine process of review/weeding of old records"* and to lighten the burden of the record room. It was done at the behest of P.N. Haskar, who was a famous diplomat and also Personal Secretary to the Prime Minister Indira Gandhi. The timing of destruction of this file clashed with the then ongoing judicial inquiry led by Justice G.D. Khosla.

It is also a fact that regarding this file, Samar Guha had raised a question in 1974 asking *'whether such a vital file has been destroyed or withheld?'* Prime Minister Indira Gandhi gave a misleading reply to Samar Guha in black and white. She wrote that *"the file was destroyed only because it contained copies ...I can assure you that this file contained only copies of certain documents which are still available in other files."*

Taking note of the above information, **the JMCI opined that 'File 12 (226)/56—PM titled as *"Investigation into circumstances leading to the death of Netaji"* could have been of *"great assistance"* in resolving the controversy surrounding Netaji's disappearance.** On questioning the rationale and the exact order related to the destroyed file, the PMO submitted that no order as such could be located. The officials could only provide *"the relevant page of the File Register showing destruction of the file in 1972."*

According to the Manual of Office Procedure in those days, there were three categories of files among which 'Class-A' included those files or the records fit for permanent preservation, or files of historical importance, or files related to well known national or international public event or cause or celebrity, or to other events which gave rise to interest or controversy on the national plane. The files of this category could not be destroyed before 25 years and with prior consultation with the National Archives of India. With such clear rules and procedures, the file '12 (226)/56—PM' seemed to have been destroyed not only hurriedly and unlawfully but **such an act had also strengthened the assumption that there might have been a motive to hide the truth and to divert the inquiry proceedings of the Khosla Commission.**

The seriousness and importance of such files could be understood with the fact that **most of the secret files about Netaji were being maintained by Jawaharlal Nehru as *'PM's Special Files'*** with the assistance of his Personal Secretary, Mohd. Yunus. Now it is very difficult to know the fate of Netaji's communications to Nehru and Nehru's letter to British Prime Minister Attlee which had been referred to in the unchallenged deposition of Shyamlal Jain, a witness who appeared before the Khosla Commission.

It was an allegation vide the status report submitted by the JMCI on December 7, 2004, that in 1954 the Ministry of External Affairs (MEA) had received Rupees two hundred along with the ashes and other remains of Netaji from the Indian Embassy in Tokyo, vide the receipt of the then Minister of External Affairs and the Prime Minister Jawaharlal Nehru under Office Note D/S 13170, dated December 2, 1954, from the secret file of the PMO's *'File 23 (11)56-57 PM-INA Treasure."* The basis of this allegation was a Note D/S 13170 dated December 2, 1954, prepared by M.O. Mathai, the then Personal Secretary and a close associate of Prime Minister Jawaharlal Nehru. The JMCI questioned when and under what circumstances the ashes were received by the MEA and where were they preserved? In this connection the MEA's vague answer was that *"the ashes were not disturbed with the understanding that they would remain (in Renkoji) until a decision has been taken by the Government of India."*

It is true that the JMCI could not unravel the core mystery and the Government of India exercised its constitutional right in rejecting the findings of the JMCI. **The JMCI concluded in its**

findings that Netaji Subhas Chandra Bose "is dead" but he did not die in the plane-crash as alleged and that the ashes in the Japanese temple "are not of Netaji". In the absence of any clinching evidence the JMCI could not give a positive answer as how, where and when Netaji died. The findings of the JMCI inferred that a secret plan was contrived to ensure Netaji's safe passage, to which Japanese military authorities and Col. Habibur Rehman were parties and the purpose of Netaji's flight was to go to the Soviet Union to continue his independence movement. According to the JMCI, it is at all not a controversial matter that Netaji had succeeded in evading the Allied Forces and escaping out of their reach as per his emplaning at Saigon on August 17, 1945, and as a camouflage thereof the entire make-believe story — of the air crash, Netaji's death therein and his cremation — was engineered by the Japanese Army authorities, including two doctors and Habibur Rehman and then the Tokyo Radio broadcast on August 23, 1945.

—o—

21

What Remains Now ...

It was Wednesday on May 17, 2006 when the United Progressive Alliance (UPA) Congress-led Government expressed its opinion about the findings of the Justice Mukherjee Inquiry Commission (JMCI). Presenting the one line Action Taken Report (ATR) along with the JMCI's report which comprised three volumes, a Dravid Munnetra Kazgam (DMK) coalition partner and the then Minister of State for Home, Sevugan Ragupathy, said in the Parliament that the incidental delay in tabling the JMCI report *"has been occasioned by the time taken in translation (in Hindi), consideration of the report by the Government, its approval by the Cabinet, and adjournment of the Parliament"* on March 22, 2006. Sevugan told the Parliament that the **Government had decided to reject the findings of the JMCI including both of its major findings about the plane-crash and the ashes kept in Renkoji Temple, Tokyo.**

The stand of the Government was challenged by three Lok Sabha MPs — Subrata Bose of the All India Forward Bloc, Major B.C. Khanduri and Raghuvir Singh Kaushal, both of the Bhartiya Janta Party—as they fielded an unstarred question and asked

Ragupathy to defend the Government's line. Simultaneously, the UPA's allies belonging to Rashtriya Janata Party and the Samajwadi Party, pleaded for a full discussion on the findings of the JMCI. Members of left parties also opposed the ATR and demanded to know reasons for turning down the panel's findings. The main contention of these parties was that the Government had failed to give any reason while disagreeing with the findings.

The Forward Bloc member Subrata Bose, the nephew of Netaji, wanted specifically the detailed reasons and explanation from the Government *"for its cryptic one line ATR disagreeing with the findings of the panel."* He said: *"Netaji was my uncle but he belonged to whole of India and whether he is alive or dead, does not matter. He lives in the heart of the people."*

Ignoring the new clues described in the report of the JMCI, the Congress-led Government was quick to propose through the leader of the Lok Sabha Pranab Mukherjee that *"a structured debate should take place during which it would reply to the issues raised by the members."* He further said that *"two commissions had been established earlier but this (Mukherjee) Commission was set up as the earlier (National Democratic Alliance) Government rejected their findings.*[1] *This is nothing new. All points will come up during the discussion which should be a structured one."*

Beyond the above governmental hitchhiking, the role played by the Indian National Army (INA) in influencing the British to leave the country depends upon the history books for us, but **the mystery surrounding Netaji's disappearance is still hidden in the secret files kept as classified documents by the Government of India, United Kingdom and Russian Federation.** Basing on the

1. It was not the NDA Government but Morarji Desai-led Government of Janata Party which had undone the decision of previous panels on August 28, 1978.

findings of the JMCI if Netaji did not die in August 1945, then *'what happened to him'* is not only a natural question but an enigmatic curiosity. In this connection the most disturbing suspicion arises against those who either do not want to reveal the documentary references being maintained as *'Top Secret'* for the last seven decades or are bent upon to hide and bury those live facts which are directly related to the most brilliant hero of our freedom struggle.

The thread of incidents related to Netaji leads us to the Indian Government which has not done what it could and should have done, by extending official and honest support to the JMCI in its investigation efforts in Russia. Answering a question related to the cooperation of the Russian authorities, Anuj Dhar said that *"No government in the world, least of all a former super-power, can be expected to release sensitive information just like that (Netaji's presence in Russia after August, 1945). So bonafide official approaches will have to be made at the highest level, just as the Swedish and the American governments did in the case of Raoul Wallenberg*[1]*. Former USSR premier Mikhail Gorbachev is reported to have said that it was up to Russian and Indian governments to resolve the issue once for all."* This fact has never been disputed that the extant records show that the Indian Government has never took up the matter related to Netaji's disappearance with the Russian Government.

The British and American Governments' declassified documents have also very expressly concluded that *'Netaji did not die in the plane accident'* and that he was keen to return to India. According to the exhibits displayed by the JMCI's it was a terrible

1. Raoul Wellenberg disappeared in 1944. The USSR had claimed that he perished during the fighting in Budapest and later said that he died of natural causes in Moscow, but lastly admitted in December, 2000, that Wallenberg was held as a suspect spy until his death in a Soviet prison.

and ironical fact that even Mahatma Gandhi did not buy the theory of plane-crash. **One year after Netaji's alleged death, Khursheed Naoroji, Personal Secretary of Gandhi, tried to use the political influence through Gandhi's American biographer Louis Fischer to prevent Netaji from coming back to his motherland.**

Considering the matter from an absolutely opposite angle and inspite of supporting the version of the Indian Government, the Chairperson of *'Netaji Research Bureau'* and a former MP, Krishna Bose, the daughter-in-law of Suresh Chandra Bose, says in an article published in 'The Times of India' on may 23, 2006: *"For Indians Netaji is a legend. Many people believe even today that if by some miracle he returned, their miseries would vanish. This is an honourable sentiment that I deeply respect. But it is time for the nation to accept his mortal end, and the circumstances of the end. Subhas Chandra Bose lives forever in millions of hearts and minds through his valiant deeds, and in the supreme sacrifice he made for freedom. None of the other leaders of our freedom struggle had such a glorious death. Let us not deprive Netaji of his martyrdom. The time has come to close the futile debate about his death. Let the nation concentrate instead on preserving and honouring his life and legacy as an eternal source of inspiration. Finally, is it not high time to bring the leader's remains home?"*

Krishna Bose began her article referring to her journey to Taipei that *"On my first visit to Taipei 27 years ago, I went looking for the historic sites related to the last days of Netaji Subhas Chandra Bose. I walked in to the old one-storey, red-brick building of Nanmon Hospital. There I was shown the emergency entrance and the wards. This old building has since been demolished and on my later visits — most recently in October 2005 — I have seen a modern hospital standing there. I also saw the Nishi Honganji Temple where the remains of Netaji were enshrined before arrangements could be made to transfer it to Tokyo. The only site I missed was the crematorium, which earlier visitors including my husband Sisir Bose had seen when he visited Taipei in 1965. It had been shifted by the time of my first visit in 1979."*

It is perhaps because of the alleged prejudicial functioning of the JMCI, Krishna Bose has said that *"The seven survivors of the air crash, including Colonel Habibur Rehman of the INA, the doctors who treated Netaji's injuries, the Japanese interpreter who was called to interpret him during his final hours (and who knew Netaji personally, since he had acted as his interpreter before) and even the ward boy at the hospital on that fateful day, have testimonies which are consistent with one another. The Japanese General Shidei, who was also on the plane, was killed instantaneously. When I met Shidei's family in Japan, his perplexed brother asked me why some Indians still insist on denying the crash: 'We were informed by our government of my brother's death. We see no reason why we should have been lied to.'"*

Referring to the ashes Krishna Bose questions that *"The young Indian cadets of the Azad Hind Movement, who were being trained in Tokyo's military academy, kept vigil over the urn. Some of these cadets are still alive, but none were called to testify by the Mukherjee Commission."*

With these observations of Krishna Bose, we can understand her sincerity but it is surprising as to why she herself has not ventured to persuade such potent witnesses to appear before the JMCI, and a more important point is why the facts which have been provided either by the Taiwanese Government or have been dug out in Russian and British archives have no mention in her article?

Similarly, Captain Lakshmi Sehgal who first rejected the plane-crash story but later on, she told on December 4, 2000 the *'Ananda Bazar Patrika'* that *"the death of Netaji occurred in the plane-crash"*, and again confirmed before the JMCI on June, 4, 2001 that *"I still believe that Netaji died on August 18, 1945 at Taipei; I also believe that the ashes kept in Japan are the ashes of Netaji."* In the same news item in the above Bengali daily, she was quoted as saying that after the fall of Japan *"we received information that Netaji would go to Taipei from Saigon and thereafter he would proceed secretly to Manchuria."* While agreeing that she made such a statement, but Captain Sehgal corrected her quote by saying that *"I have not been correctly quoted. After the fall of Japan we received information that Netaji would go to Taipei from Saigon, but we had no information then that he would go to Manchuria. We did not know whether he would go to Tokyo or Manchuria."*

The head of the Rani Jhansi Regiment, Captain Dr. Lakshmi Sehgal was 86 years old when she was deposing before the JMCI. She endorsed her statement made in Kolkata on January 23, 2001, that she unambiguously informed the journalists that the death of Netaji occurred in the plane-crash at Taipei on August 18, 1945. But she declined to have said that in her opinion *"the mystery of disappearance of Netaji is nothing but a fancied imagination of some self-seekers."* She further added that *"I am certain that Netaji died in the plane-crash at Taipei on August 18, 1945. The matter of disappearance has now become a myth."*

On a question whether she possesses any document or record or knows the existence of any such documents, records, etc., which could prove that Netaji died in the alleged plane-crash and that the ashes kept in Renkoji Temple in Japan, are ashes of Netaji, Captain Sehgal answered in the negative. In a reply to a question she also said that *"I did not believe the news of his death when I heard about it from Radio broadcast. It is not correct to say that within a day or two I came to know that the news was true. I did not believe the news until I met and talked to Habibur Rehman in India."*

When a reference from her book titled *'A Revolutionary Life — Memories of A Political Activist'* was raised during her deposition before the JMCI, she stated that *"Two days after I moved in, we heard the news that Netaji had been killed in an air crash while flying from Saigon to Japan. We took the news very cooly as we were convinced, it was incorrect, and that Netaji himself had put it out to enable him to escape. This feeling persisted for several years. In fact it was only when Netaji did not appear even after independence, then I accepted he was no more. Even today the circumstances of the air-crash remain in doubt. The fact that Col. Habibur Rehman never saw his body and was only given the urn supposedly containing his ashes added to the suspicion."* Captain Sehgal clarified that *"The book was in fact published in 1997, but I had prepared the manuscript in the 1950s when I still believed that Netaji was not dead. The manuscript was lying with me for want of a publisher. In 1995-1996 a publisher approached me. I gave him the manuscript without any alteration, updating or further editing. It is not correct to say that at the time of publication of the books I was still under the belief that Netaji had not died in the plane-crash."*

Further explaining her point of view, Captain Sehgal said that *"I believe that Netaji died in the air-crash. My belief in his death in the air-crash was first generated when I met Habibur Rehman in India. My said belief became stronger and firm by subsequent developments, namely, non-appearance of Netaji in India even when the country was passing through several crises starting from the partition of India. My firm belief is that no power on earth could prevent a man like Netaji from returning to India when the country was passing through so many crises."* In a very plain manner she accepted that the ashes kept in the Renkoji Temple in Japan were the ashes of Netaji and it is only because she believes it.

Regarding the issue of war criminal, Captain Sehgal said before the JMCI that *"I heard that Netaji was to be declared as an international war criminal but I do not know whether he was declared a war criminal or not. I have no knowledge in this respect."*

In her cross-examination before the JMCI on the presumption that Netaji might be under arrest in Russia, Captain Sehgal accepted that on July 13, 1992 she was told that there were some comrades, specially Abid Hasan, who was Personal Secretary of Netaji and who had a feeling for a long time that Netaji had been arrested, and he was in prison in Russia and such a possibility could not be ruled out. Captain Sehgal also admitted that in her interview with V.P. Saini, she referred to a letter of Jawaharlal Nehru to Lord Mountbatten in which Nehru had suggested that Netaji should not be allowed to return to India until the process of the partition of the country was completed. She disclosed that this reference was made in her presence by a British historian to the audience during an international conference in Kolkata organised by the Netaji Research Bureau.

During her deposition she also confirmed that after the end of the Second World War, in the first week of September 1945 *"I was interviewed by American war correspondents. At that time American war correspondents were mostly American intelligence people. They told me that they followed a person whose physical description answered to that of Netaji upto the Russian border."*

The statements of Captain Lakshmi Sehgal are plain and honest confessions, but the contradictory references are surprising. Her belief has two sides and both are opposed to each other. It cannot be disputed that her dedication to Netaji is pure and free from what vitiates, weakens or pollutes. Her insistence now to endorse the government's version is a sort of natural pressure on her because she was fed up and was compelled to change gradually her views about the disappearance of Netaji. Her evidence before the JMCI and her previous statements are so plain and truthful that she cannot be blamed for their contrary assertions and a proposition so related to another that if either is true or false, the other is false or true.

There was a very optimistic comment by Sharmila Ganeshan in her article published in *'The Times of India'* on May 25, 2006 that *"Sixty one years after his death, it would seem that only an extreme historian or an out-of-work fan would care to find the truth behind Netaji Subhas Chandra Bose's mysterious disappearance ... did he actually die in the 1945 Japanese plane-crash. But when the NDA Government-appointed Justice Mukherjee Commission of 1999 said that Bose did not die in the crash, one of free India's unsolved mysteries resurfaced."* The JMCI's findings had shockingly stated that Netaji did die but not in the 1945 crash. The conclusions of the JMCI are supported by legally admitted evidences and documents that *"there is no record relating to the death or cremation of Netaji or his three companions that included an important Japanese General Shidei which should have definitely been recorded."*

Due to the passage of many long years, none of those witnesses were available before the JMCI for questioning whose submissions might have unravelled the mystery. These witnesses could have helped but owing to the long passage of time, they were either dead or untraceable or too old to depose and also quite a number of documents could not be traced. But still the JMCI could collect *"robust circumstantial evidence on record"* much of which earlier inquiry panels did not get. **Inspite of the stiff opposition by the Government of India and its policy not to provide any document under its control, the JMCI had some advantages over previous panels as it was supported by such activists and research scholars who enabled it to reach some very definite conclusions.** Actually, the JMCI was the only inquiry panel to obtain information directly from the Taiwanese Government on the point of air-crash that was supposed to have taken place on its territory. The JMCI could manage to visit Taiwan despite the adverse and leg-pulling attitude of Indian government' officials. The Taiwanese authorities provided documentary evidences and **made the startling disclosure that there was no air-crash anywhere in their country on and around August 18, 1945.**

It was also equally significant that on the request of the JMCI, the Taiwanese government divulged that **the cremation register in Taipei for the period August 17 to 27, 1945, contained the names of neither Netaji nor the two pilots and the Japanese General Shidei who were claimed to have been on the same flight and died on the same day.** In the light of such evidences who can doubt the assertion of the JMCI that the *"absence of any entry relating to their cremation defeats the story of the death of Netaji and some of his co-passengers in the plane-crash."*

During the investigation, the JMCI was not only restricted and prevented by the Government from travelling overseas where the truth lay concealed, but it also gave evasive replies to many specific posers and this attitude was deliberately adopted in order to harass the inquiry panel. Mathai's note could be taken as an example in this regard along with the affidavit filed by one senior official declaring not to grant access to the files in possession of the Government. It was strange that the Government which had set up the JMCI, was trying to hide behind the provisions of the Evidence Act to suppress the truth. It was within the powers of the JMCI to overrule the government's objections but the government could always appeal to any High Court in the country or the Supreme Court against the decision of the JMCI, and thus the legal battle might have stretched on for a much longer time than expected. Instead, the JMCI's approach was to collect archival papers from the archives of the United Kingdom, and the British Government agreed to let it have about 700 documents which were available in their archives. If the same arrangement would have been possible with the Russian Government there would have been more surprises in the findings of the JMCI.

Our efforts to confront and challenge the mystery of Netaji's disapperance will continue till its final exposure. The question of disappearance is a question which is being posponed for the last seven decades. It is time when the Government of India would demonstrate its democratic maturity and the true spirit to unravel the resting points of the mystery present to the nation the truth as truth and nothing but truth.

—o—

Appendix-1

Affidavit: Dr. Purabi Roy

I, Dr. Purabi Roy, wife of the late Kalyan Roy, aged about 59 years.by occupation Research Professor residing at 47-C, Abdul Halim Lane, Calcutta - 700 016, do hereby solemnly affirm and state as follows:

1. That I have received letter No. JMCI/Meeting/99-2000/48/11 dated 4.4.2000, issued by Sri P.K. Sengupta, Secretary of Justice Mukherjee Commission of Inquiry, communicating that the Hon'ble Commission at its proceeding held on 23rd March, 2000, had entirely ordered that *"the Commission would like to have an affidavit filed by Mrs. Purabi Roy indicating the particulars of the documents which might have come to her notice in course of her research and considered by her to be relevant for the purpose of the enquiry by this Commission..."*

2. In compliance with the above mentioned direction of the Hon'ble Commission I state as follows:

(a) In pursuance of a cultural agreement signed between the Asiatic Society, Calcutta, and the Institute of Oriental Studies, Academy of Sciences, Moscow, in March 1995, a project has been undertaken to compile accessible materials, now available in the Russian Archives, pertaining to Indo-Russian Relations from the

earliest period to 1947. As a first step in working out this programme, I was deputed by the Asiatic Society to Moscow in May-September 1994 to collect archival documents. Then in May-August 1995, the Asiatic Society deputed a team of three scholars — Sobhanlal Dutta Gupta. Dr. Hari Vasudevan and myself to Moscow to collect archival documents for the period 1917-1947. The team brought back with them immensely valuable materials, virtually unknown to scholars till now. The bulk of the material is in Russian and English. Again I was deputed to Moscow and London in June-October, 1996.

(b) The period between 1917-1947 is of special interest in view of the fact that after the October Revolution, the Soviet Union became a source of inspiration to liberation movements in the countries in Asia, particularly India, under colonial rule. Many Indian revolutionaries, who were in exile, shifted their centre of activity to the Soviet Union during that period. The documents reveal unknown chapters of international Communist movernent. Some materials, in fact, contradict the hitherto known facts. From those collected materials, the selected documents were edited and published in two volumes by the Asiatic Society which are as follows:

(i) Indo-Russian Relations 1917-1947: Select Documents from the Archives of the Russian Federation. (Part-I,1917-1947), Edited and compiled by Sobhanlal Dutta-Gupta, Hari Vasudevan and myself, in April, 1999; and

(ii) Indo-Russian Relations- 1917-1947, Select Documents from the Archives of the Russian Federation (Part-II,1929-1947) Edited and compiled by Sobhanlal Dutta-Gupta, a Hari Vasudevan and myself, in May 2000.

(c) What appears to be more interesting is that the unearthed materials hinting at Netaji Subhas Chandra Bose's contact with the

Soviet leaders, asking for arms help, later recognition of' the Provisional Government of Azad Hind by USSR, Soviet agents' activities in India during and after the World War II and many other interesting informations. Some documents relating to Netaji are in former NKGB-KGB or present FSB archives and President's archives which were not accessible to the scholars. Special permission is required to scrutinise them. It is believed that examination of these materials eventually clear the mystery of Netaji's disappearance. The list of the Russian Archives from which the documents have been collected and deposited in the manuscript department of the Asiatic Society, Calcutta, are as follows:

- *(i)* State Archive of the Russian Federation
- *(ii)* Ministry of External Affairs
- *(iii)* Russian State Military Historical Archive
- *(iv)* Russian State Library Manuscript Department
- *(v)* Russian Centre for Conservation and Study of Records for Modern History
- *(vi)* Personal Archive of E. Ya. Luisternik

The List of archives which are not accessible:

- *(i)* Former NKGB-KGB present FSB Archive
- *(ii)* President's Archive
- *(iii)* Stalin's Archive
- *(iv)* Archives of the Far East of Russian Federation
- *(v)* Archives in Omsk
- *(vi)* Military Archives of Russian Ministry of Defence at Paddolsk
- *(vii)* All the archives of St. Petersburg remained totally untouched

(viii) Archives in Irkutsk

The most revealing document unearthed from the archives of' the Ministry of External Affairs (MTd) Russia: 0179, year 1946. Inventory la. file la. Number of documents 8 from l2th September to 28th October, 1946.

(d) That V.G. Sayadvants, a Soviet agent, was in India from 1943, who was engaged in selling Soviet books, periodicals and films. He was living in Bombay.

(e) In August 1946 Sayadyants left for Moscow through Teheran. In Teheran he submitted a brief report dated August 28, 1946, to the then Soviet Ambassador in Teheran, T.V. Sadchkou. Savadvants had mentioned that he is carrying a personal letter of Nehru for Stalin. Further, he gave a brief report on the political situation in India dated 1st September, 1946.

(f) It is interesting to note that some time in 1991 the National Archives of India has received a few documents from Soviet Union on Subhas Chandra Bose. It appears that a few files on Subhas Chandra Bose were declassified (which were in possession of Soviet Archives) and sent to India from the Department of Culture through the Embassy of India in Moscow. At present the papers are in possession of the National Archives of India Ref.: Acc No. 6757. S.C. Bose Group IV Serial No. 11, Total six documents. Number of pages 46, year – not mentioned.

(g) Besides archival documents there are a few provocative articles on Netaji Subhas Chandra Bose which have been published in the 1990s. It is interesting to note that during the period of' *'Glasnost"* and *'Perestroika'* many untold stories were told mainly by unravelling documents from the NKGB-KGB archives. Russian Indologist Mitrokhin remarks: 'Glasnost is removing many blank spaces in Soviet history and in the user's relations with foreign

countries and restoring the truth about Soviet Land, 1990 Nov. Indian revolutionaries like Virendranath Chattopadhaya and, Abani Mukherjee had disappeared from the Soviet society without leaving any traces. In 1989 an article published in 'Soviet Land' journal informs the destinies of the two above-named revolutionaries. Similarly, in 1990 November, 'Soviet Land' brought out an article *"Subbas Chandra Bose and Soviet Russia"* by A Raikov where the introduction indicates to search the truth of Netaji's disappearance. Similarly, in 1992 Gorbachev Foundation has released a few documents which have been brought out in brochure form related to Subhas Chandra Bose and Bhagat Ram Talwar, the activities of the German, Soviet and Italian embassies in Kabul, Afghanistan, during the period 1941-1945. The brochure: *"Marauders are Appearing from the Game"* by Yu. L. Kuznets, Moscow, interpret that the brochure reveals the role of Bhagat Ram Talwar, who escorted Netaji during his great escape and his close relation with a Soviet KGB agent called Zaman whose real name was Mikhael Andrevich Allakherdov, in Kabul. Further, it refers to the *'Silver moon'* code, and finally, all the details prove that Bhagat Ram Talwar was spying for at least four countries, i.e., Germany, British India, USSR and Japan, if not more.

(h) In 1992 former Tass correspondent in India, late A.Vinogradov wrote an article *"Life and Death of Netaji Bose"* in 'Echo Planeti' No. 22 May/June. Later, this article was translated from Russian and published in *"Netaji Subhas Chandra Bose Commemoration Volume as a tribute in his centenary year"* by Scottish Church College, in 1998.

(i) In 1993, the Journal 'Asia and Africa Today' No.8, brought out an article by A Raikov, *"Secret of Subhas Chandra Bose's Death"*. This was followed by an article in the same journal No. 9 and 10 *"Against whom Subhas Chandra Bose fought during the years of Second*

World War", by V.B. Turadzhev. Turadzhev's article has been translated from Russian and published in "Netaji Subhas Chandra Bose Commemoration Volume, a tribute in his centenary year" by Scottish Church College in 1998. Both the authors Prof Raikov and Mr. Turadzhev were interviewed by me.

Prof. Raikov suggested that the NKGB has to be consulted.

(j) V. Turadzhev, associate editor of the journal, 'Asia Africa Today', informed that from the Indian Embassy, Moscow, he has been asked to discontinue any further enquiry related to this subject. Later, he suggested that in order to reveal the truth military archives at Paddolsk and archives in Omsk should be consulted.

(k) A Kolesnikov, former Major-General of Warsaw Pact, later joined the Institute of Oriental Studies, Academy of Sciences, Moscow, where he organised the Russian Archival Committee of the Orientalists and finally has joined the diplomatic service. He has written an article in the January 1997 issue of the Russian weekly 'Patriot: Fate and Death of Chandra Bose'. This article was translated into English and published in the 'Mainstream': 'A Russian Tribute to Netaji Subhas,' July 19, 1997 Vol. XXXV No. 32.

(l) In October 1996, an Indian Parliamentary Delegation visited Russian Federation. Amongst the delegates the late Chitta Basu and Sri Jayanta Roy of the Forward Bloc were present. At that time I was also in Moscow and I could arrange two or three meetings with A. Kolesnikov and Sri Chitta Basu at Hotel President. In these meetings A. Kolesnikov confirmed that he could access few classified files on Subhas Chandra Bose with special permission where the documents reveal that upto October 1946 Netaji Subhas Chandra Bose was in the USSR.

In addition to the above, a few observations are to be considered. The its 1952 publication the Soviet Encyclopedia gave entry to Mahatma Gandhi and Jawaharlal Nehru, but there is no mention of Netaji Subhas Chandra Bose, whereas the revised edition of this Encyclopedia of 1970 keeps space for Netaji Subhas Chandra Bose.

(m) The period of Indo-Soviet Friendship and Treaties obviously started after the death of Stalin in 1953. Stalin did neither entertain the first Prime Minister of independent India nor he officially received the first ambassador of independent India to Soviet Union. Our first Prime Minister could only visit Soviet Union after the death of Stalin, and then onwards the Indo-Soviet friendship and treaties initiated and gradually grew up. During this period Soviet academics produced innumerable Indologists who engaged themselves in different spheres of research. The Indologists who worked in the field of India's freedom struggle contributed commendable research in this area but it is strange enough to understand that there is not a single mention of 'Subhas Chandra Bose' nor do they care to analyse any aspect of this great Indian revolutionary. On the other hand, it is strange enough to note that it is only during the period of Glasnost and Perestroika that the subject came into light. Keeping this in view, I interviewed the following personalities during May-June 1995 in order to know the whereabouts of Subhas Chandra Bose.

The following personalities were interviewed during May-June 1995.

(A) From the Institute of Oriental Studies, Moscow, Russian Academy of Sciences:

(i) Dr. R.B. Rybakov, Director, suggested to consult with Pikhoi, the head of the Archival Documentation Section, R.A.S.

(ii) A A Kutsenkov, Head, Indian Department, suggested that it is necessary to go through the papers of the KGB archives.

(iii) A A Kirichenko, Head of the International Section, claimed that he is rest assured that some documents related to Netaji are lying in the KGB Cell.

(iv) V.I. Kluev, Senior Professor, stated that the documents of the Institute of Law, Radio News Bulletin, Stalin's personal files and lastly, the prison papers of the city Irkhutsk are to be consulted. If possible to go though Pronin's book named, India-Moscow,1941'.

(v) V.N. Plastun, Senior Professor. stated that Soviet agent in Afghanistan believes if there are so many materials about Subhas in Kabul, there ought to be some materials in KGB archives.

(vi) Head of the Archival Studies A A Kolesnikov claimed that there was primary information about the subject. The group of scholars who are collecting the archival documents will reveal the truth.

(B) Finance Academy, Moscow, Russia:

U. L. Kuznets, former Soviet agent, served in Afghanistan as 'Pravda' correspondent, recently in 1992, with the assistance of Gorbachev Fund, published a booklet 'Marauders Appear from the Games' where a chapter deals with Bhagat Ram and Netaji.

(C) Institute of International Relations (Academy of Diplomats):

(i) A P. Gnachuk-Danielchuk, Prof. of Bengali Language and Literature, recently his son submitted M A Diploma thesis, the subject was *"Subhas Chandra Bose in Various Newspapers"*. Prof. Kluev was his opponent who remarked why Irkhutsk city prison materials in connection with Subhas were not consulted.

(ii) Academician G.L. Bondarevsky — *'immediate intervention from the government level and requested to arrange a letter from the*

Ministry of' External Affairs, Govt. of India, requesting Russian Govt. to permit the scholars to go through the documents. Letter should be addressed to the President'.

(iii) E.M. Morosov, journalist and former head of the Soviet Information Centre, Calcutta and Delhi — *'definitely some materials are in existence which will help to get a clear view of the British-USSR Policy.'*

3. After a close examination of the unearthed documents, my observations are:

(a) The general belief is that, after the formation of the Provisional Government of Free India, it was recognised by the countries belonging to the Axis Powers. But the records show that USSR have also recognised the Provisional Government. Besides, Mr. Pramod Mehra of the National Archives of India, New Delhi, in March 1999, had presented a seminar paper at the Netaji Institute of Asian Studies, Calcutta. In his paper on *"The Declassified Documents from the Ministry of Defence"* at page 6 he mentions: "The recognition of the Provisional Government by the world powers, viz., Japan, Burma. Germany, Italy, Thailand, Philippines, Russia, declared the firm resolve of the Provisional Government to prosecute their struggle for India's freedom, File No. 265/ I.N.A. (National Archives of India)"

The records refer that the Provisional Government of Free India was having its representation at Omsk and the name of the representative consul was Kato-Kochu.

(b) Further, records which are unravelled from the Russian and British archives, clearly indicate that Subhas Chandra Bose was all along trying to go to the Soviet Union, and was seeking their help because he thought that the USSR will be the ideal place for arranging India's freedom struggle. On the other hand, USSR also

all through maintained a positive attitude towards Netaji Subhas Chandra Bose and the Provisional Government of Free India.

(c) And finally, information obtained from reliable sources reveal that the classified documents on Netaji and the INA in the Russian archives confirm that Netali Subhas Chandra Bose was in the Soviet Union upto October. 1946.

4. That, considering all these records, in 1996, I approached through Kolesnikov, and the then Prime Minister of the Russian Federation, Chernomyrdin, who suggested to organise an Indo-Russian Commission in order to investigate the missing Indian nationals within the territory of the erstwhile USSR. Besides, I submitted my application to the Chief of FSB (Federal Security Service), Russian Federation Mr. Trubnikov requesting him to permit me to get an access to the relevant files, but till now I have not received any reply.

5. Recently, Mr. Rishi Ranjan Chakravorty, a resident of London, took initiative to declassify a few files on Netaji Subhas Chandra Bose and INA, which were in the custody of the British Government and finally, he could partially achieve his unending effort with the intervention of Lord Peter Archer, whose address is given at the end of this affidavit, and Malcolm Rifkind, the former Foreign Secretary of British Parliament. As a result, a few files on War Office records have been declassified and made accessible at the Public Record Office, London.

I had the opportunity to go through the India Office Library and consulted declassified files at Public Record Office, London, from where I have brought selected documents in the form of Xerox and handwritten copy with pencil.

The following is the list of declassified files at the Public Record Office, London:

(i) WO 203/515 April 1945 Japanese-Indian Forces Command guide to Activities;

(ii) WO 203/516 August 1945 Japanese-Indian Forces Command: Supplementary Guide to Indian National Army in Malaya;

(iii) WO 203/2298 August 1945 Malaya: disposal, status, brief history; of Indian National Army;

(iv) WO 203/Aug.-Dec. 1945, Indian National Army;

(v) WOP 208/804A Nov. 1942-1945, Indian traitor's fifth columnists trained by Japanese-Indian Independent League, Indian National Army, Survey of various organisations employed by Japanese for espionage, sabotage and propaganda. Reports on activities British Counter measures;

(vi) WO 208/3812 1942-1947 Subhas Chandra Bose: Activities and Death. (Cover of this file xeroxed); and

(vii) F.O. 371/56774 - 1946 Indian Soviet Relations (N227/136/38: Press Article).

6. Most of the files distinctly indicate the mysterious disappearance of notes, paragraphs, pages and references, missing information and papers; they are very abruptly arranged and most of the documents are incomplete. All these clearly prove the missing order of the documents.

7. Apart from the above mentioned files, I have received a few documents directly from Colonel Hugh Toye while I was in England in 1996, with his covering letter.

The address of Colonel Toye is given below:

5. Firm Close Lane, Wheatley, Oxford 33-1-England

Besides the Public Record Office, there are other archives in England which have many relevant papers. The following, some of which are mentioned below:

(i) Foreign and Commonwealth Office Record and Historical Department, Clive House, Pitty, France, London S.W.I. HI H.D.

(ii) E. Mountbatten in Burma, Hartly Library, Highfield, Southampton, Sol. 71 B.J.

(iii) University Southampton Library Special Collection, Highfield, Southampton.

(iv) Broad Lands Archives.

(v) Churchill Archives Centre, Churchill College,University of Cambridge. C B 30 D.S.

(vi) Cambridge University College, Oxford High Street, Oxford OXI 4 B.1.

(*vii*) Attlee Papers, Department of Western Manuscripts, Bodelian Library, Oxford OXI 3 B.G.

Address of Lord Peter Archer:

The Rt. Hon.
The Lord Arches of Sandwell
O.C. 7. Old School Court,
Wraysbury Staines, Middlesex
T.W. 19 5 B.P.

8. I state that I have already submitted to the Asiatic Society some of the documents collected by me in course of my assessment, as a member of the Research Team sent by the Asiatic Society to Moscow, for implementation of the project undertaken by the Soviet to compile accessible materials in Russian Archives pertaining to Indo-Russian relation from the earliest period to 1947.

Rest of the documents collected by me as a member of the said team are in my possession for close examination and study. These documents are to be submitted to the Asiatic Society on the completion of my work in respect of these documents.

Apart from the documents mentioned in the prceding paragraph there are a number of other documents in my possession, which in my opinion are relevant to the matters of inquiry by this Commission. These documents have been collected by me in my personal capacity as a Research Scholar and all these documents have been mentioned in my present affidavit. I shall produce all these documents before the Commission as and when I may be asked to do so.

9. That the statements in the paragraphs 1 and 7 are based on Information derived from records and those in paragraphs 2,3,4,5,6 and 7 from archival materials which I verily believe to be true and those in paragraph 8 are true to my knowledge and belief.

Identified by me: Sworn before me by the deponent who is identified to my satisfaction by Chanderyi Alam (Gupta) Advocate (Enrolment No. WB/533//1984). The Affidavit has been read out in full to the deponent who has signed it after admitting it to be correct on this the 8th day of June. 2000.

—o—

Appendix-2

Letter from British Intelligence Bureau

Secret Dated the 19th February, 1946

No.C-5

Intelligence Bureau (H.D)

New Delhi-3

My dear Young,

1. We have at last completed an examination of the information available here relating to the alleged death of Bose, and the result is not entirely satisfactory, for it reveals many discrepancies which, until clarified, make any definite conclusion on this incident a little doubtful. I would be grateful, therefore, for any possible assistance you can render in settling the points I raise in this letter.

2. Regarding the crew and passengers of the plane in which Bose travelled, the list of passengers as indicated by Capt. Habibur Rehman, seating arrangement (attached at Appendix 'A') does agree with the list, given by Capt. Yoshidha of the J.A.F. staff forwarded by SACSEA Commission No. 1 in a report dated 7 October 1945, Yoshida states.

3. The aircraft used was a K21 Heavy Bomber (Sally) and the

final destination was Tokyo. The aircraft belonged to the 3rd Air Army (H.Q. Singapore) Chief Pilot Sub./Lt. Aoyanagi

The passengers were:

1. S.C. Bose
2. One Indian Major, Lt. Col. or Col. (Capt. Habibur Rehman)
3. Lt. Gen. Shidei (former C of S Burma Army)
4. Lt. Gen. Sakai
5. Monogaki
6. Major Kawano
7. Takahashi
8. Takazawa
9. Lieut. Arai

The Japanese officers had been waiting for transport to Tokyo where they were proceeding on transfer. Yoshida's account also does not agree with a figure of 9 quoted in the Japanese Government's first report on the incident (attached as appendix B) ... In commenting on this report British Staff Section, G.H.O., AFEAC states:

".......... we have reason to believe that the Japanese Government also drew on Habibur Rehman for the information submitted to us."

This Japanese Government report states that Lt. Gen. SHIDEI (vice S.O.S. Southern Army) and two others met instantaneous death inside the plane, whereas Bose died later. Incidentally, Habibur Rehman states that 5 - not 4 - died. Can you ascertain the full names of the passengers and crew and can you possibly arrange for their detailed interrogation, because I feel sure that they will be able to settle many doubtful points concerning this affair. According to Habibur Rehman, Lt. Col. Sakamaki (or Sakai), who was seated in the turret at the time of the crash, was apparently unhurt and travelled to Fukuoka in the aircraft as Habibur Rehman on 4 September, 1945. It would appear that Sakamaki, in possession of Bose's ashes, travelled by train from Fukuoka to Tokyo. According to Habibur Rehman, Major Nagatome, a Staff Officer from Taihoku and Nakamura, Foreign Ministry official, removed Bose's ashes after the funeral on 23 August. They also merit thorough security attention.

Confined in Appendix 'C' is Southern Army signal No. 393 sent by Isoda from Saigon to the acting O.C. of the Hikari Kikan in Bangkok, instructing him to inform the Indian community of Bose's departure for Tokyo. Can you say from your records that it was usual for the Indian community to be informed of Bose's movements in this manner and in the middle of his journey? Incidentally, why was Isoda's signal of 24 August, asking certain authorities in Malaya and F.I.C. to inform the Indian communities of Bose's death, not sent to Burma and other parts of South East Asia? He certainly kept some of the Indian communities neatly in the picture regarding this last (?) journey of Bose's.

4. The disposition of Bose's remains is obscure. The Japanese Government Report referred to above states:

Aug. 20 Placed in Coffin

Aug. 21 Cremation

Aug. 23 Funeral at the Nishi Honganji Temple, Taihoku

Sept. I H.R. arrived in Tokyo

Habibur Rehman's dates are:

Aug. 20 Placed in sandalwood coffin

Aug. 22 Cremation

Aug. 23 Ashes placed in a wooden box and funeral

Sept 6 Arrived in Tokyo

Relevant to this and also contained in Appendix 'C' is Southern Army staff II Signal No. 66 dated 20 August, 1945 of which we have another version. The version quoted in Appendix 'C' states:

"...his body has flown to Tokyo by the Formosan army ...."

The alternative version states:

"...statements flown to Tokyo ....."

Our comment on version No. I is how could Southern Army have been so misinformed as to believe on 20 August that Bose's body had been flown to Tokyo, assuming of course, that the Japanese Government's report is correct? If, however, the alternative version is the correct one what "statements" were these, presumably were taken by Staff Officer TADA also mentioned in the signal, although SACSEA Commission No.1 No.68/2/10/GSI(b) dated 18 October 1945, contends that he was ordered to collect proof of Bose's death on route? The same report, incidenally, also states that in the absence of Hikari Kikan officers from Saigon, TADA used to handle their work, and was therefore, in the Hikari picture to some extent. A SACSEA Commission No. I report dated 6 November 1945 stated that Allied Headquarters, Tokyo, had been requested to fly TADA to Saigon for examination. Has he been interrogated yet? If not, would you please arrange this, for he is an important subject for interrogation in this affair.

5. We would appreciate anything you may be able to obtain from 2/Lt. Hasegawa of the General Staff, who met Habibur Rehman on his arrival from GIFU at a railway station in Tokyo and who accompanied him to Rama Murthi's house; from Rama Murthi himself, former I.I.L. Chairman in Tokyo, and from Mrs. A.M. Sahay, Kamionikubo, I-Chome 103, Tokyo, with whom Habibur Rehman stayed for a time.

6. You have probably seen the written and recorded statements of K. Watanabe formerly of the Bangkok Branch of the Hikari Kikan, forwarded by Finney on 12 November, 1945. I consider that Isoda should be severely re-interrogated on the basis of these statements. I should be grateful if you will arrange this as soon as he returns to Singapore. Incidentally, what had happened to K. Watanabe's further interrogations?

7. The SACSEA Commission No. I report dated 6 November 1945 states: *"......it is beyond doubt that he (Bose) had plans to go underground together with a number of selected friends of his movement."*

The earlier report from the Commission dated 18th October, 1945, suggested that the Japanese had undertaken to give Bose the necessary protection (to go underground). This may find confirmation through the interrogation of Chatterji and party who absconded to Hanoi with great deal of money.

8. An interesting item, which however may have no fruitful connection with this subject, is that Lt. Gen. Shideo who at one time opposed Bose's request to move his Government and part of the I.N.A. to Japan proper of China, is said by staff officers of the Japanese Army H.Q. Saigon, to have been travelling via Japan to Manchuria, where he had been posted after the surrender. In view of reports Japanese Staff Officers of H.Q. Southern Army, the Embassy staff in Bangkok, and prominent Jiffs that Bose himself was going to the Russians—was this coincidence or intention?

9. Perhaps not entirely unconnected with this research is the gold which SACSEA Commission No. I and Bhaskara Menon, Bose's former stenographer, alleged was loaded into Bose's aircraft on August 17 at Bangkok where, incidentally, he is reported as saying that he was not likely to return to that part of the world. This gold is reported to have been brought by Bose from Rangoon when he evacuated there in April, 1945. The two sources state that the gold, estimated to weigh about 200 lbs, was contained in four iron boxes. It seems unlikely that Bose took these boxes with him because there was apparently only room for two Indian passengers despite the use of turret accommodation for two Japanese officers. Habibur Rehman states that he has no knowledge of the contents of Bose's luggage, which, incidentally, was packed by Hassan (now in Singapore) and consisted of suitcase and two small attache cases. He further disclaims all knowledge of the iron boxes which is surprising as he appears to be the only person who did not see them. Perhaps Chatterji & Co., at present in Singapore, can throw more light on the whole question of the gold.

10. I enclose a copy of Habibur Rehman's CSDIC report. We find this unsatisfactory. The multitude of discrepancies in the account of the actual crash, as given first to C.I.C. in Tokyo (copy of this Appendix 'D') and later to CSDIC, is being taken up with CSDIC here but anything you can elicit through your resources welcome.

11. Incidentally, we have not been able to get anything on the conference between Bose and certain Japanese officers in the house of one Naraindass (the former local I.I.L. Chief) in Saigon on August 17.

12. I hope I have not presented you with too many posers but I do not visualise any more cropping up just yet. If you are not in possession of any of the reports I have mentioned, please wire and I shall send them to you.

13. You will understand our pressing anxiety to get to the truth of whether Bose is actually and permanently dead. Government wants to know where they stand over the matter, in view of the claims by Gandhi and others in India that he is still alive. Our examination so far only permits us to say that, unless there was a very cleverly contrived and executed deception plot, involving a very few of the highest Japanese officials, Bose is almost certainly dead. Any assistance you can give clearing up the remaining element of doubt would be greatly appreciated. In addition to the action requested in the proceeding paragraphs, we should much like to have from you a detailed paper on the measures you know have been taken to investigate the truth of the report of Bose's death, the result of these investigations and your own opinion of the evidence.

Yours sincerely,

Sd/- W. MCK Wright

Major Courtenay Young
Intelligence Division
G.I.C.B. H.Q. SACSEA
Singapore

—o—

Appendix-3

M.O. Mathai's Note

PRIME MINISTER'S SECRETARIAT

A small amount of Rs. 200/- and odd was received by the Minister of External Affairs from our Embassy in Tokyo along with the ashes and other remains of the late Shri Subhash Chandra Bose. This money is being kept in the External Affairs Ministry.

2. I have consulted the Prime Minister about this and he agrees that this amount might be transferred to the INA Relief Fund. The Ministry might get into touch with the General Secretary of the AICC, 7 Jantar Mantar Road, New Delhi, and have this money transferred to the INA Fund. A receipt might be obtained for the Ministry's record.

(M.O. Mathai)
2.12.1954.

Appendix-4

Letters from Prime Minister Nehru

Issued
16-5-62
No. 704-PMH/62

Prime Minister's House
New Delhi
My 13,1962

Dear Shri Suresh Bose,

I have your letter of the 12th May ... asked me to send you proof of the death of Netaji Subhas Chandra Bose. I cannot send any precise and direct proof. But all the circumstantial evidence that has been produced and which has been referred to in the Enquiry Committee's report has convinced us of the fact that Netaji has died. In addition to this, after a lapse of time, now, there is extreme probability of his being alive somewhere secretly. In the event of his re-appearance he would be welcome in India with great joy and affection, adds that circumstantial evidence.

Your's sincerely,

Jawaharlal Nehru

Shri suresh C. Bose,
Garia
P.O. Garia,
Distt. 24, Parganas,
West Bengal.

No.1448-PMH/62

PRIME MINISTER'S HOUSE
NEW DELHI

August 31 19

Dear Professor Sen,

Your letter of August 28th.

I have never heard of any secret protocol about Netaji Subhas Chandra Bose. Certainly the Government of India have not bound themselves to any such thing. Even if any country asks the Government of India to hand him over, it is not going to be agreed to.

Yours sincerely,

Jawaharlal Nehru

Professor Atul Sen,
[illegible],
Calcutta 2[illegible].

Appendix-5

IN THE HIGH COURT OF JUDICATURE AT ALLAHABAD
LUCKNOW BENCH, LUCKNOW.
C.M. Appln. No. 1412(W) of 1986.
In-re
Writ Petition No. 929 of 1986.

1. Miss. Lalita Bose,
2. Mr. M.A. Haleem,
3. Shri Vishwa Bandhav Tewari, ... Petitioners

Versus

1. The State of U.P.
2. The Chief Ministrer, U.P. Lucknow.
3. The Home Secretary, U.P. Council House, Lucknow.
4. The District Magistrate, Faizabad.

.... Opp.Parties.

APPLICATION FOR INTERIM RELIEF:

Lucknow Dt. 10.2.1986.

Hon'ble S.S.Ahmad,J.
Hon'ble O.B.Singh,J.

Notice on this petition has been accepted on behalf of the opposite parties by the chief standing counsel who may file counter affidavit within six weeks. The petitione may file rejoinder affidavit within 10 days thereafter. The petition shall be listed sometime in the month of April 1986. before us.

In the meantime the District Magistrate Faizabad opposite party no.4 is directed as under:

(i) An inventory of the articles left by the namele s saint at Ram Bhawan Faizabad shall be prepared or get prepared through an Accate commissioner who may be appointed either by the District Magistrate himself or he may get such an Advocate Commissioner appointed by the District Judge Faizabad and;

(ii) After the inventory has been prepared the artic les shall be shifted from Ram Bhawan Faizabad to the treasury to be kept in safe custody under his own lock and seal.

This arrangement shall continue until further orders of the Court.

Sd. S.S.Ahmad.
Sd O.B.Singh.

10.2.1986,

True Copy
14/4/86
Section Officer
Copying Department,
High Court, Lucknow Bench
LUCKNOW

IN THE HIGH COURT OF JUDICATURE AT ALLAHABAD
LUCKNOW BENCH, LUCKNOW
WRIT PETITION NO. 929 (M/B) OF 1986

1 Miss Lalita Bose, Major, daughter of late Shri Suresh Chandra Bose, resident of Netaji Research Centre, B-25, Saket, New Delhi.

2 Dr. M.A. Haleem. Vice President, All India Socialist Party, 73, Gautam Budh Marg, Lucknow.

3 Shri Vishwa Bandhav Tewari, aged about 42 years, son of Shri Inder Dutt Tewari, Vice President All India, Subhash Mukti Vahani, Tewari Nagar, Moti Nagar, Lucknow.

...............Petitioners

Versus

The State of U.P. through the Chief Secretary, Council House, Lucknow.

2 The Chief Minister, Uttar Pradesh, Lucknow.

3 The Home Secretary, Uttar Pradesh, Council House, Lucknow.

4. The District Magistrate, Faizabad.

............Opposite Parties

Lucknow Dated : 30-7-2001

Hon'ble D.K. Trivedi, J.

Hon'ble M.A. Khan, J.

It is contended by Sri Umesh Chandra that in view of The order dated 10-2-1986 passed by this Court in writ petition No. 929 (M/B) of 1986, the Commissioner appointed by Government of India will not be able to inspect the Articles. We find no such obstacle in the way of Commissioner appointed by the Governemnt of India.

However, the opposite parties are permitted to get the article inspected by the Commissioner if appointed by Government of India. (Hon. M.K. Mukherji, Former Judge of the Supreme Court appointed by the Government of India as Commissioner of Enquiry. Sd/- D.K. Trivedi

Sd/- M.A. Khan
30-7-2001

Let a certified copy of this order be handed over to parties counsel within 24 hours. Sd/- D.K. Trivedi

Sd/- M.A. Khan
30-7-2001

TRUE COPY

Printed by [signature] 31-7-01

Examined by: [signature] 31/7/2001

[signature] 31/07/2001
Section Officer
Copying Department
High Court, Lucknow Bench
LUCKNOW

Appendix-6

Missing Secret Files

Missing File Description : 1A, 2A, 3A, 6A, 8A, 12A, 16A (D.O. Note No. D/S-86 6)
File Date : August 24, 1953

Missing File Description : 17A (D.O. Note No. 3788-8EA/53)
File Date : August 27, 1953

Missing File Description : 27A (Memo No. 2/53/1971/3/601 151
File Date : October 13, 1953

Missing File Description : 33-B (Letter No. 20/62)
File Date : April, 1954

Missing File Description : 34A (**Rajya Sabha's starred Question No. 60**)
File Date : September 28, 1954

Missing File Description : 35B (**Note for Supplementaries**)
File Date : Unavailable

Missing File Description : 37A (**Lok Sabha starred Question No. 334**)
File Date : August 2, 1955

Missing File Description : 37 BCD (Enclosures to S. No. 37A) and Notes 11, 12, 13, 14, 15, 18, 19, 23, 24, 25, 26 and 29. File No. 23 (156)/51-P.M.
(Indian National Army in the Far East)

File Date : Unavailable

Missing File Description : 23 (11)-56-57 **(P.M.-INA Treasurer)**

File Date : Unavailable

Missing File Description : 12(226)/56 P.M. **(Investigation into the circumstances leading to Bose's death)**

File Date : Unavailable

Missing File Description : 249 INA-GHQ Case **(Bose and Russia)**

File Date : Unavailable

Missing File Description : 249-INA-CC (H) GHQ Case on Subhas Bose

File Date : Unavailable

Missing File Description : HQ main file 279/4 INA 10 Misc.

File Date : Unavailable

Missing File Description : 273 INA (Misc. INA)

File Date : Unavailable

Missing File Description : HQ main file 273/INA

File Date : Unavailable

Missing File Description : 138 INA and 265 INA

File Date : Unavailable

Appendix-7

UNITED NATIONS NATIONS UNIES

1 May 1997

Dear Air Vice Marshal Goyal,

I am writing in reply to your letter of 15 February 1997 to the Secretary-General, in which you seek his intervention regarding the image of 'Netaji' Subhas Chandra Bose. The Secretary-General is aware of the great regard in which Netaji is held, but he is powerless to undo references that may have been made in the past. He is confident that no United Nations agency or publication would use the term "war criminal" in reference to Netaji in the future.

Yours sincerely

Shashi Tharoor
Executive Assistant
to the Secretary-General

Air Vice Marshal S. Goyal
Chairman
Netaji Forum
New Delhi

Appendix-8

Extracts from 'Transfer of Power', Volume VI (1942-47)

(i)

Sir Robert Francis Mudie, Home member, Viceroy's Executive Council, to Sir Evan Meredith Jenkins, Private Secretary to the Viceroy. Wavell Papers.

Official Correspondence, India, January-December1945, pp 273

Top secret.

Home Department
New Delhi
23 Aug, 1945

"...whatever decision is taken in Bose's case must have the full backing of her Majesty's government. (Viceroy Wavell had been called to London for consultations by the new UK Labour Party PM Clement Attlee).

"The note has been prepared after discussion with Smith and Totterham. Smith is afraid of the agitation that his (Netaji's) *trial in this country will cause than either Totterham or I...*

3. *I have examined your suggestion that Bose be treated as a "war criminal". He is clearly not one in the ordinary sense of that word. Nor does he appear to come within the extended definition which has now been adopted by the United Nations. In this connection I would refer you to the air mail edition of The Times of August 9th."*

Yours sincerely

R.F. Mudie

(ii)

Enclosure to No. 57

Top secret

23.8.1945

Home Department

One of the most difficult questions that will confront Home Department in the near future is the treatment of Subhas Chandra Bose.

(i) Bring him back to India and try him either for waging war or under the enemy agents ordinance.

(ii) Have him tried by a court in Burma or Malaya for waging war against the king in that country.

(iii) Have him tried by a military court outside India.

(iv) Intern him in India.

(v) Intern him in some other British possession, *e.g.*, Seychelles Islands.

(vi) Leave him where he is and don't ask for his surrender.

4. I do not think that there is any chance of Bose being hanged if he were tried in India. The pressure for his release would be too great; and also his trial would result in great publicity for his doings, motives, etc. ...

5. It is extremely unlikely that the Government of Burma, which is engaged in appeasing the Burma National Army, would agree to try Bose and even more likely that if they did, they would hang him. The Government of Malaya might possibly have no such scruples and we might get a hanging if His Majesty's Government agreed to ignore agitation in India, and Parliament however strong.

But a trial in Singapore I would cause almost as much agitation in this country a trial here, unless it were held in camera and no news released till after his execution. But in that case we would be accused of judicial murder.

9. In many ways the easiest course would be to leave him where he is and not ask for his release. He might, of course, in certain circumstances, be welcomed by the Russians. This course would raise fewest immediate political difficulties, but the security authorities consider that in certain circumstances his presence in Russia would be as dangerous as to rule it out altogether.

10. The choice seems to be between deporting and interning Bose outside India or trying him in India and commuting the death sentence. The two might be combined and Bose deported (or "transported") after conviction.

There would be considerable long term advantages in a trial, but reprieve might raise the questions of why military officers who joined Bose's army should be hanged. The answer would be that their position in the Army greatly aggravated their offence, but this might not be accepted by the Army.

(iii)

II. Sir J. Colville
To Lord Penthick-Lawrence
L/PD/10/22
Private and Secret
No. 32

The Viceroy's House
New Delhi
2 Sep, 1945

"...Nehru .... is also anxious about Bose and the INA. Bose has come in for much praise as a national hero, and the nationalist press is suggesting that under international law Bose, and his followers are entitled to all the honours of war and are not liable to punishment."

(iv)

III. Note by Military Intelligence (extract)
L/WS/1/1506 : f44
Secret
No. 1005/3/GSI(b)
14 Sept. 1945

South East Asia Command and India Command Fortnightly Security Intelligence summary No. 3

6. The Japanese report of Bose's death is also a matter of considerable importance not only in the political arena but also to those concerned with security, the continued existence of "Netaji" possibly underground, would undoubtedly maintain the fervour of many Jiff's military and civilian

7. The report of Bose's death was received in most quarters in India with sympathy and regret...but in Bengal scepticism widely persists...It is generally believed that the news has been faked with Japanese connivance and that Bose has gone underground to reappear at the correct psychological moment. Political circles in the provinces have greatly interested in the recent news item which alleged that Bose had been seen alive in Saigon after the air-crash accident.

(v)

Documents No. 154
Cabinet India and Burma Committee Paper I.B. (45) 16
India and Burma Office
20 Oct. 1945

Annexture II to No. 154

B. Southe-East Asia

C. *"The prime problem is the disposal of the Far East collaborators is the action to be taken against Subhas Bose if he were found alive ..."*

—o—